The
FARMER'S WIFE
Magazine

JULY
1936

First published in 2010 by Voyageur Press, an imprint of MBI Publishing Company,
400 First Avenue North, Suite 300, Minneapolis, MN 55401 USA

Voyageur Press titles are also available at discounts in bulk quantity for industrial or sales-promotional use. For details write to Special Sales Manager at MBI Publishing Company, 400 First Avenue North, Suite 300, Minneapolis, MN 55401 USA.

To find out more about our books, visit us online at www.voyageurpress.com.

Library of Congress Cataloging-in-Publication Data

The best of the Farmer's wife cookbook : over 400 blue-ribbon recipes! /
[edited by] Lela Nargi.
     p. cm.
  Includes index.
  ISBN 978-0-7603-4052-3 (plc)
  1. Cooking, American. 2. Cookbooks. I. Nargi, Lela. II. Farmer's wife.
  TX715.B4856547 2011
  641.5973—dc22

                          2010039831

Editors: Melinda Keefe and Kari Cornell
Layout by: Helena Shimizu

Printed in China

The Best of
The Farmer's Wife
Cookbook

OVER 400 BLUE-RIBBON RECIPES!

MELINDA KEEFE AND KARI CORNELL, EDITORS

Voyageur Press

Contents

The FARMER'S WIFE

The Magazine for Farm Women

October 1935

Over a Million Copies a Month--

Commencing *Youth*

A NEW SECTION *for* YOUNG WOMEN

Introduction

The *Farmer's Wife*, a monthly magazine published in Minnesota between the years 1893 and 1939, offered rural women both practical advice and a glimpse of the larger world around them. In an era long before the Internet and high-speed travel connected us all, the magazine aimed to offer community among hard-working rural women in many parts of the country, to provide a forum for their questions and concerns, and to assist them in the day-to-day goings on about the farm—everything from raising chickens and slaughtering hogs, to managing scant funds and dressing the children, to keeping house and running the kitchen.

The kitchen is where the farmer's wife really shone. She could be creative in the kitchen, letting her imagination run wild over stews, roasts, salads, casseroles, preserves, cakes, and cookies of her own invention. She could show off her skill, whipping up a simple, delicious meal and dessert of the utmost perfection. She could exercise one of the most esteemed qualities among country women—that of thrift, using the eggs, milk, butter, preserves, and other stores abundant on any farm—while at the same time showing love and care for her family through the hearty meals and delectable treats she offered them each and every day.

Issues of the magazine portray the farmer's wife as a woman willing and able to economize her time in the kitchen; a woman bent on nourishing her family, both body and soul; and a women who understood the importance of laying up stores for the future. The farmer's wife tackled the responsibility of feeding both family and neighbors with great seriousness and strict planning, preparing filling dishes for supper as well as tasty cakes and cookies for visitors. The farm woman prepared sweet but modest offerings to gladden the hearts of hard-working family members and friends.

This indispensable volume is a collection of our favorite recipes, culled from the *Farmer's Wife* magazines. The recipes in this book have been reprinted much as they appeared on the pages of the magazine. Most recipes have been taken from issues spanning 1911–1939, and many were written by the magazine's own readers. In their language, they reflect the curious style and manners of their times, and herein lies a great deal of their charm, and the reason I have chosen to alter them as little as possible. Anyone accustomed to reading cookbooks will nevertheless feel right at home among the pages of this book. After all, the farmer's wife was nothing if not common-sensical, and so were her recipes.

Tips for Using this Book

Anyone new to cookbooks—and, more particularly, historical cookbooks—is advised to follow the golden rule of the recipe: read it thoroughly, start to finish, and preferably more than once, before embarking. Make sure you understand the instructions and the order in which they must be carried out; check that you have all the ingredients at hand and assembled; and be sure to preheat your oven a good twenty to thirty minutes before you are ready to bake. Wherever possible, I have attempted to abolish confusing, misleading, or laborious instructions. There are some guidelines to remember, however, when using this cookbook.

Farm Fresh Ingredients

First, the term *seasonings* would generally have been understood by the farmer's wife to mean salt and pepper. Efforts have been made in this book to differentiate between salt and pepper seasoning and the secondary meaning of the word, which includes other herbs, spices, and flavorings—these are listed separately on ingredients lists.

Farm women once had an ample supply of bacon and other drippings readily at hand, kept in a coffee can and used almost daily. Most contemporary cooks don't keep their drippings, so oil or butter can be substituted as appropriate. When a recipe calls for both bacon and drippings, the fat leftover from frying the bacon can, of course, be used for just this purpose.

In any recipe, shortening can be substituted for lard; "fat" can be interpreted as "butter"—use accordingly.

Aside from cottage cheese, which could be readily produced by pouring hot water over thick, sour milk (a common farm product), the farmer's wife did not make much cheese, unless she was engaged in its commercial manufacture. She had ample access to "store" cheese, though, which is how she commonly referred to cheddar. Recipes in the *Farmer's Wife* magazine sometimes referred specifically to other types of cheese, such as American or Parmesan; mostly, though, the original recipes are vague in the type of cheese to use. Experienced or adventurous cooks are encouraged to follow their instincts as to what sort of cheese might be used in any dish.

Honey was not necessarily a common farm staple—the farmer's wife more frequently used sugar in her cooking and baking. Recipes in the magazine almost always refer to "strained" honey, which is the clear, liquid version most of us buy these days, honey removed from the comb and strained free of wax and crystals. Any store-bought honey not in the comb will suffice for the recipes here.

Quite a number of the original *Farmer's Wife* baking recipes call for sour milk. According to Sandra Oliver, editor of *Food History News*, sour milk was a naturally occurring product on farms in the days before pasteurization. And it was very useful for baking. "The acidity in the sour milk interacted with the alkaline in the baking soda to make the gas that raised baked goods," she explains. I've substituted buttermilk in the recipes that call for sour milk. If you'd like to make your own sour milk, add

1 tbsp. vinegar to 1 c. "sweet" milk (a term the *Farmer's Wife* used to differentiate it from "sour" milk).

Measurements

1 pint = 2 c.	1 gill = 4 oz.
1 quart = 4 c.	1 teacup = 8 oz.
1 peck = 8 qts.	

Always sift flour once before measuring, and unless otherwise specified, use large eggs when eggs are called for in a recipe. Also, 1 square Baker's chocolate refers to the 1-ounce variety, and rolled oats should be of the old-fashioned type, not the quick-cooking. The following are some other measurements you might need:

1 pound yields:

4 c. sifted all-purpose flour	2½ c. brown sugar
4½ c. sifted cake flour	2¾ c. powdered sugar
3½ c. graham flour	1⅓ c. molasses or honey
3 c. cornmeal	2 c. milk
5½ c. rolled oats	4 c. nut meats, chopped
2¼ c. white sugar	3 c. dried fruit

Some recipes in this book do not stipulate baking times. The following guidelines can be used:

For cookies: bake until just golden.

For cakes and breads: bake until the cake begins to pull away from the sides of the pan and a toothpick inserted in the center comes out clean. Also, for breads, tap the pan and listen for a hollow sound.

For custards: bake until just set.

For single-crust, filled pies: start in a hot oven (425°F to 450°F) for the first 10 minutes to crisp up the crust, then lower the temperature to moderate (350°F) to finish.

For unfilled pie shells: bake at 425°F for 18 to 20 minutes, or until lightly brown.

For unfilled tart shells: bake at 425°F for 12 minutes.

Some recipes in this book also do not indicate exact oven temperatures. When in doubt, follow these guidelines:

Slow	Up to 300°F
Very moderate	300°F to 350°F
Moderate (Medium)	350°F to 400°F
Hot (Quick, Fast)	400°F to 450°F
Very hot (Very quick)	450°F to 500°F

More than anything, this book wants to be used, not merely perused and admired. So please use it! And know that as you do, you are cooking up a bit of farmland history.

—*Lela Nargi*

Comfort Foods

The farmer's wife, at first, might not be an obvious source of recipes for comfort foods. After all, she is—or was, during the forty-six years in which The Farmer's Wife magazine was published in Minnesota—hard-working, thrifty, and highly skilled in the kitchen. But when reading issues of The Farmer's Wife, another image comes to the fore: a woman willing and able to economize her time in the kitchen; a woman bent on nourishing her family, both body and soul; a woman with ready access to many of the ingredients we associate with "comfort."

Naturally, no two people will agree on all the ingredients that create comfort; so much of comfort is rooted in our personal circumstances and rituals peculiar to our families. But few would argue with the basics: butter, cheese, and bacon (farm staples, all), along with eggs, fruits, and vegetables—and chocolate. And few would argue with the premise that comfort food is simple food—relatively easy to prepare and not requiring sophisticated palates to enjoy.

The following recipes provide something for everyone, no matter your heritage, no matter your preferences. Perhaps you'll even discover a brand-new something to offer you comfort.

A Few Basics

❦ White Sauce
1934

1 tbsp. butter
1 tbsp. flour
1 c. milk
½ tsp. salt

Melt butter in a skillet; add flour and salt and stir to blend. Add milk and stir until thickened. This makes a thin white sauce, useful for cream soups and as a sauce for vegetables. A medium white sauce, for vegetables, meat, and fish, can be made by increasing the amount of butter and flour to 2 tbsp.; and a thick white sauce, for soufflés, by increasing the butter and flour to 3 tbsp.

❦ Gravy

If you have cooked any sort of meat in a pan or skillet, you can make gravy from the drippings. Otherwise, a simple gravy can be made by following instructions for White Sauce (above), substituting broth for milk. Stir until thick and season with salt and pepper.

❦ Buttered Crumbs
February 1932

Allow ⅛ as much butter as crumbs. To prepare crumbs, use 1 c. dry bread. Dry thoroughly in oven, then roll to crush [or pulverize in blender or food processor]. Melt butter, add crumbs, and stir until every crumb is coated.

❧ Scalded Hoecake (Delicious)

Three or four handfuls [about 2 c.] of fresh water-ground corn meal. Pour over this enough hot water to make a stiff mush; this will take about 2 c. The water, too, should be fresh and just below boiling point. Add cold water slowly to thin the mush until when it is dropped from the spoon no impression is left in the batter, or until it will slowly pour from the pan. This will require about 2½ c. cold water and will make a deliciously thin, crusty cake. If a thicker cake is desired, do not make the batter quite so thin. Two or three spoons of melted fat added to this batter will help make the crust crisp, but it is not necessary.

Drop the batter by spoonfuls for small cakes, or pour in one large cake upon a smoking hot, well-greased griddle or baker. Cover cakes closely until crisp, light, and golden brown on lower side; then remove cover, turn cakes over, and cook uncovered. Serve hot with plenty of butter and a glass of sweet milk.

You will notice that the best part of these cakes is the crust, especially the crisp, lacy edges. So you will probably like to make them thin and small so as to have more crust and more outside edge. This amount of batter will make about 12 small or 4 large cakes.

MIRIAM WILLIAMS SAYS
"Use Butter Generously"
By Annette C. Dimock
March 1925

Some women are naturally lavish. They set a good table—plenty of maple syrup and butter for the "stack o' wheats," an extra dish of sauce besides dessert, a full jar of crisp butter cookies.

Other women use creamery butter sparingly, usually buying a reliable brand of butter substitute, because it is "just as good."

The butter-saving woman is not as scientific or wise a planner as it might seem if she looks to a cream check for cash. Multiply butter-saving and butter-substituting country cooks many times and it does things to the national supply of butter. I learned that the holdings of butter in cold storage were higher last August than during 1929, which marked the record peak of 151 million pounds. Folks must use butter a bit more freely if a surplus such as this is to be reduced and the price of butter kept stable.

Fats which are competitive to butter all have their place, but one does not yearn to be particularly lavish with them.

With butter it is different. I level-measure baking powder, spice, and flour for cakes or gravy, but when it comes to measuring butter for seasoning, it's a rounding tablespoon or a generous lump. Few things make me bristle like the restaurant sandwich which isn't spread with butter, and clear to the edges, too. The dairyman who almost caused a rift in the church by his explosions over the "miserably skimpy" pats of butter which the ladies' aid served at the church supper, has my sympathy.

Let yourself go when it comes to seasoning with butter. Folks always sit up with relish to the family table where there are melting butter squares on hot porterhouse or round steak, and a golden yellow heart in the bowl of fluffy mashed potatoes. And who can resist vegetables cooked just to a tenderness, their own liquid cooked down, and seasoned with sweet flavored butter? Rich velvety cakes made with butter command a premium at the market or church bazaar.

Use generously of your own products. Set a good table. Cook well that you may live well. *The Farmer's Wife* magazine recipes support these ideas.

❦ Milk Hoecake

*You perhaps know that hoecakes were first baked on shining hoes or polished
shovels before the open fire by . . . old slave[s], and to this day it is my belief that an old
antebellum . . . mammy can "beat the world" at cooking such appetizers.*

—The Farmer's Wife

2 c. corn meal
1 scant tsp. baking soda
1 scant tsp. salt
enough fresh clabber [raw milk that has soured and thickened—an old-fashioned farm
    product] or buttermilk to make a cakelike batter
1 or more eggs or a little bacon drippings may be added to make a richer mixture

In a large bowl, mix all ingredients until just combined. Cook on a greased griddle
uncovered on top of the stove by turning like pancakes, or this is perhaps more
delicious baked in the oven.

Variation:
When baked in muffin tins, this same recipe makes delicious muffins or "egg bread."
Beat 1 egg with 1 tbsp. water and brush on top of "breads" before baking.

Fancy Breads in Loaves

❧ Peanut Butter Toast
September 1917

1 tbsp. melted fat
1 tbsp. flour
2 tbsp. peanut butter
salt and pepper to taste

milk
12 pieces of toast
crisp-fried bacon

Heat fat in saucepan, add flour, stir until smooth, add peanut butter and seasoning. Mix thoroly; add milk enough to thin to spreading consistency. Pour over thin slices of toast, place a slice of crisp bacon on each slice of toast, and serve at once.

❧ Cinnamon Toast
April 1923

Cut slices of white or raisin bread ⅓-inch thick and toast to a light brown. Spread with butter while the toast is still hot enough to melt the butter. Sprinkle the buttered side of the toast generously with a mixture of ground cinnamon and sugar. The cinnamon and sugar are used in the proportion of 1 tsp. cinnamon to ¼ c. sugar. Place in the oven to heat and dissolve some of the sugar into the butter. Cut each slice in two, diagonally, and serve while hot.

❦ Hominy Pudding
October 1933

2 c. hominy (grits)
⅔ c. chopped dates or raisins
⅔ c. maple syrup
1 c. milk
1 egg, beaten
¼ tsp. salt
juice of ½ lemon

Mix the ingredients and put in buttered custard cups. Set in a pan of water and bake in a moderate oven (350°F) till set like a custard.

❦ Baked Stuffed Apples
October 1932

Wash, pare, and core 4 apples. Fill cavity with ½ lb. mild or hot Italian sausage, casings removed. Bake in a slow oven (300°F) until apples are tender and sausage is thoroughly cooked, about 1 hour.

Soups

❦ Chicken Rice Soup
1934

2 qts. chicken stock
2 medium onions
1½ tsp. celery salt
2 tsp. salt
¼ c. uncooked rice, rinsed

½ c. uncooked chicken, minced
1 tsp. chopped parsley

In a large stock pot add onions, celery salt, salt, and rice to stock. Cook until rice is half done, about 10 minutes. Add minced chicken for last 10 minutes of cooking. Garnish with chopped parsley.

Editor's note: Adjust amounts of salt and celery salt in accordance with the saltiness of your stock. If you are using store-bought broth, you will probably need less than is called for.

❦ Egg Soup
July 1914

This is nourishing and can be used for invalids or delicate persons who cannot use vegetable soup.

Into 1 c. sifted flour loosely stir 1 egg, a bit of salt, and ¼ tsp. baking powder until all the flour is moistened. Stir the flour and egg mixture into 3 pts. hot beef stock, cook for 5 minutes, serve hot.

❦ Corn Chowder
August 1929

Corn chowder leaves nothing to be desired when served with graham bread and lettuce sandwiches, with apples for dessert. Heat 3 tbsp. fat in frying pan; add 2 tbsp. flour and 2 c. water. Slice into this 2 onions and 4 potatoes (¼-inch slices). Cook until potatoes are soft. Add 2 c. fresh corn [or canned corn, well-drained] and 3 c. milk. Cook for 10 minutes. Season to taste with salt and pepper.

HOT SOUPS FOR COLD DAYS
By Mabel K. Ray
January 1934

When days are cold, steaming hot soup seems to "strike the spot" just a little better than anything else. Whether it is the clear soup which whets the appetite and is used as a starter for the meal to follow, or the more substantial soup which makes a whole meal in itself, there is a time and place for every soup. Besides, soups are economical, easy to do, offer perfect use for odds and ends of left-overs, and make the family—like Oliver Twist—come back asking for "more."

Soups, like dresses, are made more attractive by a bit of trimming. Some cream soups are as colorless and uninteresting as a dull-colored dress. A bit of paprika sprinkled over the top of each dish, gives just that bit of dash that a red buckle can give to a colorless dress.

What a small child calls the "with-its" are as important to a soup as the right shoes and gloves and hat are to a dress. Some of the favorite "with-its" are:

Bread cut in half-inch-thick slices, spread with butter, cut in cubes or strips and toasted in the oven until dry and brown and crisp.

Cheese Straws
Roll out pie crust made from 1½ c. sifted flour, ½ tsp. salt, ½ c. lard, and 3 or 4 tbsp. ice cold water. Spread half of it with grated cheddar or Jack cheese; fold over and roll again. Repeat three or four times. Cut in strips about half an inch wide and five or six inches long and bake for 10 to 12 minutes at 475°F. Be careful not to use too heavy a hand with the rolling out—it should be done with a light, patting touch.

Corn Sticks
Unsweetened corn bread (see recipe for Mammy's Corn Bread on page 20) baked in a "finger roll" or corn stick pan until brown and crisp—about 15 minutes at 425°F.

Crackers. Salty wafers or plain crackers.

And the one absolute rule of successful soups, no matter what kind, is to have them really hot—not lukewarm! Warming the soup tureen and the dishes is almost necessary if the soup is to be at its best when served.

❦ Potato Soup
May 1931

1 slice from a large onion
2 c. diced peeled potatoes
1 c. boiling water
1 tsp. salt
¼ tsp. pepper
2 c. thin sour cream [thin store-bought sour cream with water to consistency of
   heavy cream]
1 tbsp. minced parsley

Cook potatoes and onion for 15 minutes in boiling water. Add seasonings and cream.
Heat. Garnish with chopped parsley.

*Editor's note: Puree in blender or food processor before adding seasonings and cream, if
desired. Heat gently, then garnish with parsley.*

❦ Cream of Spinach Soup
May 1911

Wash 4 c. spinach, drain, and put on to cook in a saucepan of boiling water [or boil
1 package frozen spinach]. Boil rapidly, uncovered, until tender, about 2 minutes, then
drain in a colander, run cold water through it, and chop fine. While the spinach is
cooking, prepare the soup by cooking together 1 tbsp. each of butter and flour, slowly
adding 4 c. hot milk and salt to taste. Season with ½ tsp. white pepper and ¼ tsp.
grated nutmeg. Add the spinach, run through the blender to puree. Serve hot.

❦ Cream of Tomato Soup
1934

1 pt. canned tomatoes	3 tbsp. butter
1 slice from a large onion	1 qt. milk
1 small bay leaf	1 tsp. salt
3 tbsp. flour	pepper to taste

Cook tomatoes for 10 minutes with onion and bay leaf. Remove from fire; strain
out liquid and remove bay leaf. Keep hot. Make a thin white sauce of the rest of the
ingredients (see instructions in White Sauce recipe on pg. 14). Keep hot. Just before
serving, pour tomatoes into white sauce. Serve at once. Always add hot tomatoes to
hot milk rather than milk to tomatoes.

Egg and Cheese Dishes

❧ Quick Supper Dish
October 1926

½ lb. soft cheese
2 eggs
½ tsp. salt
½ tsp. dry mustard
black pepper
paprika
1 c. milk or more

Cut or break cheese into small pieces into large greased pie pan. Break eggs on top and sprinkle with mixed seasonings. Add milk to cover cheese and mix all together with fork. Bake in a moderate oven (350°F) for about 15 minutes or until cheese is melted and mixture is set.

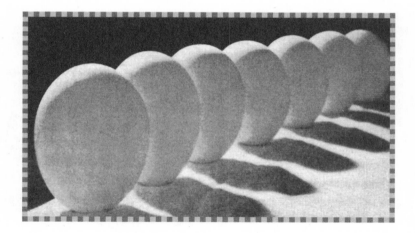

Eggs in Potato Nest
May 1926

1 qt. mashed potatoes
1 small chopped onion, cooked in butter until translucent

6 eggs
paprika
2 tbsp. chopped parsley

Left-over potatoes may be used if enough hot milk to make them soft and creamy is added. Mix potatoes with onion and arrange in greased baking dish; make six indentations in top. Into each drop an egg. Sprinkle with paprika and bake in a moderate oven (350°F) for about 15 minutes, until eggs are set. Garnish with chopped parsley.

Cheese Fondue
May 1931

1⅓ c. hot milk
1⅓ c. soft breadcrumbs (stale)
½ tsp. salt

⅓ lb. grated cheese
4 eggs, separated
1 tbsp. butter or other fat

Mix hot milk, breadcrumbs, salt, and cheese, add the yolks thoroughly beaten. Beat egg whites until stiff, then fold into first mixture. Pour into buttered baking dish and bake for 30 minutes in a moderate oven (350°F).

Cheese Soufflé
April 1937

4 tbsp. butter
¼ c. flour
1 c. milk
1 tsp. salt
1 c. grated cheese
3 egg yolks, beaten
3 egg whites, stiffly beaten

Melt butter in a saucepan over medium-low flame, add flour and cook 2–3 minutes, stirring constantly, until lightly browned. Add milk in a steady stream and continue to cook until thick and smooth, about 3 minutes, stirring frequently. Add salt and cheese and stir until melted. Allow to cool slightly. Add beaten egg yolks and mix well. Fold entire mixture into egg whites. Turn into greased baking dish. Place in pan of hot water and bake in moderate oven (350°F) for 50 minutes, or until soufflé is firm. Serves 6.

Noodles and Rice

❦ Macaroni and Cheese
October 1916

1½ c. macaroni
salt
1 c. thin White Sauce (see recipe on pg. 14)
½ c. grated cheese
1½ cupfuls Buttered Breadcrumbs (see recipe for Buttered Crumbs on pg. 14)

Prepare the macaroni by breaking into inch pieces. Drop it into boiling water to which has been added salt in the proportion of one tablespoonful to one quart. Cook until tender. Keep the water boiling rapidly and stir frequently to keep the macaroni from sticking to the bottom of the pan. When done, pour thru a strainer. Set the strainer in a pan of cold water and wash the macaroni to remove the starch that causes the pieces to stick together.

To the white sauce add the grated cheese and mix until blended and melted. Stir into this the macaroni, then pour into a buttered casserole and top with the buttered crumbs. Bake at 350°F degrees for 20 to 25 minutes, till brown and bubbly.

❦ Noodle Mixup
January 1933

1 small onion, chopped
2 tbsp. fat
1 lb. ground beef
½ c. canned tomatoes
1 c. water
3 c. cooked egg noodles
1 c. canned kidney beans, well-rinsed and drained
½ tsp. paprika
½ tsp. salt

Fry onion in fat until brown; add meat, tomatoes, and water and cook slowly until meat is done, about 25 minutes. Add egg noodles, beans, and seasoning. Heat thoroughly and serve.

❦ Scalloped Salmon and Noodles
October 1932

2 lbs. noodles
⅓ c. flour
⅓ c. butter
3 c. milk
1 tsp. salt
¼ tsp. pepper
4 eggs
1 lb. can salmon, drained and flaked with fork
¼ c. butter
1½ c. cracker crumbs rolled fine

Cook noodles in boiling salted water until tender. Drain. Make white sauce of flour, fat, and milk (see instructions in White Sauce recipe on pg. 14) and add seasoning. Add eggs to salmon and beat slightly. Add noodles and white sauce to salmon. Place in buttered baking dish and cover with buttered crumbs. Bake in a moderate oven (350°F) until golden and heated through.

❧ Italian Spaghetti with Meatballs
1934

1 lb. ground beef
½ lb. ground pork
⅓ c. breadcrumbs
1½ tsp. salt
¼ tsp. pepper
1 medium onion, chopped
flour for dredging
3 tbsp. fat
3 c. canned tomatoes, highly seasoned (with salt
   and pepper)
½ to 1 c. cream
1 lb. pkg. spaghetti
grated Parmesan cheese to taste

Mix well the first six ingredients. Shape into balls, dip in flour, and cook in rich brown fat. Add tomatoes and cook until meat is done through. Add cream to taste and stir to mix; remove from heat. Meanwhile cook spaghetti, drain. Put in center of hot platter. Arrange balls around edge and pour sauce over spaghetti. Sprinkle with cheese.

Note: After meatballs are browned, they may be placed in bottom of baking dish, covered with spaghetti, cheese, and sauce and baked until done.

❧ Baked Rice with Cheese
May 1923

2 c. boiled rice
½ c. cut cheese
1 large tomato, sliced, optional
milk to moisten, about ½ cup
buttered breadcrumbs to cover (see recipe for Buttered Crumbs on pg. 14)
sprinkle of paprika

Arrange rice and cheese in alternate layers in buttered baking dish. A layer of tomatoes may be added if desired. Pour milk over. Cover with buttered crumbs and paprika. Bake at 450°F until crumbs are brown, 10 to 15 minutes.

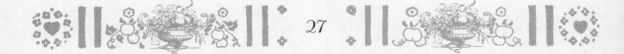

🦃 Curry with Rice
April 1926

This recipe was brought from India. Curry powder is not a common seasoning in the United States [Editor's note: It is now!], and not all Americans care for it. Those who do not may omit the curry powder and substitute any preferred pungent seasoning. Chili powder and paprika are good.

1 c. rice
2 medium onions
1 clove garlic
1 c. shredded unsweetened coconut, soaked for ½ hour in milk to cover
¼ pound veal and ¼ pound lamb previously stewed and cut into small pieces*
½ tsp. curry powder
water
milk
salt and pepper to taste

Wash the rice until the water runs clear then sprinkle it into hot salted water and boil it tender. Strain off the water and set the rice in a 350°F oven for 5 to 10 minutes—to dry. Chop onions and garlic fine and "frizzle" in a stewpan over the fire but do not brown. To this add the coconut. Add meat, curry powder, and water to cover the bottom of the pan. If the mixture seems too dry, put in a little milk. Season to taste with salt and pepper. The foreign cooks add pinches of cardamom, camino [cumin], and garam seeds [urad dal] for flavoring. Mix well and cook for 20 minutes. Pile the cooked rice around a platter, the meat and curry mixture in the center of it; garnish the edges with sprigs of parsley and serve hot.

*One half pound of either meat will do, but the combination is better. *Editor's note: ½ lb. of any leftover cooked meat, such as beef or chicken, will work as well.*

🦃 Spanish Rice
November 1929
Contributed by Mrs. O.S., Nebraska

1 lb. hamburger
2 c. tomatoes
2 c. cooked rice
2 small onions, chopped
1 tsp. salt
pepper to taste

Thoroughly mix all ingredients and bake in a hot oven—425°F to 450°F—for 1 hour. This may seem too dry without the addition of a little more liquid—either water or tomato juice—unless the tomatoes are quite juicy.

Stews and Casseroles

❧ Hot Pot
March 1926

1 lb. shoulder of beef, cut in 2-inch squares
2 tbsp. oil or butter
4 potatoes, peeled and sliced thin
1 onion, cut fine
salt and pepper to taste
water

Sear the bits of beef in oil or butter. Brown meat gives a better flavor. Butter baking dish and put in alternate layers of meat and potato and onion, having potato as the last layer. Season each layer with salt and pepper. Moisten with water, cover, and cook for 2 hours in a slow oven (325°F). If not brown enough, uncover for last ½ hour.

❦ A Stew of Distinction
September 1937

2 lbs. veal or lean lamb shoulder
3 tbsp. lard
3 c. boiling water
4 carrots
1 small stalk celery
6 small white onions, peeled
6 medium-sized potatoes
1½ tsp. salt
pepper to taste
2 tbsp. chopped parsley

Wipe the meat with a damp cloth. Cut into 2-inch cubes. Brown well in a kettle containing hot lard. Add boiling water, cover, and simmer for 45 minutes. Add the vegetables; the carrots cut in length-wise pieces, the celery in 4-inch sticks, the onions whole, and the potatoes in halves. Add salt and pepper and cook for 45 minutes more. When all are done, remove to a hot platter, piling the meat cubes in the center and arranging the vegetables in separate piles around the edge of the platter. Sprinkle meat with chopped parsley. Thicken gravy with flour, if desired; serve in separate bowl.

❦ Hasty-Tasty Stew
November 1936

2 strips salt pork (or bacon), diced
1 onion, minced
2 c. cooked, left-over pork
1 c. diced celery
2 carrots, peeled and sliced thin
2 potatoes, peeled and diced
1 10¾ oz. can condensed tomato soup
1 c. or more water
salt and pepper to taste
dumplings (see instructions in Pot Pie recipe on pg. 32) or biscuit dough
  (see instructions in Meat Pie recipe on pg. 34)

Fry out salt pork or bacon; add onion and meat. Cook until lightly browned, add other vegetables, tomato soup, and water. Season as necessary with salt and pepper; bring to a boil and simmer for 15 minutes. Drop in dumplings, cover tightly and cook for 15 minutes. Or put in a baking dish, top with biscuits, and bake in a hot oven (400°F) until biscuits are brown. If cooked vegetables are used, do not add them until the stew is ready for dumplings. Serves 4 or 5.

Boston Baked Beans
February 1935

1 qt. dried navy, pinto, or small white beans
1 small onion, peeled and chopped
¼ lb. salt pork or bacon
½ to 1 tbsp. salt
½ tbsp. prepared mustard
1 c. hot water
3 tbsp. molasses

Wash and soak beans in cold water to cover overnight. In the morning, drain, cover with fresh water and cook slowly until the skins break, 45 to 50 minutes. Drain. Place onion in bottom of earthenware bean pot; pour in beans. Score rind of salt pork (or chop bacon). Mix seasonings and hot water together. Bury pork in beans, leaving rind exposed (or mix in chopped bacon). Add molasses and hot water mixture. Cover bean pot and bake in a slow oven (250°F) for 6 to 8 hours. Add water as necessary. Bake uncovered the last hour.

❧ Smothered Chicken
February 1935

3 or 4 lbs. chicken, cut in serving pieces
flour, salt, and pepper
1 tbsp. each lard and butter
3 tbsp. flour

1 small can cream-style corn
1 c. cream
½ tsp. salt
1 tsp. paprika

Roll pieces of chicken in flour seasoned with salt and pepper, and brown lightly in hot fat. Remove chicken to baking dish. Add flour to fat, stirring till smooth; then add corn, cream, and seasonings to make a gravy. Paprika makes a rich-colored gravy. Stir and when smooth pour over chicken and bake in a moderate oven (350°F) until tender. If rather young and tender, the chicken may be baked uncovered in a very moderate oven (325°F). If less tender, cover during baking and remove cover last 20 minutes to brown.

❧ Pot Pie
February 1937

3½ lbs. chicken or veal
1 small onion, chopped
salt and pepper to taste
1 large potato, peeled and diced
¼ c. parsley, chopped

Dumplings:
2 c. sifted flour
3 tsp. baking powder
½ tsp. salt
1 tbsp. butter, plus extra for sprinkling over the top
1 egg, beaten
about ½ c. milk
pepper

Stew chicken or veal with onion in water to cover until almost done. Add salt and pepper, potato, and parsley. Boil for 10 minutes; drop in dumplings (see recipe below). Cover and cook for 15 minutes without lifting the cover.

To make dumplings:
Sift together flour, baking powder, and salt. Rub in butter; add egg and milk to make a soft dough. Roll out on floured board, spread with butter and sprinkle with pepper. Roll up like jelly roll and cut in rounds.

NEIGHBORLINESS PLUS FOR THE INVALID

By Miram J. Williams

April 1934

The thoughtful neighbor who brings over a pot of baked beans and a loaf of brown bread when mother is ill, gives it word of caution: "this is for you boys, Sonny, and your Dad. I've fixed a custard for your mother, probably beans won't be just the thing for her. Perhaps I can help get her tray ready."

That is neighborliness plus, the neighborly spirit plus thoughtfulness and good judgment. Women who attended the Illinois Farm and Home Week this year gained a lot of the "plus" part from the talk given by Harriet Barto of the Home Economics Staff, University of Illinois, on food for the sick.

"Go slow on onions," brought a smile from some who perhaps remembered how weak they felt when husband or son came in their own sick room with an offering of potatoes fried with onion. Less saltiness, less sweetness than perhaps is usual, was Miss Barto's advice. Hot things hot, and cold things cold, is not easy when the patient is many steps from the kitchen, but the use of a small preheated teapot to carry hot drinks and soup prevents both sloppy saucer or tray and undesirable lukewarmness.

Thoughtfulness is again shown by the form in which food is served—meat cut up if it takes force . . . bread or toast cut in smaller pieces and perhaps buttered in advance.

❦ Hamburger Casserole

February 19

Contributed

1 lb. ground

1 egg, beate

½ c. breadc

½ tsp. salt

¼ tsp. peppe

¼ tsp. poultr

¼ c. milk

3 or 4 thinly

2 onions, thir

¼ c. milk

Mix meat, eg   bottom of a
baking dish, th   on milk, almost
to cover. Bake

❧ Meat Pie
March 1927

Use any left-over cooked meat adding peeled and chopped potatoes, sliced onions, and peeled and chopped carrots, seasoning with left-over gravy (see recipe on pg. 14), or moistening with plain chicken broth. For the top use the following mixture.

Biscuit:
2 c. flour
5 tsp. baking powder
½ tsp. salt
2 tbsp. butter
1 c. milk

Knead into a soft dough and roll out to cover filling in casserole dish. Bake for 25 to 30 minutes (350°F) until hot and biscuit dough is nicely golden.

❧ Ham and Sour Cream Casserole
1934

2½ c. noodles
3 qts. water
1 tsp. salt
1 small onion, chopped
2 tsp. chopped parsley
3 tbsp. butter
1 lb. cooked ham, cut in small pieces
3 eggs, beaten
½ tsp. nutmeg
⅛ tsp. pepper
2 c. sour cream
1 c. breadcrumbs

Boil the noodles until tender in salted water. Drain and set aside. Brown the onion and parsley in the butter. Add the ham and remove from the stove. Beat together the eggs, nutmeg, pepper, and sour cream and add to the ham. Add the drained noodles and mix. Place in a greased baking dish and spread the breadcrumbs on top. Bake uncovered for 30 minutes at 350°F or until set.

❦ Emergency Casserole

February 1933
Contributed by Mrs. J.J.G., North Dakota

2 tbsp. butter
1 onion, sliced thin
3 carrots, diced
1 slice bacon, cut into small pieces
2 c. potatoes, diced
breadcrumbs
butter
salt and pepper to taste
water to cover

Place butter in pan, add onion, layer of carrots, layer of bacon, and diced potatoes.
Cover all with breadcrumbs dotted with butter, salt, and pepper. Add water to cover
the bottom of the pan and cover tightly with foil. Bake for 30 minutes at 350°F.
Serves 6.

❦ Escalloped Tuna and Peas

August 1931
Contributed by Mrs. G.R., Michigan

2 tbsp. butter
6 tbsp. flour
1 tsp. salt
¼ tsp. pepper
½ tsp. celery salt
3 c. milk
1 c. cooked peas
2 c. canned tuna, drained and flaked with fork
Buttered breadcrumbs to cover (see recipe for Buttered Crumbs on pg. 14)

Melt the butter; add the flour and seasonings. Blend and add the milk. Cook until thick.
Add the rest of the ingredients and when well mixed, pour into a buttered baking dish,
cover with buttered breadcrumbs. Bake in a moderate oven (350°F) for 20 minutes.

Meat and Fish

❦ Southern Fried Chicken
March 1938

Select a young spring chicken, about 2½ to 3 lbs. Dress and disjoint to prepare for pan. *[Editor's note: Wash the chicken pieces in cold water and dry on paper towels.]* Chicken should be thoroughly chilled before it is used, several hours or overnight. To prepare for frying, sprinkle the slightly moist chicken with flour. Put just a few pieces at a time so they do not touch into a skillet containing hot fat fully 1½ inches deep. (In the Country Kitchen we used a full pound of fat in our large skillet and fried only 6 pieces at a time.) Fry gently, turning once. Each piece is crusty brown on all sides, which is a characteristic of good southern fried chicken. Drain on paper towels or brown paper. In the south, peanut oil is used for frying; in the north, use lard or vegetable fat. After frying, strain fat into can or jar, where it can be used again and again if it is not overheated during use and if it is carefully strained after each using.

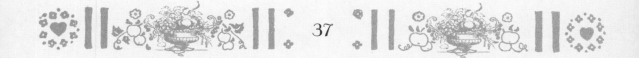

❦ Chicken Salad
April 1929

3 c. cold, left-over chicken, cubed
1½ c. chopped celery
1 tsp. salt
2 hard cooked eggs
½ to ¾ c. mayonnaise
crisp lettuce or sandwich bread

Combine chicken, celery, and salt. Cut up egg, saving three or four perfect slices for a garnish. Add egg to other ingredients and mix well with mayonnaise. Serve on crisp lettuce if available, or as a sandwich filling.

❦ Meat Balls
March 1927

Put 1 qt. canned crushed tomatoes on the stove to heat, season to taste with salt and pepper, then drop in meat balls made as follows:

Mix 1 lb. sausage, pork, or beef with a large grated onion and three slices of dry bread that has been run through a meat chopper [or blender or food processor]. Form into balls about the size of walnuts and drop into the tomatoes. Boil for about 20 minutes.

❦ Meat Loaf
April 1930

2 strips bacon or salt pork
2 lbs. ground beef
⅝ c. tapioca, uncooked
2 c. canned tomatoes
½ small onion, chopped
2½ tsp. salt
¼ tsp. pepper

Dice bacon or salt pork, fry out fat and add both bacon and dripping to the remaining ingredients. Mix thoroughly and bake in a loaf pan in a moderate oven (350°F) for 45 to 60 minutes. Serve hot or cold with a garnish of small onions, radishes, and parsley.

❦ Pot Roast and Noodles
June 1930

Use the large pieces such as the ribs. Melt a little fat in a kettle and brown the meat well on all sides. Add water to cover and cook until tender. In the meantime, cook broad noodles until tender in boiling, salted water. Drain and add a little liquid—about ½ c.—from the cooked meat. Simmer until the noodles have become well flavored with the meat juices. Serve in a border around the meat.

❦ Barbecued Ribs
February 1939
Contributed by Mrs. Cleve Butler

4 lbs. spareribs
1 onion, chopped
2 tbsp. fat or butter
¼ c. vinegar
dash cayenne
2 tbsp. Worcestershire sauce

2 tbsp. brown sugar
1 tbsp. celery salt
½ tbsp. ground mustard
1 c. tomato catsup
1 c. water

Trim spareribs free of excess fat. Put in roaster and put in a moderate oven (350°F). Cover and bake while fixing sauce by cooking onion in butter until soft and then adding remaining ingredients. Before pouring sauce over ribs, drain off excess fat from ribs. Bake meat uncovered, basting with sauce frequently, for 1½ hours or until meat is very tender.

❦ Butterfly Pork Chops
(For very hungry people)
October 1938
Contributed by Mrs. M.L.C., Kansas

Have the butcher cut double rib chops and remove the bone. Flatten out to make large oval chops, each one weighing ½ lb. or over. Mix fine dry bread or cracker crumbs with salt and pepper. Roll chops first in crumbs then in egg (1 egg beaten with 2 tbsp. milk), and again in crumbs. Place in refrigerator or cool place for half an hour to set the coating. Brown on both sides in hot lard or drippings. Add ¼ c. water, cover the skillet or Dutch oven tightly, and reduce heat. Cook very slowly on top of stove or in a moderate oven (350°F) for 45 minutes to an hour.

🌿 Fish Cakes
March 1937

6 potatoes, peeled
2 c. salt fish, cooked and chopped fine
2 tbsp. butter

4 tbsp. milk
1 egg
pepper to taste

Boil potatoes until tender, drain and mash together with the fish until very light and fine. Add the butter, milk, egg, and pepper to taste. Drop by spoonfuls into hot fat and fry brown.

🌿 Baked Ham with Pineapple
December 1927

1 slice ham, 1½ inches thick
6 slices pineapple, juice reserved

Wipe ham and place in a small roaster. Arrange slices of pineapple on top of ham. Add the juice from the can of pineapple and more water to just come ½ way up on meat. Bake in a hot oven (425°F) at first. Then more slowly (350°F) until ham is tender.

Vegetables

❧ Hot Cabbage Slaw

September 1934

2 tbsp. sugar
1 tsp. flour
¼ tsp. salt
¼ tsp. powdered mustard
1 egg
½ c. sour cream
¼ c. vinegar
1 qt. shredded cabbage cooked 5 minutes in salted boiling water and drained

Mix dry ingredients in saucepan; add egg; beat together; add sour cream and vinegar. Bring to boil, stirring constantly. Boil about 2 minutes, remove from fire and pour over cooked cabbage. Let stand in a warm place a few minutes to absorb flavor of sauce. Serve hot.

❧ Glazed Carrots

January 1931

Boil 1 lb. peeled carrots till just tender—10 to 15 minutes—drain and cut lengthwise in halves or in quarters if large. Place in a single layer in a baking dish. Over them pour a syrup of ½ c. cider boiled with ½ c. maple sugar (or brown sugar) until thickened. Bake at 350°F until brown, basting occasionally with the liquid. Serve in the syrup.

❧ Carrot and String Bean Casserole

June 1937
Contributed by N.F., Nebraska

1 small onion, minced
⅓ c. butter
3 tbsp. flour
1 tsp. salt
dash pepper
2½ c. milk
1 c. grated cheese
2 eggs
3 c. cooked carrots
3 c. cooked green beans
¾ c. soft breadcrumbs mixed with 2 tbsp. butter

Cook onion in butter until soft, add flour, seasonings, and milk, and cook until thickened, stirring to keep smooth. Add cheese, stir until melted then remove and pour over slightly beaten eggs. Arrange sauce, carrots, and green beans in layers in baking dish, top with buttered crumbs. Bake at 350°F until crumbs are brown.

❧ Sweet Corn Delicious

August 1929

8 ears corn
4 tbsp. butter
2 c. milk
1 tsp. salt
⅛ tsp. pepper

Cut corn from cob and place in frying pan with the butter. Cook for 12 minutes [or less, if you prefer crisper corn], then add the milk, salt, and pepper. Serve as soon as the milk is hot.

❦ Oven Fried Potatoes

May 1934

Pare potatoes and cut lengthwise in strips as for French fries. Let stand in cold water for 15 or 20 minutes while oven is getting hot (400°F). Melt butter or bacon fat in a flat, fairly shallow baking dish, about 1 tbsp. to a potato. Drain potatoes thoroughly, stir in the fat until they are coated, sprinkle with salt and pepper. Bake at 400°F, allowing up to 45 minutes to brown. Stir once.

❦ Potato Cheese Sticks

March 1935
Contributed by M.R., New York

2 c. warm mashed potatoes
½ c. melted butter
1 c. grated cheddar or Jack cheese
1 c. flour
1 tsp. salt
1 egg yolk
2 tbsp. milk

Mix the first five ingredients in order given. Cool. Roll into a rectangular sheet ¼ inch thick. Cut into strips 4 inches × ½ inch. Brush with egg yolk, beaten and thinned with 2 tbsp. milk. Bake for 10 to 15 minutes in a hot oven (450°F).

The Farmer's Wife editor's note: Serve hot with salads, tomato juice, etc. Makes 40 sticks. These are less crisp than pastry cheese straws, but very tasty.

❦ Potato Puffs

March 1927

4 c. hot mashed potato
1 tbsp. melted fat
2 tbsp. milk
1 tsp. salt
¼ tsp. pepper
yolks of 2 eggs
whites of 2 eggs beaten stiff

Mix all but the whites of the eggs in the order given; beat thoroughly, fold in the stiffly beaten whites, pile in a baking dish, and cook for 15 to 20 minutes (at 400°F) until the mixture puffs and is brown on the top.

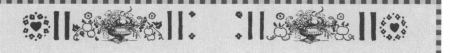

POTATOES ARE GOOD FOOD
By Jeanette Beyer and Edith Tolle
September 1929

If you are tired of potatoes in the trite forms of fried, baked, or boiled, you will enjoy them in these new designs:

Bacon Stuffed Potatoes
Put 6 large potatoes in the oven, bake (at 350°F) until done, about 1 hour. Then take out and roll slightly. Cut a slice from side and scoop out inside into a chopping bowl. Chop in small pieces and to this add 8 slices of bacon which have been previously fried and chopped fine. Add 2 tbsp. butter, and salt and pepper. Mix all together and put back in shells of potatoes. Lay in a pan and put in oven until thoroughly heated through—10 to 15 minutes.

Buttered Potatoes
Peel and slice as many potatoes as are desired, place in a kettle with boiling water to cover. Cook slowly for about 15 minutes until potatoes are soft but not mushy. Drain, add salt and pepper to taste and a generous amount of butter. Serve, garnished with paprika or bits of parsley sprinkled over the top.

Potato Au Gratin
2 c. mashed potatoes
3 tbsp. milk
pepper and salt to taste
1 tsp. butter
3 tbsp. grated cheese
1 c. breadcrumbs

Beat together the above ingredients, except the cheese and crumbs. Strew half the breadcrumbs thickly in a greased baking dish, put in the potato mixture, sprinkle with cheese and remaining breadcrumbs, dot with bits of butter, and bake for about ½ an hour in a good oven (400°F).

Baked Potato Kugel
3 c. grated raw potato
1 medium-sized onion, grated
2 tbsp. flour
salt to taste
1 egg, beaten
2 tbsp. melted butter or chicken fat
1 tsp. baking powder

Mix all ingredients together and bake (at 350°F) in a slightly greased square cake tin for about 1 hour or until quite brown.

Scalloped Potatoes with Fresh Pork
½ lb. fresh boneless pork
6 medium-sized potatoes
2 onions, sliced
2 tbsp. flour
salt and pepper to taste
1 tbsp. butter
1 qt. milk

Trim the fat from the pork, cut in small pieces and put in the bottom of a casserole. Put in a layer of sliced potatoes, a layer of onions and sprinkle with flour, salt and pepper. Dot lightly with butter. Repeat until within about 2 inches of top of dish. Lay pork on top. Sprinkle with salt and pepper and cover all with milk. Cover dish and put in a medium oven (350°F) and bake for 1 hour. The last 10 minutes, uncover dish to brown the meat.

❦ Baked Spinach with Cheese

February 1935
Contributed by H.R., Indiana

2 tbsp. butter
2 tbsp. flour
1 c. milk
½ c. cheese, diced
2 eggs, separated
2 cups chopped cooked spinach
buttered breadcrumbs for topping (see recipe for Buttered Crumbs on page 14)

Make a sauce of butter, flour, milk, and cheese. Stir and cook until thick and smooth. Remove from heat; add egg yolks beaten slightly and spinach. Beat whites and fold into mixture. Put in a baking dish, cover top with buttered crumbs and bake for 30 minutes in a moderate oven (350°F).

❦ Baked Winter Squash

October 1935

Scrub squash and cut in pieces for service, removing seeds and spongy part. Put in baking pan, skin side down; sprinkle with salt and pepper. Cover and bake for 40 minutes to 1 hour in a moderate oven (350°F). Uncover, and lay on each piece bits of butter or a thin strip of bacon or a spoonful or two of rich cream. Some like to sprinkle squash lightly with brown sugar or top with a marshmallow for a sweet vegetable dish. Return to oven and bake until lightly browned.

❦ Carameled Sweet Potatoes
October 1932

½ c. butter
1 c. brown sugar
1 lg. can sweet potatoes

Melt butter and sugar together in baking pan. Lay sweet potatoes, drained, in this syrup. Place in a hot oven (450°F); when potatoes are browned on bottom, turn and brown on other side.

❦ Sweet Potato Balls
August 1932

3 medium-size sweet potatoes
3 tbsp. milk, warmed
2 tbsp. butter
1 tbsp. brown sugar
¼ tsp. salt
1 egg, beaten
½ c. breadcrumbs

Boil potatoes with skins on until tender. Peel and mash. Add hot milk, butter, sugar, and salt. Whip until well mixed and fluffy. Form into small balls, dip in beaten egg, then crumbs. Bake in a moderate oven (350°F) for 15 minutes.

❦ Fried Green Tomatoes
September 1928

Slice firm green tomatoes into half-inch slices. Sprinkle with a little salt and a generous amount of brown sugar. Dip the slices in dry bread or cracker crumbs, patting in as many crumbs as possible. Have ready in a frying pan melted drippings, or melted butter, and lard. Brown the tomato slices well on one side then turn and brown on the other. When browned and tender remove carefully to a serving platter and make a dressing out of the drippings by adding a cupful of milk and thickening it with a scant tbsp. of flour dissolved in a little cold water. Boil to cook the flour, salt to taste and pour around the tomato slices.

Sweets

❦ Old-Fashioned Applesauce
October 1938

2½ qts. peeled, sliced apples
¾ c. water
¾ c. sugar

Put the apples and the water into a saucepan, cover tightly, and cook rapidly without stirring until they begin to boil. The apples should be cooked to a mush by this time. Add the sugar, and cook for 2 or 3 minutes longer, stirring constantly. More or less water may be used, depending on stiffness desired.

❦ Apple and Peach Sauce
September 1914

Pare, core, and cut into quarters 1 qt. apples. Skin, halve, and remove the pits from ½ qt. ripe peaches. Add just enough water to prevent burning. Put in sugar to sweeten and a little cinnamon and mixed spices (cloves, nutmeg, allspice) to taste if desired. Cover and cook until the apples are soft and the peaches tender but not broken. Serve cold with cream, either plain or whipped.

❦ Apple Crisp
October 1929

4 c. sliced apples (6 to 8 apples)
½ c. water
1 tsp. cinnamon
1 c. sugar
¾ c. flour
½ c. butter
1 pt. whipped cream
1 tsp. sugar

Cut apples in ¼-inch slices and place them in a buttered baking dish. Add water and cinnamon. Work together the sugar, flour, and butter until crumbly. Spread over apples and bake uncovered at 350°F. Serve hot with whipped cream, sweetened with sugar.

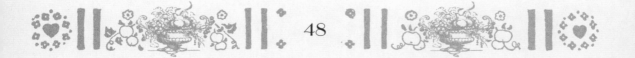

❦ Deep Dish Apple Pie
February 1929

Peel and cut 6 apples into very thin slices, pour 1 c. sugar and 2 tbsp. water over them, place in a hot oven (400°F) until they begin to steam, then cover with the following batter:

Beat an egg well and add ½ c. milk and 1 tbsp. melted butter; stir in 1 c. flour that has been sifted with a pinch of salt and 1 tsp. baking powder. Bake in a moderate oven (350°F) until the crust is thoroughly done and a rich brown. A glass dish is good to use, as it is better to see that both apples and crust are well done.

❧ Peach Pudding
September 1912

Butter a pudding dish and place canned peach halves in the bottom of it. Pour over them a batter made of 1 c. milk, 1 c. sugar, 1 egg, 2 tbsp. butter, 2 tsp. baking powder, and flour (start with ½ c. flour and add more as necessary). Drop this over the peaches and bake at 350°F until nicely browned. Serve with cream.

❧ Rhubarb Dumplings
April 1923

2 c. flour	¾ c. milk
4 tbsp. baking powder	2 c. diced and scalded rhubarb
½ tsp. salt	1½ c. sugar, divided
2 tbsp. lard or butter	2 c. water

Mix flour, baking powder, and salt. Cut in shortening as for biscuit. Add milk and mix lightly into soft dough. Divide into six equal parts and roll each into a circle ½ inch thick. Mix rhubarb and ½ c. sugar and pile uncooked in equal parts of the six circles of dough. Bring water and remaining sugar to a boil in an oven-proof dish. Bring the edges of dough around rhubarb, pinching it in place. Lay with smooth side up in the boiling syrup. Remove pan from flame and place in a hot oven (400°F) to bake for 35 to 40 minutes.

❧ Golden Custard
April 1937
Contributed by Mrs. J.A.W., Minnesota

8 egg yolks
⅔ c. sugar
sprinkle salt
1½ tsp. vanilla
¼ tsp. almond extract
3 c. milk
¼ c. cream

Beat yolks; add sugar. Mix in the rest of the ingredients. Pour into a buttered baking dish. Set in a pan of hot water. Bake for 50 minutes in a slow oven (about 325°F). Remove pan from water. Cool and chill. I often bake this custard along with my angel food, since both require the same oven.

JUST CUSTARDS
October 1935

When I suggested to the editor that an article on custards should be interesting he asked his usual question, "Why?" The temptation to say, "Because" was strong, but I thought I'd better prove it by a little experimenting in our County Kitchen. When the results were tasted and talked over by some of our staff, we were sure that a custard story would be interesting.

Can you make a perfect plain custard—smooth and even, with that delicately fine flavor of eggs and milk brought out, but not obscured, by sugar and flavoring? Here are important things:

Beat eggs for custard just long enough to mix them thoroughly, not until frothy.

A fairly moderate temperature in baking is best for smooth, tender texture. Set custard cups or baking dish on a rack, if possible, in the bottom of a pan. Then surround the custard cups or baking dish with hot water. Otherwise, the outside edges of a custard are apt to be somewhat porous and cheesy, because of too high a temperature.

A test for doneness is that a knife blade comes out clean. Remove at once from the hot water when they are taken from the oven or a custard will overcook.

Just Custards

❦ Pineapple Custard
February 1929

5 eggs
½ c. sugar
¼ tsp. salt
1 qt. scalded milk
1 tsp. flavoring (such as vanilla or pineapple extract)
1½ c. well-drained chopped pineapple

In a double boiler, beat eggs slightly and add sugar and salt; mix. Add gradually the scalded milk and cook until mixture coats the spoon. Cool, flavor with extract, and pour over pineapple. Serve very cold.

❦ Rice Pudding
February 1927

½ c. uncooked rice
1 c. water
½ c. raisins
stick cinnamon
3 c. milk
½ tsp. salt
6 tbsp. sugar

Combine the rice, water, raisins, and cinnamon in a pan; cover and cook, slowly stirring with a fork when necessary, until water has been absorbed, about 20 minutes. Add milk, salt, and sugar and cook for 1 hour in double boiler; serve hot with cream and sugar if desired.

❦ Fried Cakes
June 1910

Two cups of sugar, two eggs, and one teaspoon of salt. Three tablespoons of melted lard, one even teaspoon of grated nutmeg. Stir all together until it is like cream, then dissolve one large teaspoon of baking soda in two cups of sour milk or buttermilk and add to sugar and egg mixture. Add flour to make a stiff dough, roll out as soft as possible, cut out with a doughnut cutter, and fry in hot lard.

❦ Chocolate Mousse
December 1931

1 egg
¾ c. powdered sugar
⅛ tsp. salt
2 tbsp. cocoa paste (made with equal parts unsweetened cocoa powder and cold
　water, mixed smooth)
½ tsp. vanilla
1 pt. whipped cream

Beat egg, sugar, salt, cocoa paste, and vanilla thoroughly. Whip cream, fold into first mixture and freeze without stirring for 3 to 4 hours in bowl packed with 1 part salt/ 1 part ice, to come ½ way up side of mousse bowl. Serves 12.

❦ Honey Butter
August 1933

Blend 1 c. granulated or creamed honey with ½ c. butter. (Let butter stand at room temperature for 10 minutes so that it blends more readily.) If strained honey is used, use same proportions, beating the honey first with a strong double ball bearing type of egg beater. Then blend with warm butter. Pour in glass jar, screw cap on jar, and place in refrigerator or some place where temperature is 55 degrees or lower. Honey butter must be kept tightly covered and kept in the refrigerator just as you keep butter.

Editor's note: This is delicious as a breakfast treat, on toast or pancakes.

Buttermilk Fudge
December 1938

½ tsp. baking soda
1 c. buttermilk or sour cream thinned with milk
2 c. sugar
1 tbsp. corn syrup
1 tbsp. butter
1 tsp. grated orange rind
½ c. chopped cocoanut or nuts

Put baking soda in buttermilk and let stand for 5 minutes, then add sugar and syrup. Cook in a fairly large saucepan, since it foams up more than most candies. Boil until a light brown color (about 30 minutes) and a small amount dropped in cold water forms a ball that can be shaped in the fingers. Remove from fire; add butter and orange rind. Cool, beat until creamy. Add nuts or cocoanut.

Baked Alaska
July 1923

6 egg whites
6 tbsp. powdered sugar
1 sponge cake, sliced
1 mould ice cream (1 quart of flavor of your choice, frozen hard)

Beat egg whites until stiff and stir in sugar gradually. Wet a wooden board that will fit in your oven on both sides; shake off excess water. Cover board with parchment or wax or plain brown paper; lay the sliced cake on top. Cut the ice cream in slices to cover the cake, cover with meringue, and spread evenly over the top and down the sides. Place in the oven at 450°F and brown quickly. Slip from paper onto platter and serve at once, this dessert is most appetizing when brought to the table on the platter and served on small plates, giving a portion of cake, ice cream and meringue with each service.

❦ Hot Cocoa
1934

2 tbsp. cocoa
2 tbsp. sugar
few grains salt
1 c. boiling water
3 c. scalded milk
few drops vanilla

Mix cocoa, sugar, and salt in saucepan; add boiling water gradually. Boil for 5 minutes. Add milk and vanilla; cook for 5 minutes longer or until smooth.

❦ Fruit Lemonade
August 1919

2 lemons
1 orange
¾ c. sugar
4 c. water
4 slices pineapple
ice

Squeeze the juice from the lemons and half the orange into a bowl. Add the sugar and stir well, then add the water and stir until the sugar is all dissolved. Slice the remaining half of the orange into ¼-inch slices, cut the pineapple slices into quarters, and add to the bowl. Set the bowl into a cold place until ready to serve. Plain lemonade is made the same way, omitting the other fruits.

Harvest-Time Meals

Unlike her urban counterparts, the farmer's wife wasn't just responsible for preparing meals for her immediate family—a daunting enough task in itself, especially when added to her myriad other chores. A farm in those days was dependent upon community, and at no time was this truer than at harvest time. In the busy summer months after the crops—sometimes hundreds of acres of them—had been hauled in by the family and perhaps a few neighbors, a farmer might hire a threshing crew of up to twelve men to assist in removing the edible parts of the grain from the chaff. This process could take as long as a week, during which time the crew would expect three hot, nourishing meals a day, and possibly also smaller, cold meals to bring with them out to the fields. These meals, of course, were provided by the farmer's wife.

She tackled the event of feeding the threshing crew with great seriousness, strict planning, and, if she was experienced, a tremendous amount of opinion about what should be served and how much of it. Included in the following pages are recipes for feeding folks—and in some cases, a lot of folks—during the harvest months. Some of the recipes will help you put together a simple, informal hot meal for friends and family; others will help you figure out what to do with your own garden and farmers' market bounty when it seems that the profusion of blackberries and tomatoes will never end; and still others will help you solve the riddle of what to bring along to, or even cook over an open flame at, that happiest of summer mealtime events—the picnic.

Starting Out with a Hearty Breakfast

❦ Corn Fritters
November 1912

1 c. corn, cut off the cob
2 c. flour
pinch salt
1 tbsp. sugar
1½ tbsp. baking powder
enough water to make thick batter dough

Mix all together and drop by spoonfuls into a pan half full of hot oil. Cook until nicely browned on all sides. Drain on paper towels. Serve with maple syrup.

❧ Sour Cream Crullers
August 1916

½ c. butter
1½ c. sugar
1 small egg
1 tsp. baking soda
½ c. sour cream
2½ c. flour
a little grated nutmeg
powdered sugar

Cream the butter and sugar, add the egg, then the soda dissolved in sour cream and the flour. Mix well, adding more flour if necessary so as to make a dough that will roll out easily (it should be as soft as can be handled). Roll out to ¼ inch thickness, shape with a cutter, and fry in deep hot fat to a golden brown. Drain on thick brown paper for a moment and roll in powdered sugar while still warm. Sprinkle nutmeg on top. These crullers, when properly made, are not as liable to absorb the grease as a recipe in which more shortening is used.

❧ Sour Milk Biscuits
November 1912

1 qt. flour
1 tsp. salt
1 tsp. baking soda

Sift together then rub into this, using the tips of the fingers only, 1 large tbsp. butter. Gradually stir into this thick sour cream to make a soft dough (½ to ¾ c.). When just stiff enough to be handled, mix it well by cutting through with a broad knife until it looks spongy. Turn it out onto a floured board, pat it with a rolling pin to ½ inch thick, cut it with a big biscuit cutter, and bake immediately at 375°F until golden—about 12–20 minutes. The dough should be handled with the hands as little as possible. When properly made these will "melt in the mouth."

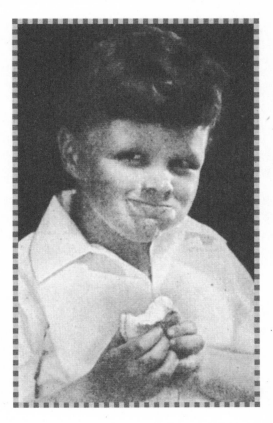

❦ Foundation Recipe for Muffins
May 1934

I

2 c. sifted flour
2 tsp. baking powder
2 tbsp. sugar
½ tsp. salt

Sift together into a large bowl

II

1 egg
1 c. milk
3 tbsp. melted butter

Beat egg till foamy, add milk and fat

III

Pour wet ingredients, all at once, into the dry and stir vigorously until dry ingredients are just dampened. The batter should not be entirely smooth. Fill buttered muffin tins two-thirds full with as little extra stirring as possible. Bake at 425°F for 20 minutes.

Variations:

With sour milk instead of sweet: decrease baking powder to 1 tsp. and sift ½ tsp. baking soda in with dry ingredients. If milk is quite thick, you might need more than 1 c.

With sour cream: Use 1 c. in place of milk, omit the butter, and follow the directions for sour milk.

For whole wheat, graham, or bran muffins: use 1 c. dark flour or bran and 1 c. sifted white flour. Increase baking powder to 3 tsp.; a little less milk is needed with coarse flour or bran. ¼ c. brown sugar may be substituted for white, or sugar may be left out and ¼ c. molasses added to the liquid ingredients.

Nut or fruit muffins: Add ½ c. chopped dates, raisins, or nuts to either plain or dark muffins. Mix thoroughly with the dry ingredients before liquids are added.

❦ Potato Muffins
May 1918

4 tbsp. butter
2 tbsp. sugar
1 egg, well beaten
1 c. mashed potato

2 c. flour
3 tsp. baking powder
1 c. milk

Cream the butter and sugar, add the well-beaten egg, then the potato, and mix thoroughly. Stir in sifted dry ingredients alternately with milk. Bake at 350°F in buttered muffin tins for 25 to 30 minutes.

❦ Two Good German Coffee Cakes

April 1913

Contributed by Sarah E. Seel

Dissolve 1½ cakes of yeast in ½ pt. equal parts warm water and milk. Beat stiff with a little flour and set to rise. Let rise to twice its height. Sift 2 qts. flour into a bowl. Salt to taste. Stir in 1 tbsp. cinnamon. Melt 2 c. butter into ¾ pt. warm milk and stir into flour, mixing thoroughly with a wooden spoon. Beat in one egg. Now pour in yeast, beating with a spoon until dough loosens from edge of bowl. Leave in bowl and set in cool place overnight. Next morning, grease two 8-inch pans. Pour dough on floured board, kneading till firm. Cut off a medium-sized piece, roll until ½ inch thick. Butter thinly, then sprinkle with cinnamon, sugar, and raisins. Roll up and place in pan to rise. Bake at 350°F for 20–30 minutes, till done.

Take another piece, roll as above, spread with good jelly, and lay flat in the bottom of a pan. Roll out another piece the same size and lay on top of first layer. Set to rise. Bake when well-up.

These recipes make an extremely good cake, which will keep fresh for 10 days.

❦ Orange Biscuits

1934

Use recipe for Baking Powder Biscuits (pg. 65), substituting orange juice for part of the milk. Roll out to ⅓ inch thick, cut, and transfer to baking sheet. On top of each biscuit put a cube of sugar that has been soaked in orange juice long enough to absorb some of it but not to dissolve. Grate orange rind over top. Bake at 450°F for about 12 minutes.

❧ Sour Milk Griddle Cakes
1934

2 c. flour
2 tbsp. cornmeal
1 tsp. salt
1 tsp. baking soda
1 tbsp. sugar
2 to 2⅓ c. buttermilk
1 egg, beaten
2 tbsp. melted butter

Mix and sift dry ingredients together. Add buttermilk, egg, and melted butter. Mix well. Drop by spoonfuls onto a buttered, hot griddle, flipping to cook on the second side when the first side is nicely browned.

❧ Rhode Island Johnny Cakes
November 1928

The meal used for these is made from white cap corn, stone ground by water power or wind because this method is slower and does not heat the meal. This is a special Rhode Island meal which is now shipped in small quantities to many localities. It must be used quickly as it soon deteriorates.

—The Farmer's Wife Magazine

Put 2 c. cornmeal into a bowl with 1 tsp. salt. Have the teakettle at the jumping boil and pour boiling water over the meal a little at a time, beating vigorously until the meal is scalded but not thinned. Then, thin with milk to the consistency of a drop batter. Drop on a well-greased, hot griddle and cook like griddle cakes. For huckleberry Johnny Cakes, add ¾ c. huckleberries to this recipe.

❧ Corn Scramble
May 1926

¼ lb. bacon
1 pt. corn kernels
6 eggs

1 c. milk
salt and pepper to taste

Cut bacon in pieces and fry with corn. Leave 2 tbsp. fat in pan. Beat eggs slightly, add milk, and cook over low heat till creamy and thick, stirring all the time. Add seasoning to taste and serve on toast or boiled noodles.

❧ Ham Omelet
April 1932

4 eggs
½ tsp. salt
¼ tsp. pepper
4 tsp. butter, melted
4 tbsp. milk
½ c. chopped ham

Separate yolks from whites. To well-beaten yolks add salt and pepper, butter, and milk. Fold in stiffly beaten egg whites and chopped ham, pour into hot, buttered skillet, and cook over low flame till bottom is golden brown and omelet puffed up. Then, set in oven at 350°F for 5–10 minutes to cook top. Crease through center and fold in half. Serve at once. Chopped ham, crisp diced bacon, dried beef, or sliced peaches, may be put between halves instead of adding when mixing.

What to Cook for the Threshing Crew

❧ Steamed Brown Bread

July–August 1921

1½ c. graham flour
2 c. cornmeal
3 tsp. baking powder
1½ tsp. salt
⅓ c. currants
⅔ c. raisins
2 c. milk
⅔ c. molasses

Mix together flour, meal, baking powder and salt, currants, and raisins. Add milk and molasses and beat well. Pour into greased loaf pans. Fill slightly over half full of batter. Steam 3 hours.

❧ Sweet Rolls

April 1938

1 c. milk, scalded
1 c. lukewarm water
2 pkgs. active dry yeast
½ c. butter
⅔ c. sugar
1 tsp. salt
2 eggs, beaten
grated rind and juice of ½ lemon
⅛ tsp. nutmeg
about 7 c. sifted flour

Scald milk and cool to lukewarm. Pour lukewarm water over yeast, stir, and let stand 10 minutes. Cream together butter, sugar, and salt, add beaten eggs, lemon juice and rind, and nutmeg. Combine liquids, add 3 c. flour, and beat smooth. Add the butter-sugar mixture and more flour to make a soft dough. Knead smooth but keep as soft as can be handled without sticking. Let dough rise in a cozy, warm place until doubled. Shape into rolls at once. Bake at 400°F for about 20 minutes.

❦ Popovers
November 1936

4 eggs, beaten slightly
1 c. milk
1 c. water
2⅓ c. sifted bread flour
1 tsp. salt
2 tsp. sugar

To eggs add two-thirds of liquid, then all of flour, salt, and sugar. (That's right, there's no baking powder.) Beat until smooth, then add rest of liquid. When blended, pour in warm, thoroughly greased pans. Fill muffin pans half full, deep custard cups or popover pan scarcely more than one-third full. Bake smaller tins, such as muffin pans, 25–30 minutes, deeper tins 35 minutes at 450–475°F, a really hot oven. Serve piping hot with butter. The popovers will pop up in 15 or 20 minutes, and the additional baking makes the thin walls crisp and brown. Serve as breakfast or hot supper bread. On occasion, fill with creamed chicken or chipped beef in cream.

❦ Baking Powder Biscuits
March 1931

2 c. flour
4 tsp. baking powder
1 tsp. salt
4 tbsp. butter or shortening
¾ c. milk

Measure and sift the dry ingredients together; work in the butter or shortening either lightly with the fingertips or by cutting it in with two spatulas or knives. Add the milk all at once to the first mixture. Stir rapidly for a few seconds, turn out on a lightly floured board, knead vigorously about half a minute. Pat or roll to ½ inch or ¾ inch. Cut, transfer to a baking sheet (or to the top of a casserole), and bake at 400°F for 12 minutes.

TABLE TALK
Hungry Harvesters Meals: Big Dinners in Hot Weather
By Jessie F. Stewart
August 1914

In these days when help is almost out of the question on the farm, it often happens that the housewife, with but a few hours' previous notice, finds herself obliged to get up a dinner for hay hands, harvesters, or threshers. And she must do it alone.

In cold weather this big dinner would not prove so formidable, for she would know that she was going to have the men sometime during the week and could prepare many eatables in advance. In summer this could not be done.

If the housekeeper is content to use only those dishes which are easiest to prepare and simple as to serving, she may get up a very nourishing and appetizing dinner with but a few hours' notice.

One of our favorite dinners on the farm was fried chicken—not the kind you are thinking of perhaps, but a much simpler dish. We used two to four old hens, depending on the crowd we were cooking for. If time was limited, we skinned them; otherwise they were scalded and plucked, cut up as for boiling, and put on to boil about nine o'clock. At eleven they were done enough for the frying.

In the oven we put a big dripping pan, or two small ones, with a generous portion of lard or drippings. When this fat was piping hot, we dipped each piece of the boiled hen in flour and placed it in the pan till all was in.

When the pan was put in the oven to fry till the chicken was brown on one side, it was then turned over and a big batch of baking powder biscuits laid over the top to bake. When the biscuits were brown on top, a gravy, made by stirring three tablespoons of flour into the boiling liquor, was poured over the pan and allowed to boil up for three minutes.

If you have timed your work correctly, you will pour the gravy over just as the men are coming to the house to wash. The chicken is heaped on large platters and the biscuits arranged about the edge. The gravy may need a bit of milk to thin. It is served in separate bowls.

With the chicken and gravy are served huge dishes of mashed potato, one of the easiest dishes to prepare, as it can be made ready after the chicken is on to cook.

As an extra vegetable, we usually had a large dish of sliced tomatoes, lots of them; sliced cucumbers with vinegar, or stewed tomatoes, all of which are easier to prepare in a hurry than string beans, corn, peas, and so forth.

Sometimes we served the chicken simply boiled with noodles or dumplings, and thus, having the oven free, baked beans as a second vegetable, since they need very little attention once they are in the oven.

Since you will have a pretty good idea that you are to have men to cook for soon, always see that your bread supply is ample. The biscuits, on meat, help out in the event of a shortage. Plenty of sweet milk and cream and nice, sweet butter should be on hand. Coffee may be ground up and kept for weeks in a closed jar. Plenty of clean towels, dish towels, and table linen may be kept always ready for the emergency dinner.

About all that is necessary is to keep calm, plan a simple dinner as you would for your own family, and multiply it by the number of extras and go at it just as for an ordinary family dinner.

❦ Chicken with Dumplings
February 1937

3½ lbs. chicken
1 small onion, chopped
salt and pepper to taste
1 large potato, peeled and diced
¼ c. parsley, chopped
2 c. sifted flour

3 tsp. baking powder
½ tsp. salt
1 tbsp. butter, plus extra for spreading
  over dough
1 egg, beaten
about ½ c. milk

Stew chicken with onion in water to cover until almost done. Add salt and pepper,
potato, and parsley. Boil 10 minutes, drop in dumplings (see below). Cover and cook
15 minutes without lifting the cover.

To make dumplings:
Sift together flour, baking powder, and salt. Rub in butter, add egg and milk to make a
soft dough. Roll out on floured board, spread with butter, and sprinkle with pepper.
Roll up like jelly roll and cut in rounds.

❦ Chicken Shortcake

April 1935
Contributed by M.C.P., New York

Muffins:
1 c. cornmeal
1 c. flour
3 tsp. baking powder
½ tsp. salt
1 egg, beaten
1 c. milk
2 tbsp. melted butter

Mix and sift dry ingredients. Combine liquids and pour all at once into dry. Stir just to dampen. Fill large, greased muffin tins two-thirds full to make eight muffins. Bake at 425°F for 20 minutes.

Filling:
3 tbsp. butter
6 tbsp. flour
1 tsp. salt
2 c. milk
1 c. chicken stock
1½ c. diced cooked chicken
8 pieces thinly sliced ham, cooked

Melt butter in double boiler, add flour and salt, and blend. Add milk and stock and stir till smooth. Add chicken and heat through. Split muffins, place a slice of cooked ham, lightly browned in butter, and a spoonful of chicken mixture on each, then put on top of muffin and another spoonful of chicken.

❦ Chicken Goulash

October 1929

1 whole chicken, 5–6 lbs.
2 c. tomatoes, chopped
2 tsp. salt
6 small onions, chopped
1 small green pepper, chopped

Boil chicken in water to cover till tender, about 2–2½ hours. When cool, remove the bones and cut the meat into small pieces. Return meat to broth, add remaining ingredients, and simmer 1 hour. Check seasoning before serving.

❦ Texas Hash

February 1921

2 c. rice
4 qts. boiling water
4 small onions, sliced
1 qt. tomatoes

2 tsp. salt
½ tsp. pepper
2 lbs. round steak, chopped fine

Cook rice in water over low flame till soft, then drain. Cook remaining ingredients together for 20 minutes. Add rice, put in buttered baking dish, and bake at 400°F for 15–20 minutes.

❦ Roast Beef Supreme

September 1937

Select two or three standing rib roasts. Wipe with a damp cloth and rub with salt and pepper. Place the roast in a dripping pan with the fat side up. Do not cover the roast and do not add any water. Place the meat in a slow oven (300°F) and roast to the desired degree of doneness. A meat thermometer will register 140°F for a rare roast, 160°F for a medium roast, and 170°F for a well-done roast. Allow 18 to 20 minutes to the pound for cooking a rare roast, 22 to 25 minutes to the pound for medium, and 27 to 30 minutes to the pound for a well-done roast. A 4-lb. roast will serve six to eight people.

Broiled Hamburgers
November 1938

2 large, mild onions
3 tbsp. butter
1 tbsp. water
1 lb. lean ground beef
¼ c. ground suet or butter
1 c. soft breadcrumbs
1 tbsp. parsley, chopped
2 tsp. Onion Juice (see below)
salt and pepper
7 bacon strips

Cut onions into seven ½-inch slices. Place flat in baking dish, add butter and water, and cover closely. Bake at 350°F. Meanwhile, mix other ingredients except bacon, then knead into seven flat cakes. Wrap each cake with a bacon strip and place on slice of onion. Broil under direct heat, 5 minutes for each side, basting occasionally.

Onion Juice:
Peel and grate an onion. Strain through a sieve and store reserved juice in a covered jar in the refrigerator.

Variation:
Cook on top of the stove, with sliced mushrooms sautéed in butter in place of onion.

Chili
October 1938

3 lbs. ground beef
3 onions
1 c. flour blended into 1 c. hot butter and browned
32 oz. thick tomato puree
3 lbs. cooked red beans
¾ lb. cooked spaghetti
salt and pepper to taste

Beef and onions are browned in fat; add tomato and beans and cook till thick. Season with salt and pepper, adding spaghetti just before serving to heat through.

❧ Loose Meat Sandwiches

October 1938

Also known these days as Sloppy Joes.

3 lbs. ground lean beef
⅓ c. fat
2 c. green tomatoes, diced
¼ c. onion, finely chopped

¼ c. celery, finely chopped
1 tbsp. salt
buns
butter

Cook ground beef in hot fat until lightly browned. Add vegetables and seasoning. Let simmer until well-cooked and slightly thick. Split buns, toast, and butter. Spread with hot mixture and serve.

❧ Beef Stew

January 1924

4 tbsp. butter
2 lbs. beef
2 c. carrots, chopped
2 onions, thinly sliced

8 medium-sized potatoes, cut in cubes
4 tbsp. flour
4 tbsp. milk or water

Heat butter in kettle. Cut meat in small pieces and brown in butter. Add enough water to cook meat and vegetables. Add carrots and onions when meat has cooked ½ hour. Add potatoes ½ hour before stew is done (usually 3 hours). Make a paste of the flour and an equal amount of cold water or milk. Add enough more cold liquid so the paste will pour. Add to stew and cook 5 minutes to thicken. Cooked rice, macaroni or hominy, cabbage, tomatoes, peas, beans, okra, and turnips may be added. Parsley, celery tops, or chopped sweet peppers add to flavor. To thicken stews allow 2 tbsp. flour to each pint of water used in making the stew.

❧ Curried Brisket with Rice Border

November 1917

2 lbs. beef brisket
2 c. onion, cut fine

2 tsp. salt
2 tbsp. flour

2 tsp. curry powder
1 tbsp. celery, chopped

Wipe the meat and cut in narrow strips. Sear on both sides in hot frying pan, then put in large stew kettle and cover with boiling water. Brown the onions in the pan where the meat was seared and add them to the meat. Season and simmer 3 hours or till tender. Mix flour and curry powder with a little cold water, add to meat, and also the celery. Boil 10–15 minutes. When celery is tender, turn onto a platter, surround with a border of cooked rice, and serve.

❦ Pork Chop Casserole
June 1927

6 pork chops
½ c. uncooked rice, rinsed
1 28-oz can tomatoes
1 small onion, chopped
salt and pepper to taste

Place pork chops in baking dish. Add rice, tomato, and chopped onion as you want. Season with salt and pepper and cover with water. Bake at 350°F for 2 hours.

❦ Stuffed Pork Tenderloin
1934

2 lbs. pork tenderloin
Sage Stuffing (see below)
2 tbsp. pickles, chopped
flour
salt and pepper to taste

Split tenderloin in half lengthwise, leaving halves joined together. Pound slightly. Fill with stuffing and pickles. Fold meat halves together and tie with twine. Sprinkle with flour, salt, and pepper. Roast at 350°F for 1 hour, basting occasionally.

❦ Sage Stuffing
November 1914

Soak a little more than 1 pt. breadcrumbs in 1 c. well-seasoned beef or chicken stock. Add 1 tbsp. powdered sage, a little more salt and pepper if necessary, and one small onion, finely chopped. Add enough melted butter or sweet cream to moisten and mix in two unbeaten eggs.

❦ Roast Stuffed Spareribs
December 1934

2 sides of spareribs
¼ c. butter
1 onion, chopped
1 pt. soft breadcrumbs
1 pt. cold cooked potatoes, chopped

1 tsp. powdered sage
2 tsp. salt
1 tsp. pepper
salt, pepper, flour

Trim spareribs so they make two neat, rectangular pieces. Wipe with a damp cloth. Sprinkle with salt and pepper and sew together on one side, using a darning needle and some string. Melt 2 tbsp. butter in a skillet, add onion, then breadcrumbs and potatoes. Cook until lightly browned and heated through (no moisture other than the potatoes is needed). Add sage, salt, and pepper; pile lightly on one rib section and sew on the other side. Rub with seasoned flour. Place on a rack over a dripping pan or a roasting pan. Bake uncovered at 450°F for the first 20 minutes, then at 375°F until well done, about an hour longer. Serve on a platter with glazed onions and baked apples. To serve, carve between ribs.

❦ Baked Southampton Ham
March 1938

Virginia hams are given a longer, more peppery cure than northern hams. Both flavor and texture are different—the fat is softer since hogs are fattened on peanuts and field peas; the flavor is much stronger than northern hams.

—The Farmer's Wife Magazine

These days it is virtually impossible to procure a raw ham like the one described below (unless you happen to be a pig farmer, or know one). Your butcher or supermarket meat section will likely offer a fully cooked bone-in ham, in which case you should proceed with the following recipe beginning with the instructions for studding the ham with cloves.

Cut off long shank end if ham is to be served whole; scrub thoroughly. Soak overnight and put skin side down in boiler, adding fresh cold water to cover. Let come to boiling point and simmer slowly, allowing 20–25 minutes per pound from time it reaches simmering boil. Add hot water as needed to keep ham covered. When done, take ham from boiler and remove skin while warm, trimming off excess fat to give the ham a neat appearance. (Some cooks let the ham cool in its liquor and then trim.) Dot the back with cloves, then sprinkle with brown sugar and cracker crumbs, mixed. Bake in oven at 350°F till brown. To carve, begin about 2½ inches from hock end, on back of the ham. Make first cut straight to bone, then cut off ⅛-inch slices with knife at angle of 45 degrees.

❦ Escalloped Ham and Potatoes
February 1923

6 medium-sized potatoes
2 thick slices raw ham
2 tbsp. flour

¼ tsp. pepper (optional)
2 c. milk

Pare and cut potatoes into thin slices. Dredge the slices of ham with flour and arrange potatoes and ham in alternate layers in a baking dish, placing one slice of ham on top. Pour on milk sufficient to reach to the top slice of ham. Bake at 375°F for 45 minutes, or until the ham is tender. Pepper, if used, should be sprinkled between layers of ham and potato. Because of the salt in the ham, added salt will not be necessary. Serve from the baking dish.

❦ Schnitz un Knepp
February 1937

A Pennsylvania Dutch dish.

1 pt. dried sweet apples
2 to 4 lbs. shank end of ham
Dumplings (see below)

2 tbsp. brown sugar
flour and water paste

Soak apples *(schnitz)* in water to cover; let stand on back of stove about 3 hours. Simmer ham till almost done, add apples, drained of part of juice, and boil ½ hour longer. Add Dumplings *(knepp,* see below) and cook 15 minutes. When done, place dumplings on a large platter around the ham, cut in serving pieces. Baking powder or raised dumplings may be used, but Miss Cole says they like raised dumplings best.

Raised Dumplings (Knepp):
¾ c. milk
about 3¼ c. sifted flour

1 tbsp. sugar
pinch salt

Scald milk, cool to lukewarm, and add 1 c. flour, sugar, and salt. Let raise till spongy, then add the rest of the flour or enough to make a dough to handle. Make into twelve dumplings like you make rolls, put on greased tin, and let raise till light. Drop into kettle of boiling broth and meat (see Schnitz, above). Cover and cook 15 minutes.

HARVEST TIME MEALS
As Planned by Farm Homemakers in 35 States
July 1935

I have just finished a "journey" to 35 states to see how farm homemakers plan and serve harvest-time meals. My "trip" took me from Maine to Oregon, and from Texas to Tennessee to Ontario, Canada. My "journey," of course, was by the letter route. In March we asked our readers to send us menus and recipes for their best harvest-time meals, and a huge box of replies came. What fun it was to read them, for those letters made me feel as though I were actually visiting in farm homes. And now I share my profitable experiences with all of you who are interested in the problem of harvest-time cookery.

—Miriam J. Williams

Yes, there are traditions when it comes to harvest meals. The theme is unmistakable: *Hungry men do not care for fancy dishes. They want plenty of good food, well cooked.* And I'm sure they're getting it in most communities, to judge from the contest letters. Many a woman said that hard-working men deserve good meals and that she enjoyed providing them. Even though many wrote of cooking and serving a crew unaided, there was no hint of complaint of hard work, only of satisfaction of a task well done.

With a few rare exceptions, dinners and suppers were built around a hearty meat dish. Meat loaf headed the list, with roast beef next. Other favorites were: baked or boiled ham, fried and stewed chicken, browned home-canned meat, roast pork, steak—smothered or Swiss-style—chicken, or meat pie. Interesting "strays" were barbecued ribs, pork chops en casserole, baked domestic rabbit, mulligan and Brunswick stew, meatballs, fried ham and cream gravy, corned beef, chop suey, casserole of sausage, and many combination dishes.

Potatoes? *Of course!* Three times a day in some cases where a hearty breakfast was served. And the men want them mashed. No other single dish chalked up a score like mashed potatoes, unless it was gravy or bread and butter, of course. Boiled or browned potatoes were popular with roast dinners where there was plenty of good brown gravy. Scalloped potatoes were a prime favorite with meat loaf and ham dinners, or with cold, sliced meats served for supper. It almost amounts to a law—don't forget potatoes.

As for other vegetables, no one could be more surprised than I was at the variety that men eat—carrots, alone and in combination with cabbage, with celery, or with

peas; Harvard-style beets and beet greens; turnips, scalloped and creamed with peas; summer squash; sauerkraut; green limas, spinach with egg slices; stewed tomatoes and green corn; creamed onions; savory mixed vegetables; broccoli. You can guess the favorites—beans, both green and baked dried beans; corn; peas; tomatoes; cabbage; cucumbers and lettuce. And when I began a list of different kinds of salad served, my skepticism, born of "harvest men don't eat salads," began to disappear. While nothing could get ahead of crisp cabbage slaw, yet the other salads must have been popular to judge from the number a recipe would serve.

The bread was mostly homemade in the form of plain and fancy rolls, dark and light sliced bread, steamed brown bread, cornbread, biscuits, and occasionally, muffins. A few mentioned buying sliced bread in town. Rolls were often baked the day before, or early in the day, to be reheated in a covered pan or paper sack before serving. Jelly or preserves of some kind usually accompanied bread and butter.

Coffee, iced tea, cold fruit drinks, and buttermilk were the accepted drinks. When it came to the drink taken to the field, it frequently was hot coffee if a lunch was served, and cold buttermilk or lemonade if sent out alone. You can guess the most popular dessert—pie, and apple pie at that. There were variations, however—apple pie with cheese crust, deep-dish apple pie with its thick, flaky crust on top, and the open-faced kind with crust beneath and cream on top. Lemon pie and sour-cream raisin pie ranked high in popularity, with chocolate, custard, and berry pies next in line. Canned or fresh fruit, served both as "sauce" or in a quivery jelly, and flanked with cake or cookies, was second to pie in popularity. Spicy cakes and cookies seem to be men's favorites, for they represented nearly 50 percent of the ninety-two cake and cookie recipes submitted. And next in number came chocolate cakes—many of these made with sour cream as a time-saving feature.

There was a surprisingly wide range of puddings and cobblers. I liked these particularly: fresh peach cobbler, Dutch apple cake with caramel sauce, a creamy rice pudding served with maple syrup from Vermont, a cocoanut-sweet potato pudding from North Carolina, spiced baked apples served with cream and a plate of creole chocolate cake, a fruited tapioca which could be made ahead, and a generous shortcake from Kansas calling for a gallon of strawberries! Homemade ice cream was looked upon as the dessert supreme, sometimes served at the last meal as a special treat.

How much do harvesters eat? Plenty of what you serve is the cue, and 486 quantity recipes submitted bear this out. A city meat loaf in my file calls for 6 lbs. of meat for twenty-five people, while the recipes submitted in this contest average 8 to 10 lbs. of meat for twenty-five servings. For baked beans, bring out the biggest crocks for harvest season. The good cooks do not agree, but it seems to take from 2 to 3 qts. dry beans to serve twenty-five. For eight men, says a neatly written recipe for Green Beans, Southern-Style, use 1 *gallon* green beans. Another for scalloped corn suggests 4 c. for eight servings. Two pies will serve eight, says one lady; others think ten. A recipe for pineapple ice cream goes like this: 3½ qts. milk, 14 eggs, 1 can crushed pineapple, 1 qt. cream, with sugar and salt, of course. It ended up, "This will make 2 gallons and will serve twenty to thirty portions." Perhaps—just perhaps, the family was extra.

❦ Sausage Pudding
April 1935

1 c. cooked oatmeal
1 c. milk
2 eggs, separated
1 c. flour
½ tsp. salt
2 tsp. baking powder
12 sausage links

Blend oatmeal with milk and yolks. Sift in dry ingredients, beat well, and fold in stiffly beaten egg whites. Pour into shallow, buttered baking pan and lay sausage links across. Bake at 400°F about 25 minutes, till firm and beginning to brown. Remove and pour off fat. Return to oven and bake 5 minutes longer, till well browned. Drain off fat again. Serve hot, plain or with a gravy made of 3 tbsp. sausage fat, 4 tbsp. flour, 2 c. milk, and ½ tsp. salt.

❦ Lamb Stew
September 1937

2 lbs. veal or lean lamb shoulder
3 tbsp. lard
3 c. boiling water
4 carrots
1 small stalk celery
6 small white onions, peeled
6 medium-sized potatoes
1½ tsp. salt
pepper to taste
2 tbsp. chopped parsley

Wipe the meat with a damp cloth. Cut into 2-inch cubes. Brown well in a kettle containing hot lard. Add boiling water, cover, and simmer for 45 minutes. Add the vegetables: the carrots cut in lengthwise pieces, the celery in 4-inch sticks, the onions whole, and the potatoes in halves. Add salt and pepper and cook for 45 minutes more. When all are done, remove to a hot platter, piling the meat cubes in the center and arranging the vegetables in separate piles around the edge of the platter. Sprinkle meat with chopped parsley. Thicken gravy with flour, if desired; serve in separate bowl.

❧ Roast Turkey
November 1938

Stuff and truss bird. Rub surface with soft fat. Place on a rack in an open roaster, breast side down, turning first on one side, then the other during roasting. Bake uncovered in a very moderate oven (300–350°F). If the bird gets too brown, cover with a clean white cloth dipped in fat. Allow 20–25 minutes per pound (dressed but undrawn weight) for a small bird (8–10 lbs.); 18–20 minutes per pound for a medium bird (10–16 lbs.); and 15–18 minutes per pound for a large bird (18–25 lbs.). A test for doneness is a loose leg joint when the drumstick is twisted.

❧ Turkey Stuffing
November 1915

1 qt. coarse breadcrumbs
½ c. salt pork, chopped, or butter
2 tsp. salt
2 tbsp. poultry spice
pepper to taste
milk or water

Mix all together, moistening slightly with the milk or water. Chestnuts shelled, skinned, and cooked tender are often added. Sausage meat is sometimes used with an equal measure of crumbs.

❦ Knedliky (Bohemian)

February 1928
Contributed by Mrs. M.V., Ohio

4 c. flour
1 ¾ c. milk
1 egg
1 tbsp. salt

½ tsp. baking powder
2 slices bacon, chopped
½ an onion, sliced

Mix together making a stiff dough that will hold the spoon upright. Have water boiling and dip the spoon first in the boiling water; then, take a spoonful of the dough and drop into the boiling water. When all the dough has been dipped in water, cover and let boil for 5 minutes, then stir from the bottom. Replace the cover and boil for 25 minutes. Remove one dumpling from kettle to see if it is done on the inside. If not, let them boil longer. Drain and place in a bowl. In a skillet, fry some bacon and onion and pour over the bowl of knedliky. Serve at once.

❦ Scalloped Potatoes

November 1922

7 lbs. potatoes
salt and pepper
½ c. flour

½ lb. butter
2–4 c. milk, scalded

Wash, pare, soak, and cut potatoes in ¼-inch slices. Put a layer in buttered baking dishes (you will probably need two) or shallow pans, sprinkle with salt and pepper, dredge with flour, and dot with butter. Repeat till pans are filled. Add hot milk to reach up to the top layer of potatoes. Bake gently at 375°F till potatoes are soft and golden.

❦ Potato Pancakes I

May 1918

6 large raw potatoes, grated
1 ½ tsp. salt
1 tbsp. milk
1 egg, beaten
3 tbsp. flour

Mix above ingredients, beat thoroughly, and cook on both sides on a hot griddle in oil or butter, flipping once.

❧ Potato Pancakes II
May 1918

1 c. boiled potatoes, mashed or ground in a ricer
½ tsp. salt
1 egg, beaten
¼ c. milk

Mix ingredients in order given, beat thoroughly, and cook as in previous recipe.

❧ Norwegian Cloob or Potato Dumplings
February 1928
Contributed by Mrs. F.M. D.W., South Dakota

1 dozen medium-sized potatoes, cooked and mashed
1 dozen medium-sized potatoes, grated
3 eggs, beaten
1 tsp. salt
3 tbsp. milk

Mix together and knead stiff like bread. Wet hands with water and knead balls with a small piece of pork fat in center. Boil in pork or chicken broth for 1 hour; drain and serve with butter.

❧ Baked Rice
November 1931

2 c. uncooked rice, rinsed
3½ c. meat stock
3–4 slices bacon
1 onion, sliced
1 tbsp. green pepper, minced
¾ c. tomato sauce, seasoned
salt and pepper to taste

Add rice gradually to the boiling stock. Place over hot water and steam 20 minutes, or till stock is absorbed. Brown bacon slightly and remove to another pan. Cook onion and pepper in bacon fat till browned. Add rice and mix well. Add tomato sauce. Cover with slices of bacon. Brown at 450°F.

❧ Creole Green Corn
October 1920

6 ears fresh corn
1 tbsp. oil or butter
1 sweet red pepper, chopped

Cut the corn from the cob and put in the frying pan with the fat. Cook 10 minutes, then add the chopped pepper and season with salt. (A small, minced onion may be added, and two ripe tomatoes.)

❧ Pea Soufflé
October 1916

1 c. fresh peas
1 tsp. salt
pepper to taste
4 tbsp. milk
4 egg whites

Wash peas and put them on to boil; boil till tender. Press through sieve, then add salt, pepper, and milk. Beat egg whites till stiff and fold into pea mixture. Butter a baking dish and bake at 350°F for 20–30 minutes. Soufflés should be served as soon as removed from the oven.

❧ Baked Stuffed Green Peppers
June 1922

12 sweet green peppers
2 c. breadcrumbs
2 c. chopped leftover meat
2 eggs, slightly beaten

2 tbsp. melted butter
milk to moisten
salt and pepper

Select large, smooth peppers, cut a round opening in stem ends, remove seeds and pulp, and soak in cold water for half an hour. Fill with mixture of breadcrumbs; leftover meat; slightly beaten eggs; butter; enough milk to form a soft, moist mixture; and seasoning. Place in a baking dish and bake at 375°F for 40 minutes, or till peppers are tender. Serve from baking dish or platter.

Cauliflower au Gratin
June 1922

Remove leaves and stalk from one large head of cauliflower and soak in cold, slightly salted water for 1 hour. Place in a kettle of boiling salted water and cook 30 minutes. (Sometimes to retain shape of head it is necessary to tie a square of cheesecloth over head.) Place whole cooked cauliflower in a shallow baking dish, sprinkle with grated cheese and Buttered Breadcrumbs (pg. 14), and brown in oven at 350°F for about 20 minutes. Remove from oven, pour 2 c. White Sauce (pg. 14) over cauliflower, and serve at table from baking dish.

Sweet Potato Puff
November 1924

6 sweet potatoes, pared and cut into cubes
2 tbsp. butter
½ tsp. salt
2 egg whites, stiffly beaten

Boil the potatoes till soft, then mash. Add butter, salt, and stiffly beaten egg whites. Fill buttered custard cups. Set in a pan of hot water and bake 20 minutes at 400°F. Serve hot, straight from the cups.

Stuffed Sweet Potatoes
January 1911

Bake large, smooth sweet potatoes at 400°F until soft through, about 1 hour. When done, cut in half length-wise and remove from skins. Mash, add ½ tbsp. butter per potato, salt and pepper to taste, and a drizzling of heavy cream, beating thoroughly. Refill skins, set back in oven, and brown before serving.

Scalloped Sweet Potato and Apple
November 1923

Into a buttered baking dish put a ½-inch layer of pared, sliced sour apples. Sprinkle with sugar. Cover with a layer of pared, sliced sweet potatoes, season with salt and pepper, dot with butter, and sprinkle generously with sugar. Repeat, having not more than three layers. Cover for the first 15 minutes of baking at 375°F, then bake uncovered until the apples are soft—45–60 minutes.

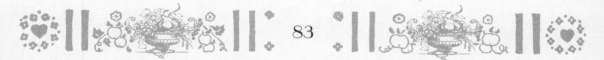

Always Serve Dessert

Steamed Chocolate Pudding with Sterling Sauce
February 1938

½ c. unsalted butter
1 c. sugar
1 egg, beaten
2 c. cake flour
¼ tsp. salt

1 tbsp. baking powder
1 c. milk
3 oz. bittersweet chocolate
1 tsp. vanilla

Cream butter, add sugar gradually, and then egg. Sift flour, salt, and baking powder, then add alternately with milk. Melt chocolate over low flame in a double boiler, then add with vanilla. Turn into twelve to fourteen small buttered molds, custard cups, or ramekins, filling two-thirds full. Cover with waxed paper and steam over gently boiling water for 1½ hours, adding more water to the steamer as necessary. Serve hot with:

Sterling Sauce:
¾ c. butter
2 c. light brown sugar

½ c. heavy cream
2 tsp. vanilla

Cream butter and sugar very thoroughly. Add cream gradually to prevent separation. The mixture will be fluffy and smooth. Put in double boiler and when sugar is dissolved, add vanilla. Serve hot or cold.

❦ Cherry Batter Pudding

June 1927

1–1½ lbs. cherries, stoned	2 tsp. baking powder
sugar	½ c. milk
1 c. flour	1 tsp. unsalted butter, melted

Fill baking dish three-quarters full of stoned cherries tossed with sugar. Sift dry ingredients, add milk and butter, beat till smooth, and spread over the fruit. Bake till brown at 350°F. Serve with Fruit Sauce:

Fruit Sauce:

2 c. fruit juice	sugar, if needed
1 tbsp. cornstarch	pinch salt
3 tbsp. flour	1 tsp. unsalted butter

Heat the juice. Mix cornstarch, flour, sugar, and salt and blend into juice. Cook 10 minutes over medium-low flame, stirring while it thickens. Remove from fire and add butter. Beat thoroughly and serve.

❦ Bread Pudding

June 1925

2 c. stale breadcrumbs	½ tsp. salt
1 qt. scalded milk	2 tbsp. butter
1 c. sugar	1 tsp. vanilla OR ¼ tsp. cinnamon and
2 eggs, well beaten	nutmeg OR grated orange or lemon rind

Soak bread in milk, cool, and add remaining ingredients. Bake at 350°F for 1 hour. Serve with any desired sauce. A much finer pudding may be made by using four eggs. Put two eggs and two yolks in the pudding. Make a meringue of the remaining whites, stiffly beaten with 2 tbsp. sugar added and beaten again. Spread this over warm pudding and return to oven till well puffed and delicately browned. This is good either hot or cold.

❦ Buttermilk Pie

September 1934
Contributed by Mrs. S.G.P., Wisconsin

2 tbsp. butter
2 tbsp. flour
2 egg yolks and 1 whole egg
1½ c. sugar

1 tbsp. lemon juice
2½ c. buttermilk
Meringue (pg. 189)

Cream the butter and flour together. Add the beaten yolks and whole egg. Add sugar, lemon juice, and buttermilk, stirring well. Pour into pie plates lined with rich pastry and bake at 450°F for 10 minutes before lowering to 350°F. Use two leftover egg whites for Meringue (pg. 189).

❦ Cocoanut Cream Pie

October 1931
Contributed by Mrs. Nora Townner

unbaked pie pastry
2 c. milk or cocoanut milk
2 eggs, separated
¼ tsp. salt

3 tbsp. sugar
1 c. grated unsweetened cocoanut
Meringue (pg. 189)

Line a pie tin with uncooked pie pastry, then add filling mixture made with milk, egg yolks, salt, sugar, and cocoanut as in regular custards. Bake at 450°F for 10 minutes, then reduce heat to 350°F and continue cooking for 30 minutes. Make Meringue with leftover egg whites (pg. 189). Spread on top of pie and bake until golden brown.

❧ Fruit Cobbler
1934

1 c. flour	1 tsp. melted butter
⅓ c sugar	1½ c. fresh stoned
¼ tsp. salt	cherries, chopped
1 tsp. baking powder	apples, cleaned
¼ c. milk	berries, etc.
1 egg, beaten	

Sift dry ingredients together and add milk, egg, and butter. Mix and pour over fruit arranged on bottom of buttered baking dish. Bake 25 minutes at 400°F till brown. Serve hot.

❧ Basic Honey Cake
August 1933

½ c. butter	2 tsp. baking soda
½ c. honey	4 tsp. baking powder
½ c. sugar	¼ tsp. salt
2 eggs, beaten	⅓ c. milk
2 c. cake flour	2 tsp. cream

Cream butter, honey, and sugar. Add beaten eggs and beat till blended. Sift dry ingredients and add alternately with milk. Do not beat, just mix slightly to blend. Add cream and pour batter into two buttered-papered-buttered 8-inch cake pans. Bake at 350°F for 20 minutes.

❧ Old-Fashioned Strawberry Shortcake
1934

2 heaping c. flour	¼ c. butter
2 tsp. baking powder	¾ c. milk
¼ tsp. salt	plenty of strawberries
2 tsp. sugar	

Mix the dry ingredients and sift. Rub in the butter with the tips of the fingers and add milk gradually. Toss on a floured board, divide into two parts, pat and roll out, and bake in buttered and floured layer cake tins at 400°F for 15 minutes. Split and butter. Sweeten strawberries to taste and place on the back of the stove till warmed. Crush slightly and put between and on top of the shortcake. Cover the top with whipped cream, sweetened and flavored with vanilla extract—to 1 c. cream add ¼ c. sugar and ½ tsp. vanilla.

❧ Blackberry Gingerbread Upside-Down Cake
September 1938

2 c. flour
½ c. sugar
1 tsp. ground ginger
1 tsp. cinnamon
½ tsp. allspice
¼ tsp. salt

½ tsp. baking soda
1½ tsp. baking powder
1 egg
¾ c. molasses
½ c. melted butter
¾ c. hot water

Sift dry ingredients together; then mix together egg, molasses, butter, and hot water; add dry ingredients. Beat till well blended. For the topping:

4 tbsp. butter
¾ c. berry juice
¾ c. brown sugar
2 c. blackberries, washed and drained

In a 9-inch cast-iron skillet, bring butter, juice, and sugar to a boil and boil 2 minutes. Add berries, then pour in batter carefully to cover all fruit. Bake at 350°F for 35 minutes. Let stand in pan 15 minutes before turning out, inverted, onto a plate or cake stand.

❧ Harvest Layer Cake
October 1933

3 c. sifted cake flour
3 tsp. baking powder
½ tsp. salt
½ c. butter
1¼ c. brown sugar, firmly packed
3 egg yolks, unbeaten
1 c. milk
1½ tsp. vanilla

Sift flour once, measure, add baking powder and salt, and sift together three times. Cream butter thoroughly, add sugar gradually, and cream together until light and fluffy. Add egg yolks; beat well. Add flour alternately with milk, a small amount at a time. Beat after each addition until smooth. Add vanilla. Bake in two greased 9-inch layer pans in moderate oven (375°F) for 30 minutes, or until done. Spread frosting between layers and on top and sides of cake. Sprinkle nuts over top and sides of cake while frosting is still soft, if desired. (*All measurements are level.*)

❦ Peach Dumplings
September 1912

Make a rich biscuit dough:
Mix and sift 2 c. flour, 3 tsp. baking powder, and 1 tsp. salt; quickly work in 4 tbsp. fat with a fork or dough blender. Add ⅔ c. milk all at once and stir lightly to make a soft dough. Turn out onto a slightly floured board and knead lightly for a few seconds.

Roll thin and cut out saucer-size. Place in each one peach peeled and sliced, sprinkle with sugar and small pieces of butter, roll up, and pinch together securely at the top. Place in a deep pan with pieces of butter, sugar, and peach slices surrounding them, pour over all 1 c. boiling water, and place in the oven at 350°F at once. Bake for half an hour. When nicely browned, serve hot with sugar and cream.

❦ Compote of Apples
October 1912

Make a syrup with 1 c. sugar, 1 c. water, 1-inch stick cinnamon, and the juice of one lemon. Boil slowly for 5 minutes. Core and pare six apples and cook them in the syrup till almost done. Drain and finish by baking at 350°F for 10–20 minutes, till very soft. Boil syrup down to a jelly. Fill apple centers with whipped cream. Pour syrup around apples; sprinkle with chopped nuts and put whipped cream around base.

❦ Apple Injun
February 1925

3 c. milk
½ c. cornmeal
1 tsp. cinnamon
1 tsp. salt
1½ c. brown sugar
1 pt. cold milk
1 qt. sweet apples, cut in eighths

Scald 3 c. milk and sift in cornmeal, stirring rapidly. Cook 5 minutes. Remove from fire and add cinnamon, salt, sugar, milk, and apples cut in eighths. Bake slowly in a deep, covered dish at 325°F for 4 hours. Serve with ice cream.

❧ Applesauce Cheese Tarts
October 1935

1 c. flour
¼ tsp. salt
⅓ c. butter
¼ c. grated cheddar cheese
2½ to 3 tbsp. ice water
Applesauce (pg. 150)

Sift flour and salt together into mixing bowl; add butter and cut in with pastry blender or two knives until particles are size of wheat grains. Stir in grated cheese. Add water by teaspoonfuls, tossing with fork till all flour is moistened. Gather into a ball and divide into four or five portions (one for each tart). Shape into balls, flatten on floured board, and roll out to fit over bottoms of inverted tart or muffin tins. Trim and prick all over with a fork. Chill for 30 minutes, then bake at 425°F for 10–15 minutes, till slightly browned. Remove from pans and cool. When cold, heap chilled applesauce into the shells and garnish with grated cheese or stiffly whipped cream.

❧ French Vanilla Ice Cream
1934

2 c. milk	⅛ tsp. salt
4 egg yolks	2 c. cream
⅔ c. sugar	½ tsp. vanilla

Scald milk in double boiler and pour slowly, whisking all the while, over egg yolks mixed with sugar and salt. Return to double boiler and simmer till the mixture coats a spoon. Chill in refrigerator, add cream and vanilla, and freeze in an ice cream maker according to manufacturer's instructions.

Variations:

Peanut Brittle Ice Cream: Grind peanut brittle to make 1 c. and add when ice cream is partially frozen.

Peppermint Ice Cream: Grind peppermint candy to equal 1 c. Omit vanilla and decrease sugar to ½ c. in foundation recipe. Add candy when ice cream is partially frozen.

Sour Cream Chocolate Ice Cream: To the foundation custard recipe add 2 oz. melted bittersweet chocolate and chill. Replace cream with 1 c. milk and 1 c. sour cream mixed with ⅓ c. sugar.

Lazy Day Late Summer Picnics

❧ Deviled Eggs
July 1914

4 hard-cooked eggs
¼ tsp. salt
½ tsp. Dijon mustard
⅛ tsp. pepper

1 tsp. vinegar
2 tsp. mayonnaise
paprika

Remove shells from eggs and cut in half lengthwise. Remove the yolks and mash them smooth with all remaining ingredients except paprika. Roll mixture into eight balls and place back in each half of egg. Garnish with sprinkle of paprika.

❧ French Salad Dressing
April 1917

2 tbsp. vinegar
6 tbsp. oil
½ tsp. salt

¼ tsp. pepper
paprika

Combine ingredients in a bowl. Beat steadily until thoroly blended and thick. Serve on fresh greens. The ingredients may be mixed, beaten, and put in a bottle. Just before using, shake the bottle hard, thoroly, to blend the ingredients.

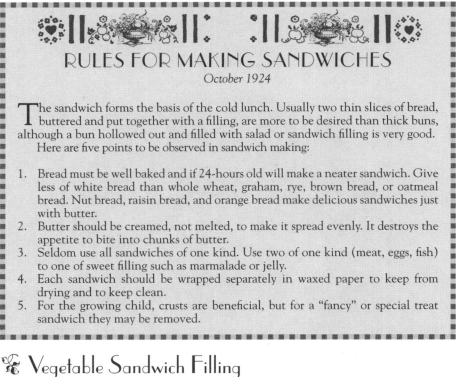

RULES FOR MAKING SANDWICHES
October 1924

The sandwich forms the basis of the cold lunch. Usually two thin slices of bread, buttered and put together with a filling, are more to be desired than thick buns, although a bun hollowed out and filled with salad or sandwich filling is very good. Here are five points to be observed in sandwich making:

1. Bread must be well baked and if 24-hours old will make a neater sandwich. Give less of white bread than whole wheat, graham, rye, brown bread, or oatmeal bread. Nut bread, raisin bread, and orange bread make delicious sandwiches just with butter.
2. Butter should be creamed, not melted, to make it spread evenly. It destroys the appetite to bite into chunks of butter.
3. Seldom use all sandwiches of one kind. Use two of one kind (meat, eggs, fish) to one of sweet filling such as marmalade or jelly.
4. Each sandwich should be wrapped separately in waxed paper to keep from drying and to keep clean.
5. For the growing child, crusts are beneficial, but for a "fancy" or special treat sandwich they may be removed.

❧ Vegetable Sandwich Filling
March 1928

1 c. sugar	12 medium red
4 tbsp. flour	peppers
1 tsp. ground mustard	1½ c. vinegar
2 tsp. salt	½ c. water
4 medium onions	

Thoroughly mix together the sugar, flour, mustard, and salt. Finely mince with peppers and onions, then drain off liquid. Mix all ingredients together, cook 20 minutes, and allow to cool before spreading on bread or toast.

❧ Sweet Chocolate Sandwiches
September 1929

2 oz. bittersweet chocolate	3 tbsp. heavy cream
2 tbsp. unsweetened butter	⅔ c. finely chopped walnuts
1 c. powdered sugar	

Melt the chocolate in a double boiler; add butter, sugar, and cream and cook gently for 5 minutes. Add nuts. Cool slightly and spread between buttered slices of bread.

❧ Country Kitchen Salad
July 1936

1 qt. cold, cooked cubed potatoes
1 tbsp. vinegar
1 tsp. salt
dash pepper and cayenne
¼ tsp. paprika
2 tbsp. oil

1 or 2 c. chopped celery, shredded
   lettuce, cucumber, sliced radishes
2 tbsp. chopped onion
4 hard-cooked eggs cut in eighths
½ c. chopped sweet pickle
2 c. salad dressing

Marinate cubed potatoes in vinegar, seasonings, and oil about 1 hour. Add the other ingredients. Blend with dressing. Part of the dressing may be mayonnaise, if desired. Salad is improved by standing, except for lettuce, which should not be added till just before serving.

Variations:
With carrots: Add ½–¾ c. finely shredded carrots to the dressing, omitting some of the other vegetables.

Marinating with sour cream: Omit oil, and instead heat ½ c. sour cream with vinegar and seasonings. Pour over potatoes and let stand until cold before mixing with other ingredients.

❧ German Potato Salad
February 1928

2 lbs. potatoes
salt
¾ lb. bacon
2 medium onions, sliced

½ c. vinegar
1 c. water
½ c. sugar

Boil potatoes without peeling. Drain, cool, peel, and chop. Salt lightly. Cut bacon into pieces and fry, then drain on paper. Cook onions in bacon fat till translucent. Add vinegar, water, and sugar. Stir to mix, bring to a boil, then add potatoes. Serve topped with bacon.

PICNIC EATS FOR A CROWD
June 1924

Every alive community has its get-together days when, as one family, the whole group plays together. The day of days seems to be Picnic Day. Instead of each family working independently, why not have the women get together and decide on a menu, estimate as nearly as possible the amount needed, and then assign the foods to the various families?

Three Suggestive Menus

1.	2.	3.
Hot wieners	Sliced meat	Sandwiches
Rolls	Buttered rolls	Potato salad
Vegetable salad	Vegetable salad	Vegetable salad
Fruit	Potato salad	Pie
Cup cakes	Fruit	Pickles
Doughnuts	Pickles	Fruit
Pickles	Sheet cake	Lemonade
Coffee	Cookies	Coffee
Lemonade	Coffee	

Fruit Sandwiches for 25

1 lb. raisins
½ lb. figs
1½ c. sugar
1 tbsp. flour

¼ c. cold water
½ c. orange juice
rind and juice of 2 lemons

Chop the raisins and figs, then combine with sugar and flour. Add water and fruit juice and cook in a double boiler until thick. Use two full slices of bread for each sandwich.

Ham Sandwiches for 25

1 lb. cooked ham
⅔ c. chopped pickle

1 c. sifted breadcrumbs
1 c. salad dressing

Mix all together, using two full slices of bread for each sandwich.

Egg Sandwich Filling for 25

24 hard-boiled eggs
1 c. sifted breadcrumbs
1½ tbsp. lemon juice

2 tsp. salt
salad dressing

Chop eggs, add crumbs and seasoning, and make into a paste with the salad dressing.

Cabbage Salad for 60

4 lbs. cabbage
½ c. chopped pimientos

1½ c. chopped pickle
3 c. salad dressing

Vegetable Salad for 60

6 qts. boiled, diced potatoes
1 qt. diced cucumbers
2 qts. cut celery
2 c. chopped onion

up to 5 tbsp. salt
2 tsp. pepper
dressing (about 4 c.)

❧ Two-Tone Meatloaf

July 1936

Part I
1 lb. ground veal
¾ lb. ground fat pork
3 crackers rolled into crumbs
1 tbsp. onion, chopped
½ tbsp. lemon juice
2 tbsp. cream
salt and pepper to taste

Part II
1 lb. ground fresh pork
½ lb. ground cured ham
2 eggs, beaten
½ c. breadcrumbs
½ c. catsup
½ tsp. salt
dash pepper

Combine each set of loaf materials separately, mixing very thoroughly. Mold the first mixture into a firm oval loaf, and over it put the second mixture in an even layer. Place on a sheet of parchment or wax paper and set on a rack in an open roasting or dripping pan. Bake uncovered at 325°F for 2 hours. Makes a 3-lb. loaf.

🍃 Angels on Horseback

August 1929

For this recipe of cheese with bacon (Angels on Horseback) we are grateful to the Girl Guides, English sisters of our own Girl Scouts. One-inch cubes of cheese are wrapped with a slice of bacon. This may be done so that the point of the green cooking stick holds the bacon firmly around the cheese during roasting. When the bacon is crisp, the "angel" is quite done and should be quickly popped into a roll. A lettuce leaf should be added to each roll. Plan for two "angels" per person.

🍃 Camp Fried Potatoes

June 1935

2 lbs. potatoes
1 or 2 onions

⅓ c. bacon or other fat
salt and pepper

Pare and slice potatoes into thin strips. Let soak in cold water till ready, then drain thoroughly. Slice onions. Put half the fat in hot skillet, add half potatoes and onions, and sprinkle with salt and pepper until beginning to brown and get clear. Push to one side, add remaining fat, potatoes, and onions and cook till all are done and nicely browned.

🍃 Rhubarb Punch

July 1932
Contributed by S.D.A.C.

3 c. rhubarb
3 c. water
1½ c. sugar

1 c. orange juice
3 tbsp. lemon juice
2 c. ice water

Cook rhubarb, cut in small pieces without peeling, in 3 c. water until very soft. Rub through a fine strainer, add sugar, and stir until it dissolves. Chill. Add fruit juice and ice water and pour into glasses. This makes six glasses.

🍃 Switchel

August 1923

This is a favorite summer drink for the eastern haymaker and harvester. Put 1 tsp. sugar, ¹⁄₁₆ tsp. powdered ginger, and 2 tsp. boiled cider in a glass and fill with water. Vinegar and molasses may be substituted for boiled cider, half and half.

Foundation Punch
August 1923

4 oranges	1 c. sugar
2 lemons	½ c. water

Squeeze the juice from the oranges and lemons. Boil the sugar and water to the thread stage. Add fruit juice and water to make 2 qts. 1 c. chopped mint leaves may be steeped in boiling water, strained, and substituted for part of the water.

Variety is gained by adding other fruit juices, sweetening if necessary with more of the syrup.

Berry Punch: Equal parts foundation punch and berry syrup.

Cherry or Currant Punch: Three parts foundation to one part cherry or currant juice.

Ginger Punch: Boil ½ lb. cut ginger in the foundation punch.

Grape Punch: Equal parts foundation punch and grape juice.

Lemonade
August 1912

Wash the lemons well before using, scrubbing them lightly with a small brush; rinse and dry. Roll them until soft and grate off the yellow rind, being careful not to get any of the bitter white skin. Cut the lemons in two and squeeze out the juice, adding 2 oz. sugar and 1 qt. water to three lemons. Let stand for half an hour and add a freshly cut slice of lemon to each glass. The water may be poured boiling hot over the lemon and sugar then cooled, if wished.

Raspberryade
July–August 1921

1 c. raspberry juice	1 tsp. sugar
2 tsp. lemon juice	3 bruised mint leaves
1 c. water	

Stir until sugar is dissolved and place on ice to cool.

Slow Cooker Fare

The farmer's wife did not have a slow cooker, but she would most assuredly have wanted one! The magazine was filled with articles extolling the virtues of time-saving devices of every stripe, especially those that would cut down on time spent in the kitchen, where the farmer's wife labored for so much of each and every day. She may have loved to cook for her family, but she also loved to spend time with them outside the kitchen, and she was always looking for ways to create more free family time. The slow cooker is perfect for preparing stress-free family meals if a small amount of time for their preparation can be set aside first thing in the morning to get the ingredients ready for the pot.

Not every recipe devised by *The Farmer's Wife* is appropriate or convenient for transferal to the domain of the slow cooker. In fact, a number of recipes tested for this section were utter fiascoes and were discarded. But casseroles, soups, and pudding-based desserts all appear in abundance on the pages of the magazine and are excellent slow-cooker fare. Almost all the recipes can be doubled or tripled with ease, either to accommodate large gatherings or to store as leftovers for later meals—exactly the sort of penny-saving foresight *The Farmer's Wife* practiced and appreciated.

About the Slow Cooker

Not all slow cookers are created equal. Nor are they all of equal size. In determining which slow cooker to use in devising and testing the recipes in this book, I opted first for large and second for reliability. Both criteria were met by the highly rated All Clad 6.5-quart model with ceramic insert. It cooks family-size meals and eliminates hot spots, cool spots, and inaccurate temperature measurements. Obviously, not every cook has this model in his or her kitchen. Be aware that cooking times, additions of liquid, and the amounts of ingredients that can be accommodated will all vary with the slow cooker used. You may find that a recipe in this book that calls for 3 hours of cooking time requires something closer to 4½ in your cooker. That 1 cup of liquid is not enough to soften your beans, or it could be the exact opposite. Get to know your slow cooker. If it is new to you, find out what its quirks and foibles are and take these into account as you become accustomed to cooking with it.

I discovered as I tested recipes that they generally tended to generate liquid in the slow cooker; the temperatures are low and the slow cooker is covered, so no liquid evaporates. Meat and vegetables give off water and juices as they cook,

which only adds to the amount of liquid in the pot. For many recipes, you will need to use less liquid than you are accustomed to when cooking on top of the stove or in the oven. Plan to keep an eye on the pot, though. If there is too little liquid to see the dish through to the end of its cooking time, add 1 tablespoon to ¼ cup at a time.

Another discovery is that vegetables take longer to cook with the slow cooker than with other methods. Be prepared for this, and also be aware that slow cooking can leach out much of a vegetable's vitamin content. Some nutritionists recommend a quick sauté on top of the stove before slow cooking to keep some of the nutrients locked inside the vegetable. If this method is not specifically called for in a recipe in this book, feel free to undertake it, if you desire.

One of the great advantages to the slow cooker is its warm function. When the dish is finished, it can remain in the pot at a consistent temperature until you and your family are ready to eat it. However, be forewarned: if it is placed for too long on warm, dishes, especially with meat, tend to dry out. If a dish is cooked many hours before you are ready to serve it, you would fare better to take the food out of the slow cooker, refrigerate it, and heat it up on top of the stove when you are ready to serve. It's an extra step, but is one that will abolish disappointment and disinterest in the food you find on your plate.

Soups are hands-down the best meals to make in the slow cooker. They are actually meant to generate liquid and they also improve with sitting—qualities that abolish at least two of the above-mentioned concerns. If you are just learning to use your slow cooker, try the soup recipes first. They are sure to be crowd pleasers! Feel free to experiment with soups. The soup recipes devised by *The Farmer's Wife* were mostly extremely simple ones and used only a few core ingredients. For example, you can easily substitute one vegetable for another when making a cream soup; the farmer's wife certainly would have.

There are some things that should never be cooked in the slow cooker, no matter how accomplished or adventurous the cook. These include chickens with skin on, particularly whole chickens or any other large, bony, and greasy pieces of meat; and red kidney beans from their raw state. In the first instance, you will discover a greasy, unappetizing, and potentially germ-laden mess awaiting you in the slow cooker. Since slow cooking is low-temperature cooking, fat from the skin of a chicken or other animal will gradually melt off into the pot, sit on its surface, and allow bacteria to grow and fester.

In the second instance, red kidney beans contain a high level of a toxin that can only be destroyed through boiling, which is never accomplished in the slow cooker. In fact, the low temperature of the slow cooker can actually increase the amount of the toxin. Precooked and/or canned kidney beans are an obvious exception, but extreme caution should be exercised if you plan to cook these beans in the slow cooker. To use dried kidney beans in the slow cooker, the FDA advises that you first soak them in fresh water for at least five hours, change the water, and boil the beans briskly for at least ten minutes.

Finally, not all recipes in this book require exceptionally long cooking. This does not abolish the usefulness of the slow cooker—far from it! In addition to the advantage of being able to walk away from a cooking meal for a period of hours, the slow cooker can boast these nifty features: it does not generate heat on a hot day (as I write this, it is a sweltering 94 degrees Fahrenheit outside, while inside my kitchen I am testing spoon corn bread in the slow cooker with no discomfort whatsoever); even on cool days, it frees up the oven and stove burner space for the preparation of other dishes. This should make the slow cooker the hands-down favorite tool of the holiday season.

Soups

🍂 Tomato Soup

August 1910

This is a simple, delicious soup that makes the most of very ripe, late-summer tomatoes. You may add a small carrot along with the onion, as The Farmer's Wife *did in the original recipe from 1910; or you can opt for a fresher tomato flavor and leave the carrot out. Beef broth was the liquid of choice in the original recipe, but chicken broth (or even water) better enhances the pungency of the main ingredient. Dill makes a lovely garnish. This recipe can easily be doubled or even tripled to feed a crowd, or to freeze until a midwinter meal requires the remembrance of a little summer sunshine.*

bouillon with toasted cheese triangles

green pea soup with minced hard-cooked egg

cream of tomato soup with chopped bacon

corn sausage chowder with French fried dumplings

vegetable soup with cheese bread roll

1 medium yellow onion, peeled, quartered, and sliced thin
1 small carrot, peeled and minced (optional)
1 tbsp. butter
½ c. chicken broth (or water or beef broth; see above note)
3 large, very ripe beefsteak tomatoes, about ¾ lb. each, washed, cored, and cut into bite-size pieces
1 tbsp. sugar
1 tsp. salt
1 tsp. chopped dill, or more to taste
2 tbsp. heavy cream, or more to taste

Sauté onion (and carrot, if using) in butter over low heat and cook until very soft, stirring occasionally. Deglaze with chicken broth and pour all into slow cooker. Add tomatoes and all their juice, salt, and sugar. Set slow cooker to low and cook 4 hours. Pour soup into blender and purée. Pour the soup through a strainer if you do not like the occasional bit of tomato skin turning up in an otherwise smooth soup. Pour into a pot to reheat when ready to serve. Add dill, stir in cream, and allow the soup to warm but do not boil. Check for seasoning and serve.

❧ Vegetable Soup
August 1910, March 1918

The farmer's wife was, most assuredly, NOT a vegetarian (except against her will in wartime, when meat shortages forced her to find ways to finagle a dinner out of beans, cheese, and eggs). Hence this recipe, which calls for the home cook to brown her vegetables in drippings. You can certainly follow this procedure or you can sweat the vegetables in olive oil before adding to the slow cooker. This recipe is equally good in winter when root vegetables are in abundance, or in late spring when the first carrots and potatoes are emerging. The Farmer's Wife would have added heavy cream to enrich the soup at the end. A more refreshing choice is a squeeze of fresh lemon juice.

2 tbsp. drippings from bacon, or olive oil
1 large yellow onion, chopped
3 garlic cloves, peeled and smashed
8 carrots, chopped
4 stalks celery, chopped
2 yellow-fleshed potatoes, such as
   Yukon gold

water
salt to taste
6 peppercorns
2 tbsp. flat parsley, washed and
   coarsely chopped
juice of 1 lemon

Wash the vegetables and chop, first peeling the carrots and potatoes. Sweat the onion in the drippings or oil with a little salt until softened. Add carrots, celery, and garlic and sweat until onion just begins to brown—about 5 minutes more. Add to slow cooker along with the potatoes, salt to taste (about 3 tsp.), peppercorns, and water to just fully cover the ingredients (about 6 c.). Set slow cooker to low and cook 4 hours until vegetables are done. If the broth is not flavorful enough, turn the slow cooker to high, remove lid, and continue to cook for ½ hour to evaporate the water and condense the flavors (if you like, a faster way is to boil the soup in a pot on top of the stove). Add parsley and stir to mix. Squeeze in lemon juice to taste—up to 1 whole lemon— and add seasonings to taste. Serve immediately.

❧ Cream of Potato Soup/Potato Chowder

August 1910, May 1918

The substitution of the whites of two leeks for onions will turn this easy American soup into a classic French vichyssoise (blend the soup after cooking and be sure to add the cream!). The farmer's wife would have approved; such a recipe would surely have enlivened her club luncheons. Or stay with the basics for a humble Sunday supper that sticks to the ribs, especially when served with a loaf of crusty bread and some butter.

6 large potatoes, scrubbed, peeled, and diced
1 large yellow onion, peeled and chopped
1 tbsp. olive oil
4 c. chicken broth

salt and pepper to taste
4 slices of bacon, chopped and fried, to garnish
OR chopped parsley or chives
½ c. heavy cream (optional)

Place the potatoes in the slow cooker. Heat the olive oil in a large skillet over a medium flame and add the onion, stirring until it is soft and beginning to brown. Add the chicken broth and stir to deglaze the bottom of the pan, then add the contents to the slow cooker. Set to low and cook 4 hours. The soup may be served hot with the potatoes left in pieces and a garnishing of bacon or parsley.

Variation:

For a smooth soup, you may let the soup cool slightly and purée it in the blender, adding cream and parsley or chives to garnish. Taste for seasoning and add salt and pepper if desired.

❧ Clam Chowder

November 1928

6 slices bacon, diced
1 qt. potatoes, peeled and diced
4 medium onions, peeled and diced
4 tbsp. butter
salt and pepper

3 c. fish stock or clam juice
1 qt. clams, removed from shells and their liquor reserved
1 c. milk
1 c. heavy cream

Fry the bacon, place in slow cooker, and fry onion in the drippings. Add to slow cooker with potatoes, butter, salt and pepper to taste, and stock. Set slow cooker to low and cook 3 to 4 hours until potatoes are tender. When potatoes are soft, add clams and their liquor, milk, and cream. Cook until heated through, about ½ hour to 1 hour. Add seasonings to taste. Serve hot with crackers on top.

❧ Black Bean Soup

January 1912

These days, when we think of black bean soup, most of us tend to think of a Cuban variety, laced with lime juice, cilantro, and coriander. But black beans were a staple for the farmer's wife from the very beginning. She certainly recognized the benefit of a bit of acidity to offset the blandness of the beans (seen here with the use of lemon rind and juice), but otherwise her soup followed along the lines of most of the dishes emanating from her kitchen: not much spice and a few vegetables to add body. You may choose to add some cayenne pepper in the cooking, you can serve it with a side of hot sauce, or you can enjoy this soup "naked" as it is prescribed below.

1 tbsp. butter
1 medium onion, chopped
6 celery stalks, chopped
2 tbsp. mustard
1 lemon

1 pt. black beans, soaked overnight
6 c. chicken broth (or water, for a
   vegetarian option)
salt and pepper
plain yogurt or sour cream to serve

Cook onion and celery in butter over medium-low heat until soft. Add beans, mustard, rind of lemon, and broth to slow cooker. Set to low and cook 6 to 8 hours until tender. Season with salt, pepper, and the juice of the lemon. Ladle some of the soup into a blender, purée, and return to the slow cooker, mixing thoroughly. Serve with a dollop of plain yogurt or sour cream.

❧ Cream of Celery Soup

October 1911

The beauty of this recipe and others of its ilk throughout the pages of The Farmer's Wife is its inherent simplicity. How can you go wrong with cream and butter? Please note that it's important to trim the tough strings from the largest celery stalks and discard them; otherwise, they'll turn up in your soup after blending with unpleasant results.

1 bunch celery, washed, trimmed of
   its tough outer strings, and
   chopped fine
15 peppercorns
1 bay leaf

4 c. salted water or vegetable broth
2 tbsp. butter
salt and pepper to taste
¼ c. heavy cream (or more, to taste)
chopped parsley to serve

Add first four ingredients to slow cooker, placing the bay leaf and peppercorns in a muslin spice bag, if desired, for easy removal after cooking. Set slow cooker to low and cook 4 to 5 hours until celery is tender. Remove peppercorns and bay leaf. Allow to cool and run celery and broth through blender. Reheat in a large pot over the stove. When the soup is heated through, season with butter, salt, and pepper; remove from flame; and add cream, stirring to mix. Ladle into bowls and garnish with chopped parsley.

Stews, Casseroles, and Sauces

the STEW'S done!

Beef Stew with Carrots

A simple Farmer's Wife classic. If you like a thick stew, dredge the beef in seasoned flour before browning; if thin, omit flour altogether.

2½ lbs. lean stewing beef cut in
  1-inch pieces
1 tbsp. olive oil
flour, if desired
salt and pepper

5 cloves garlic, smashed
5 carrots, peeled and chopped
4 to 5 sprigs fresh thyme
2 c. beef broth or water

Trim beef of fat and brown in olive oil, in batches if necessary, to prevent crowding. Or you can dredge beef in flour seasoned with salt and pepper before browning for a thickened stew. Add garlic for last 2 minutes of browning, then transfer beef and garlic to slow cooker. Drain fat from pan and deglaze with water or broth. Add liquid to slow cooker along with carrots and thyme. Set slow cooker to low and cook 7 to 8 hours until beef is tender but not dry. Serve with buttered noodles.

❧ Casserole of Fowl

October 1929

The farmer's wife would have used a whole, cut-up chicken for this dish. You can do the same or use chicken pieces. Skinning before cooking prevents too much grease from forming at the top of the dish, which creates an environment where bacteria can thrive at low heat (not to mention creating a greasy, unappetizing mess). Skinning and trimming off extra fat is recommended for all slow-cooker recipes.

3 to 4 lbs. chicken pieces, skinned	2 small potatoes, peeled and chopped
3 tbsp. olive oil	6 carrots, peeled and sliced
salt and pepper	1 c. water or chicken broth
flour for dredging, if desired	1 bay leaf
1 onion, sliced thin	parsley for garnishing
2 stalks celery, sliced	

Brown skinless chicken pieces in oil over high flame and sprinkle with salt and pepper. Or, dredge the chicken in seasoned flour then brown. Drain on paper towels and place in slow cooker. Add onion and celery to the browning skillet and cook until soft; add salt and pepper to season. Add to slow cooker. Deglaze pan with water or chicken broth and add to slow cooker along with carrots, potatoes, and bay leaf. Set slow cooker to low and cook 4 to 5 hours. A longer cooking time will result in chicken that is falling off the bone. Add seasonings to taste and serve garnished with chopped parsley.

Variations:

Chicken with Dumplings: To make an even heartier meal of this casserole, the farmer's wife added dumplings. It is a tradition many in the United States now call "Southern," but its origins date back several hundreds of years and span Europe. The technique here is adapted from Lynn Alley's excellent book, *The Gourmet Slow Cooker.*

Sift together 2 c. flour, 1 tbsp. baking powder, and ½ tsp. salt. Add 1 scant c. milk and 3 tbsp. melted butter and mix well. A half-hour before the chicken is cooked, turn up the heat on the slow cooker to high. Drop the dumplings by the teaspoonful into the chicken casserole, cover, and cook 30 minutes until dumplings are cooked through. If you are not a veteran dumpling maker, you may want to test one dumpling by dropping it into boiling salted water. If the dumpling does not hold its shape, add a small amount of flour to the dough.

Casserole de Boeuf: The Farmer's Wife mandated this variation of the above casserole stating, "Same as for Fowl, using round steak or stewing beef. Serve with tomato slices seasoned with salt and browned in butter."

Brunswick Stew

March 1938

Brunswick County, Virginia, claims to be the region where this dish originated. Legend has it that a local chef out on a hunting expedition in the early nineteenth century stewed some freshly slaughtered squirrels with onions and bread over a campfire for the evening meal. By the time The Farmer's Wife got ahold of the dish in March 1938, squirrel had morphed into chicken and quite a number of vegetables had been added to the mix. You can try out this fancier version, or stick to basics with just the chicken, breadcrumbs, seasoning, and butter to stew in the pot.

1 stewing chicken cut in pieces, skin removed	4 potatoes, washed, peeled, and diced
½ c. breadcrumbs	1 pt. lima beans, fresh
salt and pepper	8 tomatoes, chopped
2 onions, peeled and sliced	corn cut from 8 ears
2 tbsp. olive oil	lump of butter
	¾ c. water or broth

Mix the breadcrumbs with seasoning and dip the chicken in it to coat. Heat olive oil in large skillet over medium-high flame. Add chicken and brown on all sides; place in slow cooker. Add onions to skillet and cook until lightly browned; add to slow cooker along with remaining ingredients. Set slow cooker to low and cook 4 to 6 hours until chicken and vegetables are all very tender. Season to taste. Serve hot.

Lentil Stew

February 1922

Lentils were a staple of the farmer's wife's pantry, as was lentil soup, one of the magazine's recipes that was adapted to make this hearty stew—a whole meal in itself. The blandness of the grains and legumes may typically require more salt than you might originally conceive; however, start with a smaller quantity for cooking and season with more as necessary once the cooking is complete. Surprisingly, butter elevates this from humble hominess to a truly delicious repast.

1 c. brown lentils, rinsed	5 cloves
½ c. barley, rinsed	1 tsp. salt, or more, to taste
2 large carrots, washed, peeled, and finely chopped	6 c. water
2 stalks celery, washed and finely chopped	1 lb. spinach, washed and chopped
1 small onion, finely chopped	butter to serve

Place all ingredients except spinach and butter in the slow cooker. Set to low and cook 4 hours. In the last half-hour or hour of cooking, add the spinach and stir. When ready to serve, taste for seasonings, adding more salt and some pepper, as necessary. Ladle into bowls and top each serving with ½ tbsp. butter. Serve with rice, if desired.

❦ Chili con Carne

February 1926, December 1928

To The Farmer's Wife, chili con carne was high exotica. It was a dish from a hot, distant land that incorporated a strange mixture of meat and beans and (gasp!) spice. The Farmer's Wife was nothing if not bland of palate. Still, the dish makes numerous appearances in the pages of the magazine over the years, a testament to the fact that as temperate as her everyday fare may have been, the farmer's wife maintained a hearty curiosity for that which was new to her, especially if it meant the discovery of a meal that drew her away from the realm of kitchen-bound monotony. At any rate, chili con carne would have called for many items already in the farmer's wife's larder: onions, garlic, beef, tomatoes, and beans. Often, however, the recipes in the magazine more closely resembled a simple stew rather than chili. The Farmer's Wife often attempted to define and re-create this alien meal. It should be noted that not all chili powders are created equal. Some are mild, and some run very hot. Know which kind you are using before you decide how much you will add. In testing the recipe, I used a moderately spicy Indian chili powder, which gave a pleasantly spicy flavor.

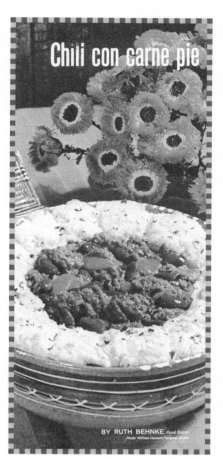

Chili con carne pie

BY RUTH BEHNKE *Food Editor*
Photo: William Hazzard/Feragnen Studio

2 c. pinto beans, soaked overnight in enough water to cover
2 c. crushed tomatoes
1½ lbs. beef, such as chuck or brisket, trimmed of fat and sliced in ½-inch slices, each then cut in half lengthwise and sliced again to make short, thin slices
2½ tsp. salt (or more, to taste)
2 tbsp. sugar or brown sugar
1 bay leaf

4 c. water
2 medium onions, quartered and thinly sliced
2 slices bacon, chopped
1 tbsp. ground cumin
1 tbsp. ground coriander
1 tsp. moderately spicy chili powder (more or less, to taste)
½ tsp. ground ginger
chopped cilantro, if desired, to garnish

Drain the beans and place them in the slow cooker with the tomatoes, beef, salt, sugar, bay leaf, and water. In a medium skillet fry the bacon with the onions over a medium-low heat until the onions are soft. Add the spices, stir to mix, and add the mixture to the slow cooker. Stir to mix, making sure all ingredients are covered with water. Set slow cooker to low and cook 8 hours. Serve over cooked rice and garnish with chopped cilantro.

Tamale Pie Dinner
October 1920

Here is a reasonable approximation of the above, so-called "Spanish" tamale pie dinner. It is, in fact, wholly American: a somewhat homier version of chili con carne. It eliminates more contemporary additions of sliced black olives and prepared chili sauce but substitutes ground beef for beef neck bone, which is a greasy challenge for the slow cooker.

1 tbsp. olive oil	½ to 1½ tsp. chili powder, to taste
1 lb. ground chuck	2½ tsp. salt
2 medium yellow onions, chopped	1 c. cornmeal
3 to 4 cloves garlic, smashed	1½ c. chicken broth
14-oz. can pinto beans, rinsed and drained	1½ c. crushed tomatoes
1 tbsp. ground cumin	⅓ c. raisins
1 tsp. ground coriander	1 c. sharp cheddar cheese, grated

Heat the oil in a large skillet over a medium flame and add the meat and onions. Cook, stirring frequently, until onions are soft and meat has lost its pink sheen. Add all the remaining ingredients except the cheese (or add the cheese to the mix, if you prefer), stir well, and evenly spread into slow cooker. Cover and cook on low for 4 hours, leaving the lid ajar for the last hour to evaporate some of the moisture. If you have not added the cheese to the mixture before cooking, sprinkle it over individual portions before serving.

Variation:
Substitute corn kernels for the raisins.

Tomato Sauce
April 1925

Here's a version of spaghetti sauce without the beef, although it's hardly a vegetarian option thanks to the salt pork. The farmer's wife didn't always eat meat with each and every meal. During wartime the magazine was rife with meatless solutions that incorporated grains, eggs, and cheese. You can make the sauce meatless, should you wish to, by merely omitting the pork and browning the vegetables in olive oil. To make this a tad more Italian, substitute 3 cloves of garlic for the cloves.

1 c. meat liquid from slow cooker	2 tbsp. unsalted butter, slightly softened
¼ c. white wine	2 tbsp. flour
2 sprigs fresh herbs, such as rosemary or thyme	salt and pepper to taste

Fry out the pork, add to the slow cooker, and lightly brown the vegetables in the drippings. Drain. Add to slow cooker along with tomato and spices. Set to low and cook 2 to 3 hours until the flavors are well incorporated. Season to taste. Serve over spaghetti and top with parmesan cheese

❧ Vegetable Stew
March 1930

In March 1930, the farmer's wife clearly found herself with a surplus of winter-stored root vegetables and canned vegetables and a deficit of ideas for what to serve for dinner. In one article, there were recommendations for four varieties of Vegetable Stew. The combinations are left intact below. You can use any of the recommendations or devise your own.

Version I	Version II	Version III	Version IV
½ c. carrot	2 sweet potatoes	1 c. potato	½ c. onion
1½ c. potatoes	1 small onion	1 c. tomatoes	½ c. potato
1 c. lima beans	1½ c. green beans	1 onion	¼ c. celery
1 c. peas	1 c. corn	½ c. celery	1½ c. tomato
¼ c. onion	4 okra pods	½ c. carrots	⅓ c. carrot
½ c. tomato	1 large tomato	½ c. peas	½ c. chopped okra
1 tbsp. butter	salt and pepper	½ c. cabbage	butter

Basic instructions for all versions: Wash all vegetables, peel those that need it, and shuck or shell corn, beans, and peas. Chop large vegetables into small pieces. Heat olive oil or bacon drippings in a large skillet and brown onions, carrots, celery, and the like. Add

to slow cooker with remaining ingredients and ½ to 1 c. water or stock. Cook 2 to 4 hours until all the vegetables are tender, stirring occasionally and making sure there is ample water at the bottom of the pot. Taste for seasonings and add salt, pepper, lemon juice, and/or any herbs you desire. Serve over rice, noodles, or cornbread..

❧ Slow Cooker Gravy

¼ c. minced salt pork, or 1 to 2 slices of
  bacon, chopped
½ c. chopped carrot
½ c. chopped celery
1 small chopped onion
1 qt. chopped tomato

1 bay leaf
5 cloves
salt and pepper to taste
parsley to garnish
cooked spaghetti and grated parmesan
  cheese to serve

After removing cooked meat from slow cooker, pour liquid into a large stockpot along with wine and herbs. Bring to a boil, then turn down flame to achieve a consistent simmer. With your fingers, on a small plate, mash together butter and flour to make small balls. Drop them one at a time into the simmering gravy and whisk until they are incorporated. Add one at a time until the gravy has achieved the desired thickness. Remove from flame, discard herbs, and taste for seasoning. Pour into a gravy boat or small pitcher to serve.

For plain meat dishes or when you need to add a little more pep, these sauces are sure to please.

MEAT SAUCES THAT MEN LIKE
A Plain Dish with a Good Taste Goes Down
By Anna Coyle
January 1923

Men's tastes in matters of food are not quite the same as women's. A study of Friend Husband's favorite meat dishes should include relishes, sauces, and spicy flavors which, added to the ordinary meat dish, transform it into something not ordinary at all.

Sauces that give variety to meat dishes are especially welcome at this season when there is likely to be an abundance of beef or pork on hand after killing.

With beef serve these sauces: parsley, mushroom, horseradish, tomato, Creole, chili, Worcestershire, chow chow, or Maître D'Hotel butter.

With lamb serve: mint sauce, caper sauce, currant jelly, or mint jelly.

With pork serve: tart apple sauce, apple jelly, or apricot sauce.

Serve cranberry sauce with turkey, currant jelly with roast chicken, and apple sauce with roast duck.

Creole Sauce

2 tbsp. onion, chopped
4 tbsp. green pepper, finely chopped
2 tbsp. butter
2 tbsp. flour
1 c. crushed tomato
1 c. brown meat stock
salt and pepper

Cook onion and pepper with the butter 5 minutes, stir in flour, and gradually add tomatoes and meat stock. Cook 15 minutes.

Horseradish Sauce

4 tbsp. grated horseradish
½ tsp. salt
⅛ tsp. pepper
½ tsp. dried mustard
1 tsp. sugar
1 tbsp. vinegar
1 c. whipped cream

Combine first 6 ingredients and fold into the whipped cream.

Mint Sauce

¼ c. mint leaves, finely chopped
1 tbsp. powdered sugar

½ c. vinegar
½ tsp. salt

Combine ingredients and let stand on the back of the stove for 15 minutes before serving.

Currant Sauce

1 c. boiling water
½ c. vinegar
½ c. currant jelly

1 c. currants, chopped
1 tbsp. flour

Heat water, vinegar, currant jelly, and currant together and simmer for 10 minutes. Thicken with flour rubbed to a smooth paste in a little cold water. Cook thoroughly.

Caper Sauce

¼ c. butter
½ tsp. salt
⅛ tsp. pepper

½ tbsp. parsley, finely chopped
¾ tbsp. lemon juice

Melt half the butter, stir in the flour, and gradually add the hot liquid, stirring constantly. Add the salt and the remaining butter and capers just before serving.

Maître D'Hotel Butter

½ c. butter
1½ c. hot water or mutton broth
2 tbsp. flour

½ tsp. salt
½ c. capers, drained

Cream the butter and mix in salt, pepper, and parsley, then lemon juice very slowly.

Main Dishes

❧ Roast Pork and Apples

October 1922

The Farmer's Wife *was big on roasts; they were a convenient way to cook up enough meat for an entire hungry family, and any leftovers had numerous practical purposes—for sandwich filling, breakfast hash, and next-day soups or casseroles. But she did not entirely eschew smaller cuts, like pork chops. This recipe pays homage to her commitment to that famous autumn combination of pork and apples, using pork chops rather than a whole pork loin to allow for easy serving (no carving!). For best results, chop apples and onion to a uniform size.*

6 boneless pork loin chops, cut
  ¾-inch thick
olive oil
salt and pepper
1 medium onion, peeled and chopped

6 sour apples, peeled, cored, and chopped
4 cloves garlic, peeled and smashed
1 tbsp. brown sugar
¼ c. apple cider
nutmeg

Brown pork chops in a large heavy-bottomed skillet in 1 tbsp. olive oil over high heat and sprinkle with salt and pepper. Place in one layer at bottom of slow cooker. Add 1 tbsp. more olive oil to skillet, add onion, and sprinkle with a little salt and pepper. Sauté onion until soft. Add apples and garlic and sauté an additional 2 minutes. Spoon mixture over pork chops, sprinkle the sugar over the mixture, and pour in cider. Cook 4 to 6 hours on low until tender (the exact time will depend greatly on the quality of meat used). A generous grating of fresh nutmeg just before serving vastly enhances this dish.

❧ Adouba

June 1938

This is a dish of Greek origin where pork is rendered especially savory with spices, vinegar, and long slow cooking.

2 lbs. boneless
  pork shoulder
1 tbsp. olive oil
dash cayenne
spice bag with:
1 tsp. whole cloves

1 tsp. whole or ½ tsp.
  ground allspice
2 sticks cinnamon
2-inch piece ginger
¾ c. cider vinegar
1 tsp. salt

Cut pork in squares, trim off fat, and brown in the oil over a high flame. Add to slow cooker with remaining ingredients. Set on low and cook for 4 hours until very tender. Serve with rice.

❧ Lamb Curry

April 1926

The Farmer's Wife *made curry with a very small amount of the mixed spice, boosting its sauce with a generous dollop of milk. It is not a combination we think much of these days, but for a time it was a very popular Americanization of Indian so-called curries of vegetables or meat cooked with a variety of spices and, often, yogurt. (If you've ever seen the 1940s film* Adam's Rib, *starring Spencer Tracy and Katharine Hepburn, you've witnessed the two main characters in their kitchen whipping up a lamb curry from a leftover roast, some curry powder, and milk on the maid's night off.) The recipe below attempts to concede to both old and new. It calls for prepackaged, nondescript curry powder instead of a more traditionally Indian breakdown of specific spices, but it is also enhanced by tomatoes (for some much-needed acidity), raisins (a little sweet to balance the acid), and cilantro, which no respectable Indian kitchen would ever do without. Serve over basmati rice for an even more authentic meal.*

2½ lbs. lamb for stew, cut in 1-inch pieces	salt
2 tbsp. olive oil	pepper
2 medium onions, chopped	1 c. chicken broth or water
2 cloves garlic, smashed	1 c. crushed tomatoes
2 to 3 tsp. curry powder (depending on the heat of the spice and your own preference)	½ c. shredded unsweetened coconut
	½ c. raisins
	chopped fresh cilantro, to garnish
8 green cardamom pods	yogurt to serve
1 tsp. ground cumin	cooked rice to serve

Trim the lamb of fat, then brown in a large skillet in the oil over a high flame and sprinkle with a little salt. Remove the meat with a slotted spoon and place in the slow cooker. Drain the skillet of fat, then add onions, garlic, and a little more olive oil, if necessary. Cook until onions are soft and slightly brown. Add curry powder, cardamom, and cumin and stir for several seconds to mix. Add to slow cooker. Deglaze skillet with chicken broth or water, add tomatoes, and stir briefly. Add to slow cooker. Set the slow cooker on low and cook for 4 to 5 hours until very tender. Add the coconut and raisins after 3 hours to preserve their flavor. Serve over rice with a dollop of yogurt and cilantro to garnish.

Variations:

You may substitute beef or chicken for lamb. Omit the crushed tomatoes for a simpler flavor.

In December 1914, The Farmer's Wife also recommended Rabbit Curry. "Europeans frequently substitute rabbit curry or rabbit pie for the Christmas fowl," she instructed. "Clean [and skin] a young rabbit. Cut into pieces as for frying. Fry in bacon fat until a light brown. Fry 3 sour apples and 2 onions, finely chopped. Add 1 tsp. curry powder and soup stock, salt, and pepper to taste." Add all to the slow cooker and follow the instructions above for Lamb Curry. Serve hot over rice or boiled, buttered noodles.

❧ Swedish Meatballs

May 1928

This is a highly traditional version of the Swedish Meatballs recipe, and one that was not originally enriched with sour cream when it ran in the magazine. If your taste buds require it, you may choose to add a small amount of sour cream after cooking.

I lb. lean ground beef
½ lb. lean ground pork
I medium potato, grated fine
I egg
¾ c. fine dry breadcrumbs
½ tsp. pepper
I tsp. salt
½ tsp. sugar

I small onion, grated
2 to 3 tbsp. milk
3 tbsp. butter
½ c. sour cream, if desired
¼ c. chopped parsley, to garnish
buttered egg noodles or boiled potatoes,
   to serve

Beat egg well and combine all ingredients, down to the milk. Form into 1-inch balls. Brown in butter. Drain and place in slow cooker. Add I c. beef broth. Set slow cooker to low and cook 2 to 3 hours until cooked through but not mushy. Be sure to stir occasionally to ensure that all sides of the meatballs are cooking in the broth so they will not dry out. Remove meatballs with a slotted spoon to a bowl. Taste the broth for seasoning and adding sour cream, if desired. Pour a little or all of the sauce over meatballs and garnish with parsley. Serve over buttered egg noodles or boiled potatoes.

❧ Ground Steak, Italian Style

November 1917

This recipe is for spaghetti and meatballs, plain and simple! Be sure to stir every now and then to ensure that the tops of the meatballs are covered with sauce so they don't dry out while cooking.

2 lbs. ground sirloin
2 tbsp. olive oil, plus extra for browning
   the meatballs
¼ c. stale breadcrumbs
I tsp. salt
pepper to taste
⅛ tsp. grated onion

2 eggs
2 28-oz. cans crushed tomatoes
I c. water
I onion
2 cloves garlic, crushed
I tsp. salt
2 tbsp. butter

Mix first seven ingredients and form into small meatballs the size of walnuts. Brown in a large skillet in enough olive oil to cover the bottom over a medium-high flame. Turn several times to brown all over. Remove browned meatballs with a slotted spoon and place on a paper towel to drain. While the meatballs are browning, mix all the remaining ingredients in the slow cooker. Add the meatballs once they are drained. Set slow cooker to low and cook 4 hours. Serve "in the center of a platter with macaroni all around and sauce over all."

❦ Limas and Lamb Stew

July 1930

Here is a flavorful ode to summer, The Farmer's Wife style. Use young lamb rather than older, tougher mutton for this dish, and sweet new potatoes freshly dug from the ground. You could even use fresh limas, which should be added to the pot about 1 or 2 hours after you've begun cooking, to prevent them from going mushy in the pot. For a true Southern flavor, serve with cornbread or biscuits.

3 lbs. lamb stew meat, trimmed of fat and
    cut in cubes
4 slices bacon, cut in pieces
1 large yellow onion, thinly sliced
4 garlic cloves, smashed and peeled
2 large carrots, washed, peeled, and cubed

1 c. water or chicken broth
2 lbs. new potatoes, scrubbed, peeled,
    and cubed
1 c. dried lima beans, rinsed
salt and pepper to taste
parsley to garnish

Place bacon in a large skillet and fry out over a medium-high flame. Add the lamb, onions, and carrots. Cook until lamb is browned and onions are softened. Add garlic just before the onions are done. Place in slow cooker, deglaze skillet with chicken broth or water, and pour contents into slow cooker. Add to pot with all remaining ingredients except parsley. Set slow cooker to low and cook 5 to 6 hours until meat is very tender. Make sure to keep an eye on the liquid, adding small additional amounts if necessary. Season to taste. Serve hot with chopped, fresh parsley for garnish.

Variation:

From November 1929 comes this simple variation on the above, for Ragout of Lamb and Early Vegetables. Substitute 1 pt. small peeled pickling onions for the yellow onion (you may brown them quickly on top of the stove before adding to the slow cooker) and omit the limas. Substitute a few sprinklings of celery salt for some of the plain salt, add 1 to 2 tbsp. Worcestershire sauce to the pot, and add the grated rind and juice of 1 lemon just before serving. One-half hour before the stew is cooked, turn up heat to high and thicken the liquid with balls made of equal parts butter and flour. Stir in before re-covering the pot. Season to taste before serving and top with croutons.

"Barbecued" Beef on Toasted Buns

Utah Club Plate Luncheon
Submitted by Mrs. P. H. Rasmussen
October 1939

You probably know them as "sloppy joes," but to the lunching ladies of Utah in 1939, these hot open-face sandwiches were considered elegant club fare. Why they were considered "barbecued" is anyone's guess, but the resulting dish is delicious and pungent, thanks to the use of green rather than red tomatoes. Hamburger buns were surely the bread of choice here, but you may substitute something more contemporary, such as ciabatta rolls or small challah buns.

⅓ c. olive oil
3 lbs. ground lean beef
1 large yellow onion, peeled
   and chopped
1 c. celery, washed and chopped

2 c. green tomatoes, chopped fine and all
   liquid reserved for the slow cooker
salt and pepper to taste
buns
butter

In a large skillet, brown beef, onion, and celery in the olive oil over a medium-high flame. Add to the slow cooker with the green tomatoes and their juice and salt and pepper to taste. Set slow cooker to low and cook 2 to 3 hours until the meat is cooked through and the tomatoes have softened into a sauce. Check for seasoning. Split the buns, toast them, spread butter on them, and top with the beef mixture.

"Barbecued" Ribs

February 1939

As long as men have been hunting, they have been throwing meat over an open fire to cook it. Barbecue, as food historian Alan Davidson points out, is and always has been a supremely male activity. This explains why The Farmer's Wife *put the name of this recipe in quotes—a woman was assumed to be the cook. She was also going to do the cooking in the oven rather than over a pit of coals or bundle of kindling.*

3 to 4 lbs. spareribs, cut into
   individual pieces
2 tbsp. butter, melted
¼ c. vinegar
1 tbsp. Worcestershire sauce

1 tbsp. brown sugar
1 tsp. celery salt (or regular salt, if
   you prefer)
½ tbsp. mustard
2 tbsp. ketchup

In a large skillet, brown the spareribs on all sides over a medium-high flame. Meanwhile, mix up all the remaining ingredients in a bowl. When the ribs are browned on all sides, transfer them to the slow cooker and spoon the sauce over them, turning to coat on all sides. Set the slow cooker to low and cook 3 to 4 hours until the meat is very tender. Turn the ribs now and again to make sure all sides are immersed in the sauce to prevent them from drying out. Serve at once.

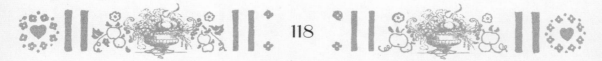

❦ Veal Casserole

February 1939

This unthrillingly titled dish is actually a take on two Franco-Russian classics: Beef Stroganoff and Veal Soblianka (a standby at the Russian Tea Room restaurant in New York City). Both dishes make use of meat, mushrooms, and sour cream. No matter which meat you choose to use, you can't go wrong. Since sour cream will break apart from long cooking, mix it into the sauce after cooking for best results.

6 tbsp. butter
1 small yellow onion, chopped
1 lb. mushrooms, stemmed and sliced
2 lbs. veal steak, cubed or sirloin, cut into
   1-inch-thick strips

1 tsp. salt
1 tsp. paprika
¼ c. water or chicken broth
1 c. sour cream at room temperature
noodles to serve

In a large skillet, melt butter over a medium heat. Add the onions and cook until just translucent. Add the mushrooms, then the meat, and stir until the meat has lost its pink sheen. Add all to the slow cooker along with the seasonings and water or chicken broth. Set to low and cook 2 to 3 hours until the meat is very tender. Stir in the sour cream and mix well to incorporate. Season to taste and serve hot over buttered noodles.

FOR YOUR KITCHEN
Some of the Devices That Are True Economies for the Farm Woman
By Wenonah Stevens Abbott
November 1914

The farm wife owes it to her family as well as to herself to have time to devote to the side of life that brings joy to the home circle. She can obtain this time only through better planning and better equipment of her workshop—the kitchen.

The farm wife needs to cultivate a conscience as to the amount of strength she can afford to expend in the general routine of housework. The failures in properly learning to estimate values in woman's work are the cause of the false economics in kitchen appliances.

To escape from the drudgery of life, the housewife must select the best procurable time- and labor-saving tools, so group them as to be able to use them without waste of motion, and adopt a system that will reduce many of the mechanical tasks to automatic process.

[Editor's note: In 1924 some of these devices would have been:]

The three-burner stove [which] cooks dinner over a quick, safe, economical fire.

The tea wagon [which] saves countless steps to and from the dining table.

A bread maker to take the place of hand-kneading.

And, one of the housewife's truest allies, the fireless cooker, [which] "prevents worry and nerve strain, and saves fuel and food values. It automatically attends to the cooking while the housewife looks after other matters. Even with the cheap models, breakfast may be prepared the previous evening and the cooking of dinner and supper got out of the way before breakfast dishes are washed."

❧ Delicious Ham Dishes

Contributed by Anna Coyle
February 1923

"No other meat food lends itself to quite the variety of dishes as does the ham now hanging in the smokehouse. There are many ways of using ham besides the usual boiled or fried ways. These ways include delicious combinations in casserole dishes, creamed dishes . . . and ham á la King." So said The Farmer's Wife in February 1923. Indeed, ham was then and continued to be a mainstay of the farm kitchen throughout the tenure of the magazine. The following recipe for "baked" ham is simple and familiar—just the anticipated clove-studding, a bit of brown sugar, and some apple cider to sweeten.

1 ham, with bone in	1 c. apple cider
15 cloves	½ c. raisins (optional)
¼ c. brown sugar	

Rub the ham all over with the brown sugar and then stud with cloves. Place in slow cooker and add apple cider. Set slow cooker to low and cook approximately 6 hours until ham is tender. Add raisins if desired and cook an additional ½ hour. Slice to serve.

☙ Pot Roast
May 1933

Tough, inexpensive cuts of meat, like the chuck used in this recipe, are perfect fodder for the slow cooker, which breaks down the sinews of the meat so that a soft, flavorful sort of stew emerges at the end of cooking. The Farmer's Wife never used alcohol of any sort in her cooking, but you may use a bit of red wine instead of vinegar to acidulate the dish. Any sort of root vegetable may be used or excluded here. The Farmer's Wife favored turnips, but carrots and potatoes are the only two vegetables that may be considered a requirement. If you desire, you may thicken the sauce before or after cooking by rolling the meat in flour before browning or after cooking the meat by making balls of equal parts flour and butter and stirring them into the slow cooker on the high setting.

3 to 4 lbs. boneless chuck roast, trimmed of fat
2 tbsp. olive oil
salt and pepper to taste
4 carrots, washed, peeled, and chopped
4 ribs celery, washed and chopped
6 potatoes, washed, peeled, and chopped

1 medium turnip, washed, peeled, and chopped (optional)
2 large yellow onions, peeled and thinly sliced
1½ c. beef broth
¼ c. cider vinegar or red wine
chopped Italian parsley, to garnish

In a large skillet, brown the meat in the olive oil over medium-high flame and sprinkle with salt and pepper, turning the meat as you go. Place in slow cooker with all remaining ingredients except parsley. Set slow cooker to low and cook 7 to 9 hours until meat is very tender. Taste for seasoning and serve hot over buttered noodles. Garnish with chopped parsley, if desired.

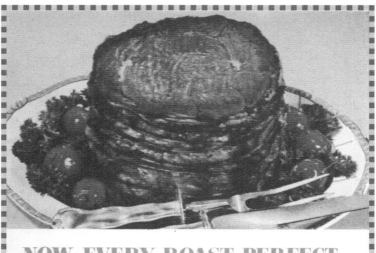

NOW, EVERY ROAST PERFECT
EVERY TIME . . .

Side Dishes

❦ Turkish Pilaf

March 1934

Rice is oh-so-easy to cook in the slow cooker, especially if you do not possess a rice cooker. It doesn't take long: only about half an hour, which is the same time you would spend cooking rice on top of the stove. But perfect rice is easier to accomplish in the slow cooker, especially if you resist the urge to open the cover and stir the rice around. The Farmer's Wife added ground beef to her pilaf, but this is a vegetarian version, unless you choose to add chicken stock.

1 small yellow onion, thinly sliced	1 tsp. salt
1 tbsp. olive oil	2 tbsp. butter
2 c. long-grain rice, such as basmati, rinsed	Parmesan cheese, to serve
2 c. tomatoes, finely chopped	parsley or cilantro, to garnish
4 c. water or stock	

In a large skillet, heat the olive oil over medium flame and cook the onion until it is translucent. Add the rice and stir to mix. Add to the slow cooker along with the remaining ingredients except the cheese and garnish. Set slow cooker to low and cook about 30 minutes until all the liquid is absorbed. Allow the rice to sit covered for an additional 15 to 30 minutes. Serve hot out of the pot, topped with grated Parmesan cheese, if you desire, and chopped Italian parsley, or chopped cilantro.

❦ Corn Pudding

November 1912

2 heaping c. corn kernels, fresh or frozen
3 eggs
2 tbsp. sugar
1 tbsp. butter, plus extra for greasing the
   slow cooker
1½ c. milk
large pinch salt

Heavily butter the inside of the slow cooker. Add 1½ c. of corn into slow cooker; finely chop remaining ½ c. corn and add. Mix remaining ingredients in a large bowl. Add to corn. Set slow cooker to low and cook 2 hours until just set. Serve hot.

❦ Scalloped Tomatoes

April 1910

There is very little variation necessary to adapt the sidebar recipe for scalloped tomatoes for the slow cooker. A little minced garlic is added for pungency, and Parmesan cheese is added to the breadcrumbs to aid in the flavoring. Breadcrumbs are sprinkled on the top layer of the dish only, as they have a tendency to become gluey in between layers. This is a great summer treat. Be sure to serve hot.

1 tbsp. plus 1 tsp. butter
3 to 4 large beefsteak tomatoes (enough to make 3 layers), ripe but still firm
¾ tsp. salt
⅓ tsp. sugar

1 tsp. minced fresh garlic
freshly ground black pepper
⅓ c. breadcrumbs
2 tbsp. grated Parmesan cheese

Butter the inside of the slow cooker with 1 tsp. of butter. Core the tomatoes, cut them in half, and slice in ¼-inch slices. Place them in one slightly overlapping layer at the bottom of the slow cooker and sprinkle with ⅓ of the salt and sugar, half the garlic, and a little black pepper. Repeat with a second layer, then a third. Mix the breadcrumbs with the cheese and sprinkle over the top of the tomatoes. Dot with the remaining butter and set to cook on low for 2½ hours and uncover for the last ½ hour of cooking. Serve immediately.

❦ Escalloped Eggplant with Tomatoes and Onions

August 1927

This is an easy, hearty, late-summer dish that can be cooked up in the slow cooker without adding heat to your already hot house or apartment. Use ripe but firm beefsteak tomatoes and large eggplants, which contain fewer seeds than the small ones.

2 large yellow onions, thinly sliced
2 tbsp. olive oil
2 large purple eggplants, peeled and cut into ½-inch slices

4 to 6 large, ripe but firm beefsteak tomatoes, sliced
salt and pepper
unsalted butter

Heat the olive oil in a large skillet and cook the onions till they are translucent and just beginning to turn golden. Butter the inside of the slow cooker. Place a layer of eggplant on the bottom and top with a layer of tomatoes then a coating of onions, sprinkle with salt and pepper, and dot with butter at each layer. Continue until all the vegetables are used. Sprinkle on a final bit of salt and pepper, and a dotting of butter. Set slow cooker to low and cook 2 to 3 hours until the vegetables are tender but still hold their shape. If they begin to stick to the bottom of the dish during cooking, you may add 1 tbsp. of water.

❦ Cauliflower in Tomato Sauce
October 1918

Here's a simple cauliflower dish, which can be made slightly fancier with the addition of herbs—fresh thyme, rosemary, or sage. Be sure to serve with chopped parsley and a lot of buttered bread.

1 large head cauliflower, broken
  into florets
1 small onion, peeled and thinly sliced
2 tbsp. olive oil

1 c. crushed tomatoes
salt and pepper to taste
fresh herbs, if desired, plus fresh
  chopped parsley to garnish

Cut cauliflower into florets and parboil in salted water for 2 minutes (this will help preserve some of the vegetable's vitamin content, but is not absolutely necessary if you are strapped for time). Drain and put in slow cooker. Meanwhile, cook onion in olive oil until lightly browned. Add to slow cooker with remaining ingredients except parsley. Set slow cooker to low and cook 2 to 3 hours until cauliflower is nicely tender. Check for seasonings and serve. Garnish with parsley.

❦ Succotash
February 1922

Alan Davidson points out that this classic old American dish, thought by most to be a vegetarian offering, included two chickens, plus corned beef and pork in its first recorded recipe; bear meat was included in a slightly later recipe. Although recipes with salt pork or bacon still turn up from time to time, it is still generally accepted that succotash, no matter what else is added to it, is a dish consisting of lima beans and corn. In fact, its name is taken from a Narragansett word (msickquatash, according to Merriam-Webster) meaning "boiled corn kernels." Fresh lima beans and corn would be ideal ingredients for this dish, but frozen limas and corn or dried limas may be substituted, although expect a longer cooking time for the latter. Succotash was a great favorite of The Farmer's Wife—*this is one of only ten or twelve varieties she published over the years.*

1 pt. shelled fresh lima beans
1 pt. corn, cut from the cob (about
  4 ears)
4 tbsp. unsalted butter

1 tbsp. water
1 tsp. sugar
salt and pepper to taste
¼ c. half-and-half

Place all ingredients except half-and-half in slow cooker. Set slow cooker to low and cook 2 to 2½ hours until vegetables are almost tender. Season to taste, add half-and-half, and stir to mix. Cook an additional ½ hour. Serve hot.

Spoon Corn Bread

November 1911

This is a classic American dish with roots in many directions: south to the Aztecs and east to England. Traditionally, it is soft and light thanks to the addition of baking powder. Fine-ground cornmeal also helps keep it on the delicate side. As a rule it also generally eschews the use of sugar, although contemporary corn bread lovers who have grown accustomed to more sweetish stuff may wish to add a bit of sweetener.

2 c. milk
½ c. fine-ground cornmeal
2 eggs
1 tbsp. melted butter or oil, plus extra for
  greasing the slow cooker

1 tsp. baking powder
½ tsp. salt
1 to 2 tbsp. sugar, if desired

Butter the inside of the slow cooker. Add all ingredients to the slow cooker and whisk very well to incorporate. Make sure that the eggs and baking powder especially are beaten in. Set slow cooker to low and cook about 3 hours until just set. To serve, spoon onto plates right from the pot, nice and hot.

Candied Orange Sweet Potatoes

April 1931

The important thing in this recipe is not how thick the sweet potatoes are sliced (although the thicker they are the longer they take to cook) but that the slices are of a uniform thickness for even cooking. The vegetable mandolin is a perfect tool for this. These sweet potatoes can be enjoyed in the cool of autumn when sweet potatoes are just ripening or even in late summer. The slow cooker means no hot oven to contend with. The Farmer's Wife favored casseroles of this sort, and here two recipes have been spliced together. One is simple and seasoned with salt, pepper, and butter. The other incorporates orange for a slightly zestier flavor. You can also add firm, tart apples that are peeled and sliced in equal proportion to sweet potatoes. Add the apples and sweet potatoes to the slow cooker in alternating layers.

2 large sweet potatoes, peeled and sliced
  ¼-inch thick
1 tsp. salt
¼ c. melted unsalted butter, plus extra for
  buttering the inside of the slow cooker

¼ c. brown sugar
½ tsp. grated orange zest

Butter the inside of the slow cooker and arrange sweet potatoes inside it in layers, overlapping slightly. Sprinkle with salt, pour butter over evenly, then sprinkle with sugar and orange zest. Set slow cooker to low and cook 4 hours. Serve immediately.

❦ Normandy Carrots

November 1931

This sweet-and-sour dish, once popular with lunching ladies, has fallen out of favor in recent years. There is scant reference to it in cookbooks or food histories, which leaves some speculation as to its origins. This writer's best guess: Normandy, a region in northern France famous for apples and butter, once inspired numbers of recipes using both products. This recipe incorporated butter, of course, and vinegar—no doubt originally apple cider vinegar— the sharpness of which was cut by the addition of sugar. It is a nice complement to a roast or pork chops.

1 lb. (approximately 4 c.) carrots, washed, peeled, and cut thinly in 2-inch strips	¼ c. vinegar 2 tbsp. butter
¼ c. sugar	¼ tsp. salt

Add all ingredients to the slow cooker. Mix well. Set slow cooker to low and cook 3 to 4 hours (depending on the age and thickness of the carrots), until carrots are tender all the way through.

❦ Spiced Cranberries

December 1931

During the holidays when stove space is at a premium, the slow cooker is perfect for dishes such as this one, especially when the whole meal must be put together at the same time.

4 c. cranberries	1 tsp. paprika
1½ c. brown sugar	1 tsp. cinnamon
½ c. mild vinegar	½ tsp. ground cloves
¼ c. water	½ tsp. salt

Add all ingredients to the slow cooker. Set to low and cook 2 hours. Raise the temperature to high, remove cover, and cook an additional ½ to 1 hour to reduce cooking liquid. Serve hot or cold.

Variation:

Stewed Cranberries, a bare-bones holiday dish from November 1910: Stew 4 c. cranberries with 2 c. sugar and ½ c. water in slow cooker on low for 2 to 2½ hours. Remove cover and cook on high for ½ to 1 hour, if necessary, to reduce cooking liquid.

Desserts

✺ Coconut Bread Pudding

September 1923

This is a wonderful way to use up leftover bread, which is something nearly every household seems to accumulate in one form or another. It certainly did in the household of The Farmer's Wife. Recipes for bread pudding appear in the magazine with amazing frequency. Heels from sliced loaves, half a baguette left a day too long in the bag, and even bits of pumpernickel bagel can be stored in a resealable bag in the freezer until enough has accumulated to translate into this classic American dessert. Thaw thoroughly before attempting to cube the bread!

unsalted butter
4 c. stale bread cubes
1 c. shredded unsweetened coconut
2 eggs

1½ c. milk
½ c. heavy cream
1 c. sugar
1 tbsp. vanilla extract

Butter the inside of the slow cooker, add bread and coconut, and mix together. In a bowl, whisk up the remaining ingredients and pour over bread and coconut. (Note: the custard should thoroughly soak the bread. If it does not, add extra cream and milk until all the bread cubes can be moistened.) Set the slow cooker on low and cook for 2½ hours. Remove the lid for the last ½ hour to enhance the crust. Best served warm right out of the slow cooker with a little heavy cream poured over or a small scoop of ice cream.

✺ Caramel Bread Pudding

December 1911

unsalted butter
4 c. stale bread cubes
2 eggs
1½ c. milk

½ c. heavy cream
1 c. brown sugar
1 tbsp. cinnamon

Follow directions for Coconut Bread Pudding. Serve hot.

❧ Brown Betty
May 1929

The Farmer's Wife did not let much go to waste in her kitchen. She used and reused as much as she could, turning leftover once-fresh bread into breadcrumbs, which turn up again and again in her chops and casseroles and desserts. She and her family gobbled up fresh fruit in season from her garden and orchard, but she also never failed to cook up the less gorgeous produce (windfall apples, for example) with its knobs and bumps and bruises. This is not to say that her aim was thrift alone. As this recipe attests, a decidedly delicious dessert can be made from the dregs, along with a few staples from the larder.

1 c. breadcrumbs	1 tsp. cinnamon
2 tbsp. melted butter, plus more (unmelted) for buttering the slow cooker	5 sour windfall apples, such as Granny Smith
1 c. sugar	juice of 1 lemon
grated zest of 1 lemon	heavy cream

Butter the inside of the slow cooker. In a bowl, mix the breadcrumbs with the melted butter, ½ c. of the sugar, zest, and cinnamon. Peel and chop the apples into ½-inch cubes, place in a bowl, and mix with the lemon juice and remaining sugar. Spread half the breadcrumb mixture on the bottom of the slow cooker. Top with the apples and then the remaining breadcrumbs. Set the slow cooker to low and cook covered for 2 hours, then cook uncovered for an additional ½ hour. Serve hot with a drizzling of heavy cream.

❧ Lemon Rice Pudding
February 1910

Basmati rice is used in this version of rice pudding for a delicate texture. For a pudding in which the grains are distinct, you may shorten the cooking time. For a more porridgelike consistency, lengthen the cooking time. Whichever type of pudding you prefer, be sure to serve it hot.

unsalted butter	1 egg
¾ c. basmati rice, rinsed and drained	grated zest of 1 lemon
½ c. sugar	3 c. milk

Butter the inside of the slow cooker, then add all the ingredients. Whisk well, making sure the egg is well beaten-in. Set slow cooker to low and cook 2 to 3 hours, till desired consistency. Serve hot.

❧ Indian Pudding

February 1910

This dessert is a classic American dish that originated with colonial cooks in the mid-1700s. Not surprisingly, it appears on the pages of The Farmer's Wife *with great frequency, as it was already considered a "classic" dish, even at the turn of the nineteenth century. Some food historians claim it is a variation of the English hasty pudding, with cornmeal ("Indian meal," hence the name Indian pudding) replacing wheat or oats here in the New World. Those who could afford sugar used it to sweeten this dish, but less-expensive molasses was more common. These days it is usually baked, although originally it was often boiled in cloth bags, as ovens were scarce.*

⅔ c. cornmeal
1 qt. milk
½ tsp. salt
1 tsp. powdered ginger
2 eggs
pinch baking soda

½ c. molasses
1 tbsp. butter, plus extra for greasing the
    slow cooker
1 c. mixed dried chopped raisins, currants,
    dates, and figs

Butter the slow cooker, add all the ingredients, and whisk. Make sure the eggs are well beaten. Set the slow cooker on low and cook 2 to 3 hours until set. Overcooking will result in a wet, curdled mess. This pudding may not be sweet enough for some, in which case you may serve with vanilla ice cream or a sprinkling of brown sugar.

❧ Banana Pudding

May 1913

Warm, sweet banana pudding will surely appeal to every member of your family on hot or cool nights. An important factor is texture; the banana must be mashed smooth (or puréed in the blender with a little of the milk you will use for cooking) or the ensuing lumps will detract from the satisfaction of the pudding. This recipe  *makes enough to feed a crowd.* The Farmer's Wife *would have used the leftover egg whites for a meringue topping, but this tends to get soggy in the slow cooker. You can make meringue cookies in the conventional oven or serve the pudding with 'Nilla Wafers.*

⅔ c. grated breadcrumbs
2 c. well-mashed banana (about 6 small
    or 4 medium bananas)
finely grated rind of 2 lemons

4 egg yolks
2 c. milk
1 c. sugar

Butter the inside of the slow cooker. Add all ingredients and mix well to incorporate. Set slow cooker to low and cook 2 to 3 hours until set. Serve hot.

❦ Graham Pudding

September 1926

This so-called "pudding" is more of a cake and may be accomplished in much the same way as the English Gingerbread Cake that follows it. Graham flour is a type of coarsely ground whole wheat flour that is readily available in health and specialty stores (not to be confused with gram flour, which refers to a flour made from ground chickpeas).

¼ c. butter, plus extra for buttering the inside of the slow cooker
½ c. molasses
1 c. graham flour
½ c. cornmeal
3 tsp. baking powder

½ tsp. baking soda
1 tsp. salt
1 tsp. cinnamon
½ tsp. each mace, cloves, allspice, ginger
½ c. buttermilk
⅔ c. raisins

Cream butter, add molasses, and stir. Mix and sift dry ingredients; add alternately with buttermilk to butter mixture. Stir in raisins. Heavily butter the inside of the slow cooker. Pour in batter and set slow cooker to low. Cook 2 to 3 hours until the pudding is set. Serve hot with whipped cream, if desired.

❦ Poached Pears

January 1926

This is a rather gentrified departure for The Farmer's Wife in the realm of desserts. It can be served any time pears are in season, for any occasion whatsoever. You can even skip the whipped cream for a more refreshing effect.

4 ripe but firm pears, such as Bosc, peeled, cored, and halved
2 c. water
1 c. sugar
1 tbsp. lemon rind, grated

In a pot on top of the stove, make a syrup of the water, sugar, and lemon rind by boiling all together until it just begins to thicken. Add to slow cooker along with pears and set to low. Cook 2 to 3 hours until the pears are just tender, stirring occasionally to ensure that the fruit sits in the syrup on all sides. Serve hot with the syrup and sweetened, freshly whipped cream.

Variation:
From November 1931, Crème de Menthe Pears: Substitute ½ tsp. mint oil for the lemon rind.

❧ English Gingerbread Cake

March 1916

Baked goods are a wonderful category of foods to make in the slow cooker. I tested this recipe on a blisteringly hot July day, without ever turning on my oven. The result? A lovely cake in a still-cool summer apartment. The Farmer's Wife was a huge proponent of gingerbread. She had dozens and dozens of recipes for it—in cake and cookie form hard and soft, frosted and not. This recipe includes raisins and nuts for a rich, chewy variety.

Take note: The gingerbread in the oblong slow cooker tends to cook first at the edges and last in the center. So, be sure to keep a close eye on the cake, turning it off and removing it from the slow cooker just as soon as the center is set, otherwise you will end up with very dry edges. Also helpful is wrapping a thin dishtowel around the underside of the cover and tucking it up over the top edges, to catch any condensation that develops during cooking.

1¾ c. flour

½ c. raisins

½ c. chopped walnuts

½ tsp. baking soda

½ c. unsalted butter, plus more for buttering the inside of the slow cooker

1 c. molasses

½ c. sugar

2 eggs

1½ tsp. cinnamon

1½ tsp. cloves

1 tsp. ground ginger

Heavily butter the inside of the slow cooker. Mix all ingredients together in a large bowl and pour into the slow cooker. Set to low and cook 2½ to 3 hours, stirring a bit before the mixture sets. Keeping a close eye on the cake, remove it just as soon as the center is set. Immediately remove with a spatula and place on a rack to cool.

GOOD THINGS TO EAT ARE MADE WITH BAKING SODA

DESSERT GINGERBREAD

1½ cups all-purpose flour
1 teaspoon Arm & Hammer or Cow Brand Baking Soda
¼ teaspoon salt
1 teaspoon ginger
¼ cup shortening
½ cup sugar
1 egg
½ cup molasses
¾ cup boiling water

1. Sift, then measure the flour. Sift three times with the baking soda, salt and ginger.

2. Cream the shortening until it is light and fluffy. Add the sugar gradually, beating after each addition.

3. Next, add the unbeaten egg, beating briskly.

4. Add the molasses. Then add the dry ingredients, beating until smooth. Stir in boiling water.

5. Turn into greased loaf pan. Bake.
   Amount: 8x8-inch pan
   Temperature: 350° F.
   Time: 30-40 min.

BUY WAR BONDS

ARM & HAMMER
CHURCH & CO'S
BICARBONATE of SC or COW
BAKING SODA BRAND

Cranberry Pudding

January 1911

This is a pudding in the English tradition—as Dr. Johnson defined it, containing flour, milk, and eggs—rather than the now-strictly American interpretation (i.e., rice pudding, tapioca pudding, chocolate pudding) that the English would define as a "milk pudding." It is technically steamed in the slow cooker and is quite delicate and sweet. Contemporary cooks may be inclined to make this during the holiday season, due to the presence of cranberries. However, it is worth noting that The Farmer's Wife made this in January 1911, and another variation (see below) appeared in September 1926. This writer tested both recipes in late sweltering July, which was possible thanks to the modern convenience of frozen foods. It made a very welcome conclusion to a light summer meal, especially since any such confection baked in the oven would have been out of the question during that season.

7 tbsp. unsalted butter, plus extra for
    greasing the slow cooker
2 eggs
¾ c. plus 1 tbsp. milk

1 8-oz. package (approximately 2 c.)
    cranberries, fresh or frozen
1½ c. sugar
3 c. flour
2 tsp. baking powder

Cream together the butter, milk, and sugar in a blender. Pour the mixture over the cranberries, add the sugar, and sift in the flour and baking powder. Mix very well and turn out into the well-buttered slow cooker. Set to low and cook 3 to 4 hours until just set in the center. Serve with heavy cream and dust with nutmeg.

Variation:

In this version of Cranberry Pudding from September 1926, substitute buttermilk for whole milk, and ½ tsp. baking soda for an equal amount of the baking powder to neutralize the acid in the buttermilk.

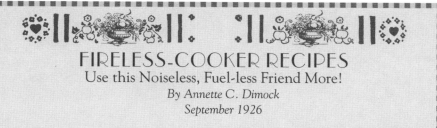

FIRELESS-COOKER RECIPES
Use this Noiseless, Fuel-less Friend More!
By Annette C. Dimock
September 1926

The fireless cooker is perfect for all foods that need long, slow cooking in the presence of moist heat, such as tough cuts of meat, dried beans and peas, pot roast, chicken fricassee, boiled chowders, soups, stews, and casseroles. Steamed breads and puddings from one's favorite recipe are most satisfactorily cooked in the fireless.

❦ Caramel Raisin Apple
February 1922

Baked apples are a classic winter treat, and they are so easily made in the slow cooker. They will take quite a bit longer to slow-cook than to bake, but as always with the slow cooker, this means you will have oven space readily available for another baking task.

6 large, firm, tart apples, well washed
½ c. raisins
1 c. light brown sugar
2 tbsp. unsalted butter, plus extra for buttering the slow cooker
½ c. apple juice

Core the apples and peel a bit of the skin from the top. Mix the raisins and sugar together and pack the mixture into the apples. Top each apple with a pat of butter. Butter the slow cooker and arrange the apples inside. Add the apple juice to cover the bottom of the pot. Set the slow cooker to low and cook 4 to 6 hours until the apples are softened through. According to *The Farmer's Wife*, these "may be served hot or cold, with or without cream."

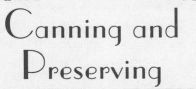

Canning and Preserving

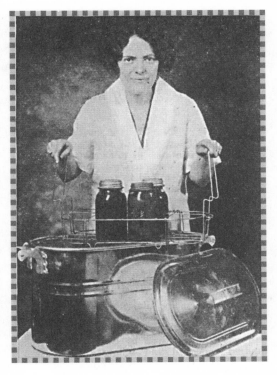

Decades before the advent of *Cook's Illustrated* and its monthly doses of kitchen science, there was *The Farmer's Wife* and its own science-based methodology, culled from staff experts, bulletins issued by the U.S. Department of Agriculture (USDA), and various extension services across the country. On no kitchen topic was the magazine's expertise more critical than on preserving.

Preserving then required (and most assuredly still does) precise procedures in order to yield wholesome, safe foodstuffs. And a farmer's wife had plenty to preserve. She put up myriad stores from her gardens, fields, and orchards—not just the niceties of jams and jellies and pickles but the fundamentals of plain fruits, vegetables, sauces, and soups that formed the backbone of meals during the long, cold months when nothing grew.

Nothing would have signified a greater failure of farmer's wifery than a scantly stocked canning cupboard, By following some of the recipes in this chapter, contemporary canning enthusiasts may experience for themselves the delightfully industrious stockpiling that made the farmer's wife prepared for just about anything, but most of all, for winter.

How to Get Started

A large number of recipes and procedures for preserving a variety of fruits and vegetables, in a whole host of ways, appear in this section. To ensure success and safety in preserving, it is important to understand a bit about how preserving works and why.

Some of the preserved foods in this book, such as jams, jellies, and other sweet spreads, lend themselves to preservation because they are made up of high-acid foods (fruits) cooked with high concentrations of sugar. Some of them, such as chutneys and certain pickles, are combinations of high-acid and low-acid foods (which include meats, all vegetables, and sometimes tomatoes) that are preserved by precise additions of sugar, salt, and/or vinegar. Still others—fruits and vegetables canned without sugar, salt, or vinegar—are rendered free of potential toxins and therefore safe to eat by processing for prescribed periods of time at high temperatures.

In fact, these days, unlike during the era of *The Farmer's Wife*, it is recommended that *all* canned foods be processed after packing in jars to eliminate any risk of contamination with molds and bacteria. There are two ways to do this, and nowadays, they are the *only* ways recommended by the U.S. Department of Agriculture (USDA) and food safety experts:

The *boiling water bath*, in which jars of food are immersed in water in a boiling water canner or large stockpot and the water brought to a boil for a prescribed time, and the *pressure canner*, which heats water to a number of degrees above boiling. These two methods are not created equal, and it is important to be aware of the differences between them and when it is appropriate to use one or the other.

A note about sterilizing and processing times given in this book: They are for altitudes of 0 to 1,000 feet *only*. If you live at an altitude above 1,000 feet, you *must* consult one of the sources listed at the end of this book or your local extension service to ascertain the correct processing time for your altitude. Failure to make adjustments for altitude will result in products that are potentially unsafe to eat.

The boiling water bath, as indicated by its name, processes food at the temperature of boiling water. It is recommended *only* for high-acid foods, which include all fruit products, all pickled products, and sometimes, tomatoes. The tomato, once considered a high-acid food, is now known to be inconsistent in its acidity levels. This is why it is recommended that lemon juice be added to certain tomato products (this topic is covered in greater detail in the section titled "Preserved Tomatoes and Tomato Products").

The pressure canner processes foods at a higher temperature than the boiling water canner and is required for everything else: namely, all vegetables that are not pickled, anything that contains meat, poultry, or seafood, and sometimes, tomatoes.

In order to can fruit and vegetable products using either of these methods, you will need some specialized equipment and some other items that can readily be found around the house. These things vary a little depending on what you are canning, so consult the "The Basics" section in each chapter to make sure you have everything you need before getting started. All canning equipment must be scrupulously clean and, in some instances, sterilized, so be sure you are clear about these methods (see page 140 for more information).

The USDA has published a set of guidelines that list methods and processing times for certain products. Invariably, these are products that have been tested by experts in land-grant universities. The methods and times should be followed exactly to minimize any risk of food-borne illness. For example, if a tested method for canning tomatoes calls for you to wash them, remove their cores, then plunge them in boiling water in order to remove their skins, this set of instructions is as critical to ensuring the safety of the tomatoes as the instructions that call for you to add a tablespoon of bottled lemon juice to each pint jar and for you to process the filled jars for forty minutes in a boiling water bath. Any deviation will result in a product that is potentially unsafe for long-term storage.

Every attempt has been made here to conform to these standards in all applicable recipes. If you have any questions whatsoever about a method or processing time, however, consult the USDA-supported website for the National Center for Home Food Preservation (NCHFP) (**www.uga.edu/nchfp**), the USDA's excellent "Complete Guide to Home Canning," which can be downloaded from this website, or contact a food safety expert at your local cooperative extension service (**www.csrees.usda.gov/ Extension**) will help you locate the extension service that is right for your area.

Obviously, it would take an untold number of centuries to test every canning recipe ever created, and certainly not every recipe that ever appeared in *The Farmer's Wife* has been tested for safety. Nevertheless, many excellent and *untested* recipes have been included in this book. Pickles, relishes, chutneys, and other such products that have not yet been evaluated in a lab for safety can still be enjoyed for short-term use: that is, they may be cooked up, packed in jars, and stored in the refrigerator to be consumed within a week or two. These recipes appear in a gray box and are marked with a snowflake icon. Other recipes may be preserved by freezing. Only tested recipes should be canned. In this way, the myriad delicious recipes devised by *The Farmer's Wife* may continue to be enjoyed by contemporary cooks. The recipes are especially useful in cooking up small batches of produce from the home garden and farmers' market, when full canner loads would have been unfeasible to begin with.

Whatever your needs—for small or large batches of jams or jellies, pickles, or condiments—*The Farmer's Wife* offers something for everyone.

Sweet Spreads

Sweet spreads exist in abundance on the pages of *The Farmer's Wife*. They were and still are a wonderful way to treat fruit abundance from the garden and to insert a little summer sunshine into winter's gloom. Some sweet spreads are jellied, others (namely, the butters and honeys in this chapter) do not necessarily need to jell in order to be considered a success.

For the most part, *The Farmer's Wife* made jellied spreads without the use of commercial pectin, although a few recipes that use commercial pectin exist on the pages of the magazine. Some have been included here.

All methods and procedures in this section, except for untested, "refrigerator" recipes, have been checked for safety against the following sources: The NCHFP website, the Clemson University Extension Service website, and the University of Minnesota Extension Service website.

The Basics

Jellies are made by extracting juice from fruit then cooking the juice with sugar. They are clear, or translucent, and firm enough to hold their shape when they are turned out of the container.

Jams are thick, sweet spreads that are made by cooking crushed or chopped fruits with sugar. They hold their shape, too, but are usually less firm than jellies.

Conserves are jam-like spreads made from mixtures that may include citrus fruits, nuts, raisins, and coconut.

Marmalades are jellies that contain bits of fruit or peel. They are traditionally citrus, but other types of marmalades appear throughout the pages of the magazine.

Fruit butters and *honeys*, which are not jellied products, were also favored by *The Farmer's Wife* and are covered in this chapter. Fruit butters are a thick sort of fruit puree, and fruit honeys are a clear condiment with a drizzling consistency. Their treatment and processing are a bit different from jellied products, so pay close attention to variations in directions.

In order to jell properly, jellied spreads require high concentrations of pectin (which occurs naturally in fruit, to varying degrees; see chart on page 144), acid, and sugar. In order to make these spreads without the addition of commercial pectin, all these elements must exist in proper amounts. For this reason, it is recommended that at least one-quarter of the fruit used for these products be unripe (unripe fruit contains more pectin) and to be either of a high-pectin variety or a combination of high and low. As you read on, you will notice that instructions for extracting juice and cooking it down recommend that you boil rapidly; this method is also intended to preserve pectin content, which breaks down at a simmer or slow boil. Sometimes it will be necessary to add lemon juice to jellies to raise their acid content.

To use all-ripe fruit or fruit of a low-pectin variety, commercial pectin must be added to the juice or fruit mixture, as directed by the individual manufacturer (directions vary with pectin brand and also between powdered and liquid types). From time to time, the farmer's wife certainly found herself with a quantity of ripe, end-of-season strawberries, for example, to cook into jam. For this reason, recipes calling for commercial pectin have not been dismissed out of hand for the purposes of this book. You should know, however, that commercial pectin products will be a far sight sweeter than those made without.

Once upon a time, it was deemed safe to preserve sweet spreads without processing them. This is no longer the case. All sweet spreads should be packed in sterilized half-pint jars and processed in a boiling water bath for five minutes (except for fruit butters and honeys, which may be packed in clean jars but then must be processed for fifteen minutes or according to specific instructions in each recipe). They must also be sealed with brand-new, two-piece lids; paraffin is no longer considered appropriate for sealing jars. These new recommendations discourage mold growth on sweet spreads.

Here is a list of the equipment you will need to make the recipes in this section:

- Canning jars in half-pint sizes. Jars may be reused from one canning season to the next. However, you must make sure that they are in good shape, with no nicks or chips or signs of wear. Old or new, before using, they must be washed thoroughly in very hot water with soap or in the dishwasher. If the products they will hold are to be processed for fewer than ten minutes (such as all the jellied spreads), they must also be sterilized, instructions for which appear on page 140. Jars with pop-top lids and any other sorts of jars are no longer recommended for use in home canning.
- Two-part canning lids. These are available from grocery stores or canning supply stores and they are good for ONE USE ONLY. Follow the individual manufacturer's directions for cleaning and sterilizing to prepare the jars for use.
- A boiling water canner or a large stock-pot. It should be deep enough to allow at least 1 to 2 inches of water to boil over the tops of the jars and have a rack to keep jars off the bottom.
- An 8- or 10-quart saucepan for cooking fruit and juices. A larger pan is better, as jellies and jams have a tendency to boil over. A heavy metal pan is preferred because it allows for even heat distribution.
- A jelly bag, or a firm unbleached muslin or cotton flannel with the napped side turned in, or four thicknesses of closely woven cheesecloth, as well as a rack or colander for hanging. This is to extract juice from fruit after cooking. Dampen jelly bags or cloths before using them to extract the juice.
- Measuring cups and spoons.
- Stainless-steel cooking spoons.
- Large bowls for collecting juice.
- A jelly, candy, or deep-fat thermometer to determine doneness in sweet spreads that have no added commercial pectin.
- A jar lifter to remove hot jars from the canner.
- Clean dishtowels and paper towels for wiping jar rims and general cleanup.

- Timer or clock to determine the end of processing time.
- Dishtowels and racks for cooling jars after processing.
- A permanent marker for labeling the type of product and the date of its making on the jars.

Getting Started

Once you have assembled all this equipment and your ingredients, you are ready to begin. Follow these steps, as outlined on the NCHFP's website (**www.uga.edu/nchfp/publications/uga/uga_processing_j_j.pdf**), before proceeding.

Note: All times, for sterilizing and processing, are for altitudes of between 0 and 1,000 feet. If you live at a higher altitude, additional times are necessary. Please consult your local extension agent for information about the sterilizing and processing times that are right for your area.

1. Wash half-pint canning jars in hot water with detergent and rinse well, or wash in the dishwasher. Sterilize by submerging 10 minutes in boiling water. (Butters and honeys, which will be processed for 15 minutes, can be packed into *clean* jars that have not been sterilized before use.) The easiest way to do this is to stand the empty jars upright on a rack in a boiling water canner filled with clean water. There should be enough water to fill the jars and still reach 1 to 2 inches above the tops of them. Bring the water to a boil and boil for 10 minutes. Leave the jars in the hot water until they are ready to be filled.

2. Prepare two-piece canning lids according to the manufacturer's recommendations.

3. Prepare sweet spread according to recipe and follow these general principles, adapted from the Clemson University Extension Service website:

   To extract juice: Use only firm fruits naturally high in pectin. Select a mixture of about ¾ ripe and ¼ underripe fruit. Wash all fruits thoroughly. Crush soft fruits or berries; cut firmer fruits into small pieces. Using the peels and cores adds pectin to the juice during cooking. Put fruit and water (as instructed) in a large saucepan and bring to a boil. Then simmer according to times given or until fruit is soft. Stir to prevent scorching. One pound of fruit should yield at least 1 cup of clear juice.

   When fruit is tender, strain through a colander into a bowl to remove seeds and skins, then strain juice again through four layers of cheesecloth or a jelly bag. Allow juice to drip through, using a stand or colander to hold the bag. Pressing or squeezing the bag or cloth will result in cloudy jelly.

   To make jelly: Use 6 to 8 c. of extracted fruit juice at a time; double batches do not always jell properly. Measure juice and sugar. When a recipe is not available, try using ¾ c. sugar for each cup of juice. Test for pectin content using one of the following methods.

4. Remove the sterilized jars from the hot water one at a time, tilting to empty. To make sure they are completely drained, turn them upside down on a clean towel

on the countertop. Turn right-side up and fill quickly with jelly mixture, leaving ¼ inch of head space. Wipe the sealing surface of the jars with a clean paper towel dampened with hot water to remove any of the mixture or sugar crystals. Work quickly to ensure that the filled jars stay as hot as possible until all are filled and ready to load into the canner for processing. Adjust lids.

5. Load the jars into the canner one at a time, using a jar lifter. Make sure to keep the jars upright at all times; tilting may cause the mixture to spill into the sealing area of the lid, which should remain clean and undisturbed. The water in the

TEST FOR DONENESS

Cooking test: Measure ⅓ c. of juice and ¼ c. of sugar into a small saucepan. Heat slowly, stirring constantly until all sugar is dissolved. Bring the mixture to a boil and boil rapidly until it passes the sheeting test: syrup forms two drops that flow together and "sheet," or hang, off the edge of the spoon. Pour the jelly into a clean hot jelly glass or a small bowl and let it cool. If the cooled mixture is jellylike, your fruit juice will jell.

Alcohol test: Add 1 tsp. of juice to 1 tbsp. of rubbing alcohol. To mix, gently stir or shake the mixture in a closed container so that all the juice comes in contact with the alcohol. DO NOT TASTE. The mixture is poisonous. Fruit high in pectin will form a solid jellylike mass that can be picked up with a fork.

Acid test: Test for acid using a simple taste test for tartness by mixing 1 tsp. lemon juice, 3 tbsp. water, and ½ tsp. sugar. If your fruit juice does not taste as tart as this mixture, it is not tart enough. Add 1 tbsp. lemon juice or ⅛ tsp. citric acid to each cup of fruit juice.

Temperature test: This is the most reliable of the doneness tests. First test the accuracy of the jelly or candy thermometer by placing it in boiling water to see if it measures 212 degrees F. Then place it in a vertical position into the boiling jelly mixture and read at eye level. The bulb of the thermometer must be completely covered with the jelly but must not touch the bottom of the saucepot. Boil mixture until it reaches 220 degrees F, which is 8 degrees F above the boiling point of water. *[Editor's note: This is for altitudes of 0 to 1,000 feet.]*

Sheet or spoon test: Dip a cool, metal spoon into the boiling jelly mixture. Raise the spoon about 12 inches above the pan, out of the steam. Turn the spoon so the liquid runs off the side. When the mixture first starts to boil, the drops will be light and syrupy. As the syrup continues to boil, the drops will become heavier and will drop off the spoon two at a time. The jelly is done when the syrup forms two drops that flow together and sheet, or hang off, the edge of the spoon.

Refrigerator/freezer test: Pour a small amount of boiling jelly on a plate and put it in the freezer for a few minutes. If the mixture jells, it should be done. During the test, the rest of the jelly mixture should be removed from the heat to prevent overcooking.

Editor's note: The procedures for making jellied spreads with commercial pectin vary somewhat from the above. With the addition of commercial pectin, it is not necessary to test for pectin, acid, or doneness. All-ripe fruit may be used for best flavor. Be sure to follow the manufacturer's directions carefully.

canner can be close to boiling when the jars are added, if the mixture has remained hot all the while.

6. Turn the heat under the canner to its highest setting, cover the canner with its lid, and heat until the water boils vigorously. Then boil 5 minutes (altitudes of 0 to 1,000 feet). Butters and honey must be boiled for 15 minutes unless otherwise instructed (again, altitudes of 0 to 1,000 feet). The water level in the canner should be 1 to 2 inches above the tops of the jars and must remain boiling during the entire 5 (or 15) minutes of processing. Keep the flame high and the lid on.

7. When the jars have been processed in boiling water for the recommended time, turn off the heat and remove the canner lid. Wait 5 minutes. Remove jars from the canner using a jar lifter, again making sure to keep the jars upright. Place them on a towel or cooling rack, leaving at least 1 inch of space between them. Do not place jars on a cold surface or in a cold draft.

8. Cool jars upright for 12 to 24 hours to make sure they properly seal and that the mixture sets. Let the jars sit undisturbed during this time. Do not tighten ring bands on the lids or push down on the center of the flat metal lid until the jar is completely cooled, as this may cause seal failures.

9. Remove ring bands from the jars. Check to make sure the jars are properly sealed using one of the following methods recommended by the National Center for Home Food Preservation:

- Press the middle of the lid with your finger. If the lid pops up when you release your finger, the lid is unsealed.
- Tap the lid with the bottom of a teaspoon. If it makes a dull sound, the lid is not sealed. If the jar is sealed correctly, it will make a ringing, high-pitched sound.
- Hold the jar at eye level and look across the lid. The lid should be concave in the center. If it is flat or convex, it may not be properly sealed.

You may opt to reprocess unsealed jars within 24 hours, using the original processing time. Or you may store them in the refrigerator, to use up within a few days, or the freezer, stored in freezer-safe plastic containers.

10. Wash jars and lids to remove all residues. Label, date, and store in a cool, dark, dry place out of direct sunlight. For best results, store between 50°F and 70°F; do not store at temperatures above 95°F or near heat sources like radiators. Likewise, do not store in any damp place or expose jars to freezing temperatures.

If a jellied spread is too soft after processing, you may remake it. Clemson University Extension lists these steps (Note: This is not applicable to sweet, unjellied spreads like butters and honeys, which are meant to be soft):

To remake cooked jelly or jam without added pectin: If the fruit juice was not acidic enough, add 1½ tsp. of lemon juice per cup of jelly before boiling. Heat the jelly to boiling and boil until the jellying point is reached. Remove jelly from heat, skim, pour immediately into sterilized hot jars, and seal and process for 5 minutes.

To remake cooked jelly or jam with powdered pectin: For each cup of jelly or jam, measure 2 tbsp. sugar, 1 tbsp. water, and 1½ tsp. of powdered pectin. (Stir the package contents well before measuring.) Mix the pectin and water and bring to a boil, stirring constantly. Add jelly or jam and sugar. Stir thoroughly. Bring to a full rolling boil over high heat, stirring constantly. Boil hard ½ minute. Remove from heat, quickly skim foam off jelly and fill hot, sterile jars, leaving ¼-inch head space. Adjust new lids and process in a boiling water bath for 5 minutes.

To remake cooked jelly or jam with liquid pectin: For each cup of jelly or jam, measure 3 tbsp. sugar, 1½ tsp. lemon juice, and 1½ tsp. of liquid fruit pectin. Place jelly or jam in a saucepan and bring to a boil, stirring constantly. Quickly add the sugar, lemon juice, and pectin. Bring to a full rolling boil, stirring constantly. Boil hard for 1 minute. Remove from heat. Quickly skim off foam and fill hot, sterile jars, leaving ¼-inch head space. Wipe jar rims. Adjust new lids and process in a boiling water bath for 5 minutes.

It is always good practice to carefully examine all home-canned jars of food for signs of spoilage prior to opening and eating. If there is any mold on a jar of jam or jelly, or signs of other spoilage, discard the entire contents of the jar or container. Visit the National Center for Home Food Preservation website, **www.uga.edu/nchfp**, or call your local extension service agent if you have any questions at all about the safety of your home-canned products.

A final note about fruits for sweet spreads: Use only those that are high-quality, freshly picked, and blemish-free. This is a good rule to follow for both fruits and vegetables in all canned products.

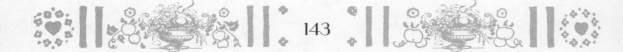

PECTIN CONTENT IN FRUITS

To make successful jellies and jams, you must use at least some fruits in the mix that are high in pectin if you prefer not to use commercial pectin in order to achieve the proper jelling consistency. Some fruits also require the addition of acid, in the form of lemon juice, in order to jell.

Here is a chart of fruits high and low in pectin:

Group I

If not overripe, these fruits have enough natural pectin and acid for gel formation with only added sugar:

Apples (sour)   Crabapples
Currants   Grapes (Eastern Concord)
Loganberries   Quinces
Blackberries (sour)   Cranberries
Gooseberries   Lemons
Plums (all but Italian)

Group II

These fruits are low in natural acid or pectin and may need the addition of either acid or pectin (or pectin-rich fruits):

Apples (ripe)   Cherries (sour)
Elderberries   Grapes (California)
Loquats   Chokecherries
Blackberries (ripe)   Grape juice (bottle Eastern
Grapefruit   Concord)
Oranges

Group III

These fruits always need added acid, pectin (or pectin-rich fruits), or both in order to jell:

Apricots   Figs
Guavas   Pears
Rhubarb   Strawberries
Blueberries   Grapes (Western Concord)
Peaches   Plums (Italian)
Raspberries

❦ Grape Jelly
August 1912

Take part-ripe Eastern Concord grapes, wash well, and add water in the amount of ¼ c. per cup of fruit. Bring slowly to a boil, crushing fruit, then boil rapidly until soft, strain, and let drip through a jelly bag. Test for pectin and acid. Rapidly boil juice 30 minutes, add a pound of sugar to a pint of juice, boil 8 minutes longer until done. Skim, pack, seal, and process.

Variations:
Substitute currants (¼ of which should be unripe), apples, or cranberries for the grapes.

Venison jelly, a spiced jelly that is particularly good with wild game, makes a pleasant change from ordinary grape jelly. To the recipe above add 1 small piece of cinnamon and 24 whole cloves tied in a spice bag. Boil in juice and remove before packing.

❦ Apple and Plum Jam
June 1924

2 c. tart apples, diced
1 c. plums, stoned and cut
3 c. water
¾ c. sugar

Place the fruit in equal measure of water, crushing slightly to free part of the juice and prevent scorching. Slowly bring to a boil, then boil quickly until fruit is tender. Remove from heat to add sugar, then return quickly to a boil and cook until desired thickness, or until jelly test is achieved. Pack, seal, and process.

❦ Strawberry Jam
June 1914

To every 2 pt. of very ripe strawberries add 1½ pt. of sugar. Mash together, stir well, and set over the fire to boil rapidly with an equal measure of water to fruit. Cook until thick, stirring to prevent scorching. Add lemon juice according to the directions on page 141. Pack, seal, and process.

Variation:
For those who like more tart strawberry jam, some housewives would add currant juice, extracted from fresh currants instead of water to the above amount of fruit. Cook until jelly test is achieved. The addition of lemon juice will not be necessary.

❦ Spiced Blueberry Jam
June 1938

4½ c. washed, stemmed blueberries
¼ tsp. each cinnamon, cloves, and allspice
4½ c. water

7 c. sugar
liquid pectin, according to
    manufacturer's directions

Crush or grind fully ripe blueberries, add spices, and mix well. Bring to a rapid boil over a hot flame with an equal measure of water to fruit, stirring constantly. Add sugar and pectin according to manufacturer's instructions. Pack, seal, and process.

❦ Apple-Peach Conserve

3 c. peeled and diced tart apples
3 c. sugar
juice of 1 lemon

2 c. peaches that have already been
    washed, stoned, chopped, and cooked
    til tender

Mix all ingredients and simmer until thick and clear, stirring to prevent scorching. Pack, seal, and process.

❦ Strawberry Conserve
August 1918

1 qt. strawberries,
    washed and hulled
½ lb. raisins

2 lbs. sugar
1 lemon
½ c. nuts, chopped

Grate the lemon peel and chop the pulp. Place all ingredients minus the nuts in a pan and cook over a slow, even fire until as thick as jam, adding a little water if necessary to avoid scorching. Add the nuts and cook 5 minutes longer. Pack, seal, and process.

❦ Pear Honey
November 1929

Pare and core 8 lbs. of pears. Cook in water to cover til soft, then strain through a jelly bag or cheesecloth. Measure juice and return to stove; bring to a rapid boil. Add ½ measure of sugar as juice, then boil again til of a honey-like consistency. Pack, seal, and process for 15 minutes.

❧ English Orange Marmalade
April 1913

6 Navel oranges
1 lemon
3 qt. water

Wash the oranges and lemon, slice very thin, removing and retaining seeds, then soak in 2 qt. of the water. Soak the seeds in the other quart of water. Next morning remove the seeds and mix the soaking water with the fruit in its water. Bring to a boil and boil 2 hours. Add 3 qt. sugar and boil 1 more hour, stirring gently. Pack, seal, and process.

❧ Harlequin Marmalade
June 1935

1 qt. strawberries, hulled and sliced
1 qt. cherries, pitted
1 qt. currants
1 qt. red raspberries
1 qt. gooseberries
5 lbs. sugar

Bring to a slow boil, crushing as you go; once juice forms and sugar dissolves, boil rapidly til clear and thick, about 10 to 20 minutes. Pack, seal, and process.

❧ Apple Butter
July 1924
Adapted from the NCHFP website

8 lbs. apples, chopped but not
    peeled or cored
2 c. sweet cider
2 c. vinegar (5 percent acidity)
2 tsp. ground cloves
2 tsp. ground allspice
3 tsp. ground
    cinnamon
2½ c. white sugar
2½ c. brown sugar

Cook apples slowly in cider and vinegar until tender. Press through colander, then cook pulp slowly with spices and sugars until very thick. Pack, seal, and process for 5 minutes.

Other Preserved Fruits and Fruit Products

The farmer's wife canned fruit in abundance, from her own fields and orchards. And she canned them immediately after picking, to ensure peak flavor and freshness. A fine solution for contemporary canners with no gardens of their own is to purchase fruit in-season from local farmers at area farmers' markets, and to can it within twenty-four hours. Make sure you select fresh, firm fruits at the peak of ripeness, in excellent condition. Do not use moldy or spotty fruit. Also make sure that fruit is carefully washed free of all dirt. *Note:* In this section, all methods,

procedures, and recipes (except refrigerator recipes) have been checked for safety against the following sources: NCHFP website, University of Georgia Extension Service website and Clemson University Extension Service website.

The Basics

There are all sorts of ways to can fruit: cooked or raw, hot or cold, or in water, juice, or syrup. *The Farmer's Wife*, most assuredly, favored syrup, as evidenced by the recipes in this chapter. But you can try your hand at other, less sweet, methods. Below is a chart of syrups from the NCHFP's website as well as methods for packing fruit, in syrup or not, from the University of Georgia Extension Service home canning.

The equipment you will need for preserving fruits and fruit products is similar to that for sweet spreads (page 139). Please consult that list. However, you will not need such specialized equipment as a thermometer or a jelly bag. Pint and quart jars, rather than

half-pint jars, are the preferred size here. Likewise, please consult the sweet spreads section for notes on how to clean and sterilize jars, pack the canner, remove jars from it, and cool and store jars (pages 140–143).

Note: The processing times outlined in this chapter are for hot water bath canners, used at altitudes of 0 to 1,000 feet. If you live at an altitude of above 1,000 feet, please consult the National Center for Home Food Preservation website (**www.uga.edu**) or your own local extension service for recommended processing times.

Since fruit products are processed for longer times than sweet spreads, it will be necessary to occasionally check the boiling water canner to make sure that the jars inside are completely covered. Add more BOILING water as necessary to ensure this.

Before eating any food that you have canned, it is important to check jars for signs of spoilage. A bulging lid or leaking jar is a sign of spoilage. So is spurting liquid, a bad odor, or mold. Dispose of all spoiled canned fruit in a place where it will not be eaten by children or pets.

Adding syrup to canned fruit helps to retain its flavor, color, and shape. Although it does not prevent its spoilage, which is why it is important to follow packing methods and processing times exactly. A "very light" syrup approximates the natural sugar content of many fruits. The quantities of water and sugar listed below make enough syrup for a whole canner load of pint or quart jars. This means nine pint jars or seven quart jars.

To make the syrups for hot packs of fruit (the preferred method of *The Farmer's Wife*), bring water and sugar to boil, add fruit, reheat to boil, and pack immediately into clean jars that have been kept hot in hot water. Empty the canner according to instructions on page 142 (jams and jellies).

Very light syrup: ½ c. sugar per quart of liquid = 4½ c. syrup

Light: 1 c. sugar per quart liquid = 4¾ c. syrup, for already very sweet fruit

Medium: 1¾ c. sugar per quart liquid = 5 c. syrup, for sweet apples, berries, cherries, grapes

Heavy: 2¾ c. sugar per quart liquid = 5⅓ c. syrup, for tart apples, apricots, sour cherries, gooseberries, nectarines, peaches, pears, plums

Very heavy: 4 c. sugar per quart liquid = 6 c. syrup, for very sour fruit

The following list of processes with process times is taken from the University of Georgia Cooperative Extension website (**www.fcs.uga.edu/ext/pubs/fdns/FDNS-E-43-01.pdf**) unless otherwise indicated. All these fruits were favored by *The Farmer's Wife* and appeared on its pages over the years; this list, however, updates procedures for safety.

Apple Juice, Hot Pack

For best results, buy fresh juice from a local cider maker within 24 hours after it has been pressed, or press your own. Refrigerate juice for 24 to 48 hours. Without mixing, carefully pour off clear liquid and discard sediment. Strain clear liquid through a paper coffee filter or double layer of damp cheesecloth. Sterilize jars and keep hot. Heat juice, stirring occasionally, until juice begins to boil. Pour into hot jars, leaving ¼ inch of head space.

Pints and quarts: 5 minutes

Apples, Hot Pack

Make a very light, light, or medium syrup. Wash, peel, core, and slice apples. Place in a large saucepan. Add 1 pint syrup, water, or juice per 5 lbs. apples. Boil 5 minutes, stirring occasionally. Pack hot apples into hot jars, leaving ½ inch of head space. Fill jar to ½ inch from top with hot syrup.

    Pints and quarts: 20 minutes

Applesauce, Hot Pack

Wash, peel, and core apples. Place in an 8- to 10-quart pot. Add ½ c. water. Stirring occasionally to prevent burning, heat quickly, and cook until tender (5 to 20 minutes, depending on maturity and variety). Press through a sieve or food mill, if desired. If you prefer chunk-style sauce, omit the pressing step. If desired, add ⅛ c. sugar per quart of sauce. Reheat sauce to boiling. Pack into hot jars, leaving ½ inch of head space.

    Pints: 15 minutes; quarts: 20 minutes

Apricots

Apricots can be packed in very light, light, or medium syrup. They can also be packed in water, apple juice, or white grape juice. Prepare the liquid and keep it hot. Dip fruit in boiling water for 30 to 60 seconds until skins loosen. Dip quickly in cold water and slip off skins. Cut in half, remove pits, and slice if desired.

Hot Pack: In a large saucepan heat fruit in syrup, water, or juice to a boil. Pack hot fruit into hot jars leaving ½ inch of head space. When packing halves, place them cut-side down. Fill jars to ½ inch from the top with hot liquid.

    Pints: 20 minutes; quarts: 25 minutes

Raw Pack: Pack raw, sliced fruit into hot jars, leaving ½ inch of head space. When packing halves, place them cut-side down. Fill jars with hot liquid, to ½ inch from the top.

    Pints: 25 minutes; quarts: 30 minutes

Berries (not cranberries or strawberries)

Berries may be canned in water, juice, or syrup. Prepare and heat the liquid of your choice. Wash, drain, cap, and stem berries. For gooseberries, snip off heads and tails with scissors. See specific instructions for canning cranberries, below. Strawberries are thought these days to keep much better frozen, so there are no standard recommendations for canning them.

Hot Pack (blueberries, currants, elderberries, gooseberries, and huckleberries): Heat to boiling about 1 gallon of water for each pound of berries. Blanch berries in boiling water for 30 seconds. Drain. Place ½ c. of hot syrup, juice, or water in each hot jar. Pack hot berries into hot jars, leaving ½ inch head space. Fill jars to ½ inch from top, with more hot syrup, juice, or water.

    Pints and quarts: 15 minutes

Raw (use for any of the berries): Place ½ c. of hot syrup, juice, or water in each hot jar. Fill jars to ½ inch from the top with raw berries, shaking gently while filling. Add more hot syrup, juice, or water, leaving ½ inch head space.

    Pints: 15 minutes; quarts: 20 minutes

Cherries

Stem and wash cherries. Remove pits if desired. If pitted, treat with a little lemon juice to prevent darkening. If cherries are canned unpitted, prick skins on opposite sides with a clean needle to prevent splitting. Cherries may be canned in water, apple juice, white grape juice, or syrup. Heat to boiling the liquid of your choice.

Hot Pack: In a large saucepan add ½ c. water, juice, or syrup to each quart of drained fruit. Bring to a boil. Pack cherries in hot jars, leaving ½ inch head space. Fill jar to ½ inch from top with hot liquid.

    Pints: 15 minutes; quarts: 20 minutes

Raw Pack: Add ½ c. hot water, juice, or syrup to each hot jar. Fill jars to ½ inch from the top with drained cherries, shaking down gently as you fill. Add more hot liquid, leaving ½ inch of head space.

    Pints and quarts: 25 minutes

Cranberries, Hot Pack
Adapted from the NCHFP website

Make a heavy syrup. Wash and remove stems from cranberries. Carefully but quickly add cranberries to boiling syrup. Boil 3 minutes. Fill fruit into hot, clean jars, leaving ½ inch of head space. Cover with boiling syrup, leaving ½ inch of head space. Remove air bubbles and adjust head space if needed. Wipe rims of jars with a dampened clean paper towel; adjust two-piece metal canning lids.

    Pints and quarts: 15 minutes

Peaches: Follow directions and processing times for apricots, on page 150.

Pears, Hot Pack

Prepare a very light, light, or medium syrup, or heat apple juice, white grape juice, or water. Wash and peel pears. Cut lengthwise in halves and remove core with a melon baller or metal measuring spoon. Boil pears 5 minutes in syrup, juice, or water. Pack hot into hot jars, leaving ½ inch of head space. Fill jars to ½ inch from top with hot liquid.

    Pints: 20 minutes; quarts: 25 minutes

Plums

Prepare a very light, light, or medium syrup. Stem and wash plums. To can whole, prick skin on two sides of plums with fork to prevent splitting. Freestone varieties may be halved and pitted.

Hot Pack: Add plums to hot syrup and boil 2 minutes. Cover saucepan and let stand 20 to 30 minutes. Pack hot plums into hot jars, leaving ½ inch of head space. Fill jars with hot syrup to ½ inch from the top.

    Pints: 20 minutes; quarts: 25 minutes

Raw Pack: Pack raw plums firmly into hot jars, leaving ½ inch of head space. Fill jars with hot syrup to ½ inch from the top.

    Pints: 20 minutes; quarts: 25 minutes

❧ Cherry Preserves

June 1935
Adapted from the NCHFP website

2 pt. pitted cherries
3 pt. sugar
2 qt. water

Rinse cherries and put in kettle, cover with sugar and add 2 qt. water. Heat very slowly at first to bring to a boil. Then boil rapidly 12 minutes. Pack fruit in hot, clean pint jars, pouring over hot syrup to cover and leaving ½ inch of head space. Process for 15 minutes.

❧ Canned Rhubarb for Sauce and Pies

June 1918

Wash rhubarb and cut in ½-inch pieces. Cook with sugar in a ratio of ½ c. sugar per 4 c. fruit, bringing to a boil. Pack at once into hot, clean pint or quart jars, leaving ½ inch of head space. Seal and process for 15 minutes.

❦ Pear Preserves
1934
Adapted from the NCHFP website

16 c. diced pears

13 c. sugar

2 tbsp. almond extract

Pare and halve pears and scoop out cores. Make syrup of a ratio of ½ c. sugar to 4 c. water per pound of pears. Boil syrup, then add pears and extract, and boil all together for 5 minutes. Remove from stove and pack hot into clean, hot pint jars, leaving ½ inch of head space. Seal and process for 20 minutes.

❦ Apple Pie Filling

6 qt. firm, crisp, tart apples, such as
 Stayman, Golden Delicious, or Rome

5½ c. sugar

1½ c. Clear Jel

1 tbsp. cinnamon

2½ c. cold water

5 c. apple juice

¾ tbsp. bottled lemon juice (or more, up
 to 1 c., to taste)

Wash, peel, and core apples then slice in ½-inch slices; blanch 6 c. apples at a time in 1 gallon boiling water for 1 minute. Drain, keeping hot fruit in covered bowl while remainder is blanched. Combine sugar, Clear Jel, cinnamon, water, and apple juice in a large kettle. Cook on medium-high heat until mixture thickens and bubbles. Add lemon juice and boil 1 minute, stirring constantly. Mix in apples then pack immediately in hot, clean pint or quart jars, leaving 1 inch of head space. Seal and process for 25 minutes.

❦ Cherry Pie Filling

6 qt. fresh cherries, washed, stemmed,
 and pitted

7 c. sugar

1¾ c. Clear Jel

9⅓ c. cold water

½ c. bottled lemon juice

2 tsp. almond extract, if desired

1 tsp. cinnamon, if desired

Blanch cherries, 6 c. at a time, in 1 gallon of boiling water for 1 minute. Drain, keeping blanched fruit in covered bowl. Combine Clear Jel, water, and flavorings in a large kettle and cook over medium-high heat until thick and bubbly. Add lemon juice and boil one minute, stirring constantly. Mix in cherries then pack immediately in hot, clean pint or quart jars, leaving 1 inch of head space. Seal and process for 30 minutes.

Preserved Tomatoes and Tomato Products

The tomato was one of the most important crops in a farmer's wife's garden. She canned it whole or in pieces to use in later, winter-bound recipes; she canned it in the form of soups and sauces; she canned it as catsups and spicy condiments to serve along with roasts.

The Basics

Tomatoes canned alone can be processed either in a hot water bath or a pressure canner. Pressure canner times are shorter and yield a more nutritious product, but a full load must be packed into the canner at one time, which makes small-batch canning impossible. A full canner load is comprised of 7 quarts or 9 pints. An average of 21 pounds of whole or halved tomatoes (and 22 pounds of crushed tomatoes) is needed for 7 quarts. An average of 13 pounds (and 14 pounds of crushed tomatoes) is needed for 9 pints. A bushel weighs 53 pounds and yields 15 to 21 quarts, an average of 3 pounds per quart.

If you only want to can a few pints or quarts of tomatoes, a boiling water bath is the clear choice. However, all tomato products that are packed with another vegetable MUST be processed in a pressure canner to ensure safety. A bit further on in this chapter you will find recommendations and recipes from the NCHFP website to start off that great late-summer tradition of canning "Friend Tomato." They are similar to tomato products from *The Farmer's Wife's* own kitchen, with updates for safety.

Only vine-ripened tomatoes in perfect condition should be used for canning. Further, the USDA recommends that you DO NOT use tomatoes from dead or frost-killed vines. To ensure the proper acidity of canned whole, crushed, and juiced tomatoes, add BOTTLED lemon juice: 2 tbsp. per quart and 1 tbsp. per pint, which can be added to the jars just before packing. You can substitute double that amount of vinegar with a 5 percent acidity, although you may not like the flavor. You can add ½ tsp. per pint and 1 tsp. per quart of salt for flavor.

Remember that the processing times listed in this book are for altitudes of 0 to 1,000 feet. If you live at a higher altitude, contact your local extension service agent for the processing times that are correct for your altitude.

Following are some notes on pressure canners, adapted from the Clemson University Extension Service website:

The *Clostridium botulinum* microorganism is the main reason pressure canning is necessary for processing some tomato products, as well as all vegetables and products

that contain meat, poultry, and fish. Though the bacterial cells are killed at boiling temperatures, they can form spores that can withstand these temperatures. These spores grow well in low-acid canned foods in the absence of air. When the spores begin to grow, they produce deadly *botulinum* toxins. These spores can be destroyed by canning food at a temperature of 240 degrees Fahrenheit or above for the correct length of time. This temperature is above the boiling point of water so it can only be reached in a pressure canner.

A pressure canner is a specially made heavy pot with a lid that can be closed to prevent steam from escaping. The lid is fitted with a vent (or petcock), a dial- or weighted-pressure gauge, and a safety fuse. Newer models have an extra cover lock as an added precaution. It may or may not have a gasket. The pressure canner also has a rack. Because each type of canner is different, be sure to read the directions for operating your canner and keep them for future reference. Two types of pressure canners are recommended for home use: the weighted-gauge pressure canner and the dial-gauge pressure canner. Make sure you know what type you have and that it is clean and in good working order. If you are uncertain how to test, maintain, or use your pressure canner, be sure to contact your local extension service agent for assistance.

Here is how Clemson University recommends canning and processing tomatoes and tomato products:

> Gather tomatoes early, when they are at their peak of quality. Do not use overripe, decayed, or damaged tomatoes, or tomatoes picked from frost-killed vines. Gather or purchase only as many as you can handle within two or three hours. Wash the tomatoes carefully, handling small amounts at a time. Lift them out of the water, drain the water, and continue rinsing until the water is clear and free of dirt. Dirt contains some of the bacteria that are most difficult to kill. Don't let the tomatoes soak, though; they will lose flavor and nutrients. The cleaner the raw tomatoes, the more effective the canning process.
>
> Examine jars and discard those with nicks, cracks, and rough edges. These defects will not permit an airtight seal on the jar, and food spoilage will result. All canning jars should be washed in soapy water, rinsed well, and then kept hot. This could be done in the dishwasher or by placing the jars in the water that is heating in your canner. The jars need to be kept hot to prevent breakage when they're filled with a hot product and placed in the canner for processing. Jars that will be filled with food and processed for fewer than 10 minutes in a boiling water bath canner need to be sterilized by boiling them for 10 minutes. *Note:* If you are at an altitude of 1,000 feet or more, boil an additional minute for each 1,000 feet of additional altitude. Jars processed in a boiling water bath canner for 10 minutes or more or in a pressure canner will be sterilized during processing. Be sure to use new two-piece lids. Follow the manufacturer's instructions for treating them. Some need to be brought almost to a boil and then left in hot water, while others need to be boiled for a period of time. (See directions on pages 23–24 (the sweet spreads chapter) for more detailed instructions.)

Tomatoes may be packed raw, or they may be preheated before packing. The hot pack yields better color and flavor, especially when the tomatoes are processed in a boiling water bath. For both raw pack and hot pack, there should be enough syrup, water, or juice to fill in around the tomatoes in the jar and to cover them. If not covered by liquid, the tomatoes at the top tend to darken and develop unnatural flavors. It takes from ½ to 1½ c. of liquid to adequately fill a quart jar.

A bubble freer is a useful tool for tomato and vegetable packing, allowing you to remove air from jars before sealing.

Raw pack: For this method put raw, unheated food directly in jars. Pour boiling water, juice, or syrup over the food to obtain the head space specified in recipe. Tomatoes packed raw should be packed tightly because they will shrink during processing.

Hot pack: For this method, heat the tomatoes to boiling (or for specified time) and then pack along with boiling hot liquid in hot jars. Tomatoes packed hot should be packed fairly loosely, as shrinkage has already taken place.

Steps for Boiling Water Bath Method

Fill the canner about halfway with hot water. Turn on the burner and heat the water.

For raw-packed jars, have the water in the canner hot but not boiling to prevent breakage of the jars when they're placed in the canner. For hot-packed jars, use hot or gently boiling water.

Fill the jars as described in raw pack or hot pack methods above.

Allow the proper head space, as indicated in each recipe. This is necessary so that all the extra air will be removed during processing, and a tight vacuum seal will be formed.

To make sure that air bubbles have not been trapped inside the jar, run a bubble freer or any plastic or rubber utensil around the edges of the jar, gently shifting the food, so that any trapped air is released. After the air bubbles have been removed, more liquid may need to be added to the jar to ensure proper head space.

Wipe off the rims of the jars with a clean, damp cloth.

Screw on the lids, but not too tightly. Air needs to escape during processing.

Put filled glass jars on the rack in the canner. Add more boiling water or take out some as needed so that the water is at least 1 inch over the tops of the jars. (If you add more water, pour it between the jars, not directly on them, to prevent breakage.) Put the lid on the canner.

When the water in the canner reaches a rolling boil, begin timing. Boil gently and steadily for the recommended time, adjusting the heat and adding more boiling water as necessary.

Use a jar lifter to carefully remove the jars as soon as the processing time is up. Place the hot jars right-side up on a rack, dry towels, boards, or newspapers to prevent the jars from breaking on contact with a cold surface. Leave at least 1 inch of space between jars.

Do not tighten the lids.

Allow the jars to cool untouched for 12 to 14 hours.

Steps for Pressure Canner Method

Be sure to read your manufacturer's instructions on the use of your pressure canner.

Place 2 to 3 inches of water in the canner. It should be hot but not boiling when canning raw-packed food; hot or gently boiling for hot-packed foods.

Fill the jars as described in raw pack or hot pack methods on page 156.

Allow proper head space, remove air bubbles, wipe jar rims, and put on lids.

Process:

Set the jars of food on the rack in the canner so steam can flow around each jar. Fasten the canner lid so that no steam begins to escape except through the vent. Turn heat to high and watch until steam begins to escape from the vent. Let the steam escape steadily for 10 minutes.

Close the vent using a weight, valve, or screw, depending on the type of canner you have. If you have a weighted-gauge canner that has a weight of varying pressures, be sure you are using the correct pressure.

For a dial-gauge canner, let the pressure rise quickly to 8 pounds of pressure. Adjust the burner temperature down slightly and let the pressure continue to rise to the correct pressure. (If the burner were left on high, the pressure would be hard to regulate when the correct pressure is reached.) Start counting the processing time as soon as the pressure is reached.

For weighted-gauge canners, let the canner heat quickly at first and then adjust the heat down slightly until the weight begins to rock gently or "jiggle" two to three times per minute, depending on the type of canner you have. Start counting the processing time as soon as the weight does either of these.

Keep the pressure constant by regulating the heat under the canner. *Do not lower the pressure by opening the vent or lifting the weight.* Keep drafts from blowing on the canner to prevent lowering the temperature of the contents. Fluctuating pressure causes underprocessing and the loss of liquid from jars.

When the processing is completed, carefully remove the canner from the heat. If the canner is too heavy to lift, simply turn it off.

Let the pressure in the canner drop to zero. This will take 30 to 45 minutes in a standard heavy-walled canner and nearly an hour for a larger 22-quart canner. Newer thin-walled canners depressurize more quickly. Do not rush the cooling by setting the canner in water or by running cold water over the canner. *Never lift the weight or open the vent to hasten the reduction in pressure.*

Older canners are depressurized when the gauge on a dial-gauge canner registers zero or when a gentle nudge to the weight on a weighted gauge canner does not produce steam or resistance. New canners are equipped with a safety lock. These canners are depressurized when the safety lock drops to normal position. When a

canner is depressurized, open the vent or remove the weight. Wait two minutes and then open the canner.

Note: Sometimes safety locks that are located in the handle of a canner will stick. If a nudge to a canner weight shows that it is depressurized, remove the weight, wait two minutes and then run a knife blade between the handles to release the lock.

Unfasten the lid and tilt the far side up, so the steam escapes away from you. Do not leave the canner unopened, or the food inside could begin to spoil. Use a jar lifter to carefully remove the jars from the canner. Place the hot jars on a rack, dry towels, boards, or newspaper right-side up to prevent the jars from breaking on contact with a cold surface. Leave at least 1 inch of space between the jars.

Do not tighten the lids. Allow the jars to cool untouched for 12 to 24 hours.

Test the lids to make sure they are correctly sealed (see page 142). If a jar is not sealed, refrigerate it and use the unspoiled food within two to three days, reprocess the food within 24 hours at the original processing time (see page 143), or freeze it in a plastic freezer-proof container. If liquid has been lost from sealed jars do not open them to replace it; simply plan to use these jars first. The food may discolor but if the jars are sealed, the food is safe. The screw bands should be removed from the sealed jars to prevent them from rusting on. The screw bands should then be washed, dried, and stored for later use. Wash food residue from the jars and rinse. Label with contents, date, and lot number (if you canned more than one canner load that day). It is important to write down the lot number so that if one jar spoils, you can identify the others from that canner load. Store in a clean, cool, dark, dry place. The best temperature is between 50 and 70°F. Avoid storing canned foods in a warm place near hot pipes, a range or a furnace, or in direct sunlight. They lose quality in a few weeks or months, depending on the temperature and may even spoil. Keep canned goods dry. Dampness may corrode metal lids and cause leakage so food will spoil. For best quality, use canned foods within one year.

Do not taste or use canned food that shows any sign of spoilage! Look closely at all jars before opening them. A bulging lid or leaking jar is a sign of spoilage. When you open the jar, look for other signs such as spurting liquid, an off-odor, or mold. Spoiled canned foods should be discarded in a place where they will not be eaten by humans or pets. If you have any questions concerning food safety, do not hesitate to contact your local extension service agent.

Whole or Halved Tomatoes, Packed Raw without Liquid
Adapted from Clemson University Extension Service website
Wash tomatoes. Dip in boiling water for 30 to 60 seconds or until skins split, then dip in cold water. Slip off skins and remove cores. Leave whole or halve. Add 1 tbsp. bottled lemon juice per pint to the jars and ½ tsp. of salt per quart, if desired. Fill jars with raw tomatoes; press pieces in until spaces between them fill with juice. Leave ½ inch of head space. Wipe jar rims. Adjust lids and process:

Boiling water bath, pints or quarts: 85 minutes

Dial-gauge pressure canner at 11 pounds pressure or weighted-gauge pressure canner at 10 pounds pressure, pints or quarts: 25 minutes

Whole or Halved Tomatoes, Packed in Water
Adapted from Clemson University Extension Service website
Wash tomatoes. Dip in boiling water for 30 to 60 seconds or until skins split; then dip in cold water. Slip off skins and remove cores. Leave whole or halve. Add 1 tbsp. bottled lemon juice per pint to jars.

Hot pack: Add enough water to cover the tomatoes and boil them gently for 5 minutes. Fill jars with hot tomatoes or with raw peeled tomatoes. Add the hot cooking liquid to the hot pack, leaving ½ inch of head space. Adjust lids and process (see below).

Raw pack: Heat water for packing tomatoes to a boil. Add 1 tsp. salt to each quart, ½ tsp. to each pint jar, if desired. Pack prepared tomatoes in hot jars, leaving ½ inch of head space. Fill hot jars to ½ inch from top with boiling water. Adjust lids and process:

Boiling water bath, pints: 40 minutes; quarts: 45 minutes

Dial-gauge pressure canner at 11 pounds pressure, or weighted-gauge pressure canner at 10 pounds pressure, pints or quarts: 10 minutes

Crushed Tomatoes with No Added Liquid
Adapted from Clemson University Extension Service website
Wash tomatoes and dip in boiling water for 30 to 60 seconds or until skins split. Then dip in cold water, slip off skins, and remove cores. Trim off any bruised or discolored portions and quarter. Heat ⅙ of the quarters quickly in a large pot, crushing them with a wooden mallet or spoon as they are added. This will draw out the juice. Continue heating the tomatoes, stirring to prevent burning. Once the tomatoes are boiling, gradually add remaining quartered tomatoes, stirring constantly. These remaining tomatoes do not need to be crushed. They will soften with heating and stirring. Continue until all tomatoes are added. Then boil gently 5 minutes. Add 1 tbsp. bottled lemon juice per pint to jars (2 tbsp. per quart) and ½ tsp. salt per pint, if desired. Fill jars immediately with hot tomatoes, leaving ½ inch of head space. Wipe jar rims. Adjust lids and process:

Boiling water bath, pints: 35 minutes; quarts: 45 minutes

Dial-gauge pressure canner at 11 pounds pressure or weighted-gauge pressure canner at 10 pounds pressure, pints or quarts: 15 minutes

❧ Tomato Sauce for Spaghetti

February 1929

Adapted from the NCHFP website

This sauce may be used for seasoning meats or soups or for macaroni and spaghetti dishes.

30 lbs. tomatoes, washed, skins and
  cores removed
1 c. onion, chopped
1 c. chopped celery
4 tbsp. minced parsley

2 tbsp. salt
4 tbsp. sugar
2 bay leaves
¼ c. olive oil

Cook tomatoes 20 minutes, uncovered, then put through a food mill to remove seeds. Chop onions and soften in a little oil with celery in a kettle over a low flame. Add tomatoes, parsley, and seasonings, bring to a boil, then cook at moderate heat until reduced by one-half. Remove bay leaves and pack in hot, clean jars, adding bottled lemon juice following instructions on page 155. Leave 1 inch of head space. Seal and process.

Dial-gauge canner at 11 pounds pressure or a weighted-gauge pressure canner at 10 pounds pressure. Pints: 20 minutes; quarts: 25 minutes

❧ Stewed Tomatoes

Adapted from the Clemson University Extension Service website

2 qt. chopped tomatoes
¼ c. chopped green peppers
¼ c. chopped onions

2 tsp. celery salt
2 tsp. sugar
¼ tsp. salt

Combine ingredients, cover, and cook 10 minutes, stirring often. Pour hot into hot, clean pint or quart jars, leaving ½ inch of head space. Remove air bubbles with a bubble freer, wipe jar rims, adjust lids, and process.

Dial-gauge pressure canner at 11 pounds pressure or in a weighted-gauge pressure canner at 10 pounds pressure. Pints: 15 minutes; quarts: 20 minutes

❧ Tomato Catsup
Adapted from the NCHFP website

24 lbs. ripe tomatoes
3 c. onions, chopped
¾ tsp. cayenne
4 tsp. whole cloves
2 sticks cinnamon, crushed into small
   pieces under a knife handle

1½ tsp. whole allspice
2 tbsp. celery seeds
3 c. vinegar (5 percent acidity)
1½ c. sugar
¼ c. canning or pickling salt

Wash tomatoes. Dip in boiling water for 30 to 60 seconds or until skins split. Then dip in cold water, slip off skins, and remove cores. Quarter tomatoes and place in a 4-gallon pot. Add onions. Bring to boil and simmer 20 minutes, uncovered. Combine spices in a spice bag. Place spices in a spice bag and vinegar in a 2-quart saucepan. Bring to boil. Cover, turn off heat, and let stand for 20 minutes. Remove spice bag from the vinegar and add the vinegar to the tomato mixture. Boil about 30 minutes. Press boiled mixture through a food mill or sieve. Return to the pot. Add sugar and salt and boil gently, stirring frequently until volume is reduced by one-half or until mixture rounds up on spoon without separation. Pour into clean, hot pint jars, leaving ⅛ inch of head space. Wipe jar rims. Adjust lids. Process 15 minutes in a boiling water canner.

❧ Spiced Green Tomatoes
Adapted from the NCHFP website

6 lbs. small, whole green tomatoes, such
   as plum tomatoes
9 c. sugar
1 pt. cider vinegar (5 percent acidity)

2 sticks cinnamon
1 tbsp. whole cloves
1 tbsp. whole allspice
1 tbsp. whole mace or ½ tbsp. ground

Wash, scald, and peel tomatoes. Make a syrup of the sugar, vinegar, and spices. Drop the tomatoes into the syrup and boil until they become clear. Pack into hot, clean pint jars, leaving ½ inch of head space. Strain syrup and pour over tomatoes with the syrup, again leaving ½ inch of head space. Remove air bubbles and adjust head space if needed. Wipe rims of jars with a dampened clean paper towel; seal and process 15 minutes in a boiling water bath.

🌿 Chili Sauce I

September 1910
Adapted from the NCHFP website

8 c. canned diced tomatoes
1½ c. Serrano peppers, seeded
  and chopped
4 c. white vinegar (5 percent acidity)

2 tsp. canning or pickling salt
2 tbsp. whole mixed pickling spice in
  spice bag

Bring all ingredients to a boil. Lower heat and simmer 20 minutes. Press through foodmill, then return to boil for 15 minutes. Pack into clean, hot pint jars, leaving ¼ inch of head space. Process for 10 minutes.

🌿 Chili Sauce II

June 1917
Adapted from the NCHFP website

3 lbs. hot peppers, washed,
  trimmed, and sliced into rings
⅓ c. garlic, minced
4 c. onions, sliced
⅓ c. cilantro leaves, chopped
3 28-oz. cans diced tomatoes
3 c. cider vinegar (5 percent
  acidity)
2½ c. water

Bring all ingredients to a boil and boil 1 hour. Remove from heat and cool slightly. Puree in blender in batches, then return to boil. Pack into hot, clean pint jars, leaving ½ inch of head space. Process for 10 minutes.

TABLE TALK
Home Canning of Vegetables and Fruit
By Ellen Shafroth
April 1912

At the first suggestion of spring and the thought of the good things to come in the garden, we realize that we are somewhat tired of our winter diet. This is especially so if dry vegetables or those bought from the grocer have been the only supply of "green stuff" during the winter months. And at the appearance of that "best seller of the year"—which comes without cost—the seed catalog, we eagerly scan its inviting pages in making the selection of our garden. Given a moderate amount of ground, a few packages of seeds and a half hour of time each day, on the average, plenty of delicious green vegetables and fresh fruits of the smaller varieties may be had for the average family's use, and a goodly supply for canning and preserving for the winter months to follow.

In foreign countries, large amounts of canned goods, both fruits and vegetables, are put up at home as a matter of course, and we are fast reaching that stage in this country. The canning of fruit has been quite largely undertaken by us; vegetables have been considered a more difficult matter, but there is really nothing mysterious about them and we may soon expect that every family having even a small garden, and certainly every farmer with land a-plenty, will "put up" all the fruits and vegetables the family will require, and perhaps more. Many people are so situated that it is impossible to do this and in the supplying of their needs there is a large field for work, at a good profit, for the woman obliged to earn her own living, for the farmer's daughter, or for any other woman having a little spare time during the summer months, for many people will pay a trifle more than the price for store goods for the home-canned article.

On too many farms no attention is paid to the garden. Then men think they are too busy to plow and cultivate the garden plot and the women of the household often have plenty to do without this additional work; but once a garden is established nothing will induce the owners to give it up—if they are made of the right stuff.

A good garden and the canning of its products mean wholesome meals and consequently better health for the family, and a saving not only on doctor's bills but on the grocery bill as well. If the saving on the grocery bill alone is carefully considered, the intelligent farmer will realize that it really pays to take the time to plow and fertilize and cultivate that small garden plot for his family's use, and no one enjoys the luscious green corn, green peas, and string beans, the crisp cucumbers, lettuce and radishes, the sweet musk melons, more than the "boss of the ranch" himself.

Preserved Vegetables and Vegetable Products

The farmer's wife canned all manner of vegetables by the bushel—everything from corn and beans to greens and potatoes.

The Basics

Mostly, the farmer's wife canned her vegetables in a boiling water bath, a method that back in 1939 was considered perfectly safe but is now known to be extremely dangerous, since it does not necessarily kill off the deadly *Clostridium botulinum* microorganism. If you plan to can vegetables, you MUST be prepared to process them in a pressure canner. All methods and recipes in this chapter (except for refrigerator recipes) have been adapted from or checked against tested recipes from the following sources to ensure that they follow the latest standards for using pressure canners, most notably, the preparation of the particular vegetable and amount of time it should be processed: NCHFP website, Clemson University Extension Service website, and University of Georgia Extension Service website. [To process, follow directions on pages 157 and 158 for using a pressure canner.] Times are for altitudes of 0 to 1,000 feet. As always, use only high-quality, freshly picked produce in excellent condition. Pint and quart jars are standard, and a bubble freer is a useful implement for removing air bubbles from jars before sealing.

Canning Vegetables

In April 1925 The Farmer's Wife canned a whole bounty of vegetables and shared the techniques with its readers. Below are updated directions for preparing and processing these farmer's wife staples, using the hot-pack method and adapted from the NCHFP website, a division of the USDA. Remember: All vegetables must be processed in a pressure canner in order to be safe! A full-canner load is comprised of 7 quarts or 9 pints, and amounts needed for each vegetable are given along with the recipes. Add ½ tsp. canning salt per clean, hot pint jar and 1 tsp. salt per quart.

❦ Asparagus

You need about 24½ pounds of asparagus to make 7 quarts.

Wash tender, fresh, tightly tipped asparagus and trim off scales. Break off tough stems and wash again. Leave whole or break into 1-inch pieces. Blanch in boiling water for 3 minutes, then loosely pack into hot, clean jars, leaving 1 inch of head space. Add salt to jars then add boiling blanching water, again leaving 1 inch of head space. Seal and process: in a dial-gauge pressure canner at 11 pounds pressure or in a weighted-gauge pressure canner at 10 pounds pressure: 40 minutes.

❦ Beans, Green and Wax

You need about 14 pounds to make 7 quarts and 9 pounds to make 9 pints.

Wash fresh, tender beans and snap off ends. Blanch in boiling water for 5 minutes, then loosely pack into hot, clean jars, leaving 1 inch of head space. Add salt to jars then add boiling blanching water, again leaving 1 inch of head space. Seal and process: in a dial-gauge pressure canner at 11 pounds pressure or in a weighted-gauge pressure canner at 10 pounds pressure, pints: 20 minutes; quarts: 25 minutes.

❦ Beans, Lima

You will need about 28 pounds to make 7 quarts and 18 pounds to make 9 pints.

Shell fresh, well-filled pods and wash the beans. Cover with boiling water then return to a boil. Pack loosely into hot, clean jars, leaving 1 inch of head space. Add salt to jars then add boiling blanching water, again leaving 1 inch of head space. Seal and process: in a dial-gauge pressure canner at 11 pounds pressure or in a weighted-gauge pressure canner at 10 pounds pressure, pints: 40 minutes; quarts: 50 minutes.

❦ Beets

About 21 pounds of beets without their tops are needed to make 7 quarts, and 13½ pounds are needed to make 9 pints.

Trim small, fresh beets, leaving the roots and an inch of stem and scrub well. Blanch in boiling water 15 to 25 minutes til skins will slip off easily. Cool, remove skins, and cut off stems and roots. Cut into ½-inch cubes or slices. Add salt to hot, clean jars and pack with beets. Cover with boiling water, leaving 1 inch of head space. Seal and process: in a dial-gauge pressure canner at 11 pounds pressure or in a weighted-gauge pressure canner at 10 pounds pressure, pints: 30 minutes; quarts: 35 minutes.

❧ Carrots

You will need about 17½ pounds of carrots without their tops to make 7 quarts and 11 pounds to make 9 pints.

Wash, peel, and rewash fresh, tender carrots. Slice and blanch 5 minutes in boiling water. Add salt to jars then pack with carrots, leaving 1 inch of head space. Cover with boiling blanching water, again leaving 1 inch of head space. Seal and process: in a dial-gauge pressure canner at 11 pounds pressure or in a weighted-gauge pressure canner at 10 pounds pressure, pints: 25 minutes; quarts: 30 minutes.

❧ Corn

You will need about 31½ pounds of perfectly ripe corn still in the husk to make 7 quarts and 20 pounds to make 9 pints.

Husk ripe or slightly unripe ears of corn, remove silk, and wash. Blanch 3 minutes in boiling water, then cut off kernels about ¼ inch above the cob, taking care not to scrape the cob. To each quart of kernels add 1 quart of hot water, bring to a boil, and simmer 5 minutes. Add salt to jars then fill with the corn and water mixture, leaving 1 inch of head space. Seal and process: in a dial-gauge pressure canner at 11 pounds pressure or in a weighted-gauge pressure canner at 10 pounds pressure, pints: 55 minutes; quarts: 85 minutes.

❧ Cream-Style Corn

You will need about 20 pounds of corn still in the husk to make 9 pints. Do not can this in quarts!

Husk ripe or slightly unripe ears of corn, remove silk, and wash. Blanch 4 minutes in boiling water, then cut off kernels at their centers and scrape remaining corn from cob with a knife. To each quart of scraped-off corn add 2 c. boiling water and return to boil. Add salt to hot, clean jars then fill with corn mixture, leaving 1 inch of head space. Seal and process: in a dial-gauge pressure canner at 11 pounds pressure or in a weighted-gauge pressure canner at 10 pounds pressure, pints: 85 minutes.

❦ Greens: Spinach, Turnip, or Mustard

You will need about 28 pounds of greens to make 7 quarts and 18 pounds to make 9 pints.

Use very fresh greens in perfect condition. Wash small amounts of greens at a time, rinsing until completely free of dirt. Cut leaves from stems and midribs then place 1 lb. at a time in a basket or colander and steam 3 to 5 minutes until very wilted. Add salt to jars then pack loosely with greens, adding boiling water to cover and leaving 1 inch of head space. Seal and process: in a dial-gauge pressure canner at 11 pounds pressure or in a weighted-gauge pressure canner at 10 pounds pressure, pints: 70 minutes; quarts: 90 minutes.

❦ Peas

You will need about 31½ pounds of peas in pods to make 7 quarts and about 20 pounds to make 9 pints.

Shell fresh, young, well-filled pea pods and wash peas. Blanch 2 minutes in boiling water. Add salt to jars then pack loosely with hot peas; cover with boiling blanching water, leaving 1 inch of head space. Seal and process: in a dial-gauge pressure canner at 11 pounds pressure or in a weighted-gauge pressure canner at 10 pounds pressure, pints or quarts: 40 minutes.

❦ Peppers (Hot or Sweet)

About 9 pounds are needed to make 9 pints. Do not use quarts.

Select fresh, firm peppers in perfect condition. Wash and remove seeds and cores. Small peppers may be canned whole, large peppers may be cut in quarters. Cut a few slits in the skin of each pepper and blanch 2 minutes in boiling water. Allow to cool then peel; flatten whole peppers. Add salt to jars then pack loosely with peppers; cover with boiling water, leaving 1 inch of head space. Seal and process: in a dial-gauge pressure canner at 11 pounds pressure or in a weighted-gauge pressure canner at 10 pounds pressure, pints: 35 minutes.

❦ Pumpkin

You need about 16 pounds to make 7 quarts and 10 pounds to make 9 pints.

Wash and peel fresh, small sugar pumpkins. Remove seeds and strings and cut in 1-inch cubes. Blanch for 2 minutes in boiling water. Add salt to clean, hot jars then pack with pumpkin cubes. DO NOT MASH OR PUREE. Cover with boiling blanching water, leaving 1 inch of head space. Seal and process: in a dial-gauge pressure canner at 11 pounds pressure or in a weighted-gauge pressure canner at 10 pounds pressure, pints: 55 minutes; quarts: 90 minutes.

❦ Sweet Potatoes

You need about 17½ pounds to make 7 quarts and 11 pounds to make 9 pints.

Wash small, mature, freshly harvested sweet potatoes and steam 15 to 20 minutes til somewhat soft. Remove skins and cut into bite-sized pieces. DO NOT MASH OR PUREE. Add salt to jars then pack with sweet potatoes, leaving 1 inch of head space. Pour over boiling water or syrup (see chart on page 149), again leaving 1 inch of head space. Seal and process: in a dial-gauge pressure canner at 11 pounds pressure or in a weighted-gauge pressure canner at 10 pounds pressure, pints: 65 minutes; quarts: 90 minutes.

❦ Succotash

March 1925

This recipe, a favorite of The Farmer's Wife, *is adapted here from the NCHFP. It will yield 7 quarts of succotash.*

3 qt. whole corn kernels, washed and cut as directed on page 166.
4 qt. shelled lima beans (prepared as directed on page 165)
2 qt. whole tomatoes (prepared as directed on page 159)

Combine vegetables in a large kettle with just enough water to cover. Boil 5 minutes. Add salt to hot, clean jars, then pack with vegetables and cooking liquid, leaving 1 inch of head space. Seal and process in a dial-gauge pressure canner at 11 pounds pressure or in a weighted-gauge pressure canner at 10 pounds pressure, quarts: 85 minutes.

❦ Mixed Vegetables

February 1929

The farmer's wife loved to can mixed vegetables. They added a touch of élan to her pantry. This mixture is adapted from the NCHFP. All vegetables should be prepared as directed on the preceding pages.

4 c. zucchini
6 c. sliced carrots
5 c. whole-kernel corn

6 c. green beans
6 c. lima beans
4 c. crushed tomatoes

Wash, trim, and cube zucchini. Prepare carrots, corn, green beans, lima beans, and tomatoes as directed on pages 159, 165, and 166. Combine all vegetables in a large kettle, adding just enough water to cover. Boil 5 minutes. Add salt to hot, clean jars, then pack with vegetables and cooking liquid, leaving 1 inch of head space. Seal and process: in a dial-gauge pressure canner at 11 pounds pressure or in a weighted-gauge pressure canner at 10 pounds pressure, pints: 75 minutes; quarts: 90 minutes.

I Can Vegetable Soup

August 1922

Contributed by Anna L. Mark

When fresh vegetables are plentiful, I can vegetable soup for winter use. We have been doing this for the past eight years, and find it advantageous to do so at a time when varieties of vegetables are plentiful and cheap. When winter comes, we can have a deliciously flavored soup that is not skimped in varieties of vegetables, some of which are not obtainable during that season. It has found favor with all our friends who have eaten it at our table and many of them are now canning it by the same recipe for home use.

We started canning vegetable soup as a method of utilizing surplus produce sometimes left over after supplying a retail trade. It was so well liked by the entire family that it has become one of our regularly canned products for home use each season.

Various combinations were tried at first, but the one always used now contains the following:

½ peck green beans (4 qt., or 16 c.)

12 ears sweet corn

12 medium-sized carrots

6 sweet mango peppers

6 red cayenne peppers

6 large onions

½ bushel ripe tomatoes

Editor's note: To update this recipe and make it safe for contemporary canning, it has been adapted from the NCHFP website and several vegetables have been removed for which no current processing recommendations exist: celery, cabbage, and turnips. Proceed as follows:

Prepare beans, corn, and peppers as instructed on pages 165–167 and tomatoes as instructed for Crushed Tomatoes with No Added Liquid, on page 159. Select small, tender carrots, wash, peel, rewash, then slice and blanch in boiling water for 5 minutes. Select onions that are 1 inch in diameter or smaller, then wash, peel, and blanch in boiling water for 5 minutes. Combine all together and boil 5 minutes. DO NOT THICKEN or add rice or pasta. Season with salt to taste. Pack hot, clean pint or quart jars halfway with vegetables, then cover with remaining liquid, leaving 1 inch of head space. Seal and process: in a dial-gauge pressure canner at 11 pounds pressure or in a weighted-gauge pressure canner at 10 pounds pressure, pints: 60 minutes; quarts: 75 minutes.

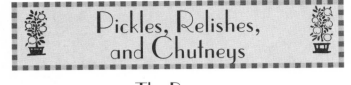

Pickles, Relishes, and Chutneys

The Basics

All of these methods and recipes have been adapted and checked for safety against the NCHFP and the Clemson University Extension Service websites.

Following is general information on fermented and pickled foods from the NCHFP website.

The many varieties of pickled and fermented foods are classified by ingredients and method of preparation. Regular dill pickles and sauerkraut are fermented and cured for about three weeks. Refrigerator dills are fermented for about one week. During curing, colors and flavors change and acidity increases. Fresh-pack or quick-process pickles are not fermented; some are brined several hours or overnight, then drained and covered with vinegar and seasonings. Fruit pickles usually are prepared by heating fruit in a seasoned syrup acidified with either lemon juice or vinegar. Relishes are made from chopped fruits and vegetables that are cooked with seasonings and vinegar. Be sure to remove and discard a $\frac{1}{16}$-inch slice from the blossom end of fresh cucumbers. Blossoms may contain an enzyme that causes excessive softening of pickles.

Caution: The level of acidity in a pickled product is as important to its safety as it is to taste and texture.

Do not alter vinegar, food, or water proportions in a recipe or use a vinegar with unknown acidity. It is recommended that only vinegar with a 5 percent acidity level be used. White distilled and cider vinegars of 5 percent acidity (50 grain) are recommended. White vinegar is usually preferred when light color is desirable, as is the case with fruits and cauliflower.

Use only recipes with tested proportions of ingredients.

There must be a minimum, uniform level of acid throughout the mixed product to prevent the growth of botulinum bacteria.

Select fresh, firm fruits or vegetables free of spoilage. Measure or weigh amounts carefully because the proportion of fresh food to other ingredients will affect flavor and, in many instances, safety.

Use canning or pickling salt. The noncaking material added to other salts may make the brine cloudy. Since flake salt varies in density, it is not recommended for making pickled and fermented foods.

White granulated and brown sugars are most often used. Corn syrup and honey, unless called for in reliable recipes, may produce undesirable flavors.

Pickle products are subject to spoilage from microorganisms, particularly yeasts and molds, as well as enzymes that may affect flavor, color, and texture. Processing the pickles in a boiling-water canner will prevent both of these problems. Standard canning jars and self-sealing lids are recommended. Processing times and procedures will vary according to food acidity and the size of food pieces.

For cucumber pickles, select firm cucumbers of the appropriate size: about 1½ inches for gherkins and 4 inches for dills. Use odd-shaped and more mature cucumbers for relishes and bread-and-butter style pickles, when they will be sliced or chopped.

For fermenting products, a 1-gallon container is needed for every 5 pounds of fresh vegetables. Therefore, a 5-gallon stone crock is the ideal size for fermenting about 25 pounds of fresh cabbage or cucumbers. Food-grade plastic and glass containers are excellent substitutes for stone crocks. Other 1- to 3-gallon nonfood-grade plastic containers may be used if lined inside with a clean food-grade plastic bag. Caution: Be certain that foods contact only food-grade plastics. Do not use garbage bags or trash liners. Fermenting sauerkraut in quart and half-gallon canning jars is an acceptable practice, but may result in more spoilage losses.

Cabbage and cucumbers must be kept 1 to 2 inches under brine while fermenting. After adding prepared vegetables and brine, insert a suitably sized dinner plate or glass pie plate inside the fermentation container. The plate must be slightly smaller than the container opening, yet large enough to cover most of the shredded cabbage or cucumbers. To keep the plate under the brine, weight it down with two to three sealed quart jars filled with water. Covering the container opening with a clean, heavy bath towel helps to prevent contamination from insects and molds while the vegetables are fermenting. Fine quality fermented vegetables are also obtained when the plate is weighted down with a very large clean, plastic bag filled with 3 quarts of water containing 4½ tbsp. of salt. Be sure to seal the plastic bag. Freezer bags sold for packaging turkeys are suitable for use with 5-gallon containers.

The fermentation container, plate, and jars must be washed in hot, sudsy water and rinsed well with very hot water before use.

All pickle products may be processed in a boiling water canner. See detailed instructions on pages 140–143 (jelly section), but follow specific recipe instructions in this section for processing times.

❦ Bread and Butter Pickles

August 1930

Adapted from the NCHFP website

Wash cucumber and cut in slices (USDA recommends ³⁄₁₆ inch), discarding blossom ends.

6 lbs. pickling cucumbers, 4 to 5 inches long	4½ c. sugar
	2 tbsp. mustard seed
8 c. onion, thinly sliced	1½ tbsp. celery seed
½ c. canning or pickling salt	1 tbsp. ground turmeric
4 c. vinegar at 5 percent acidity	3 tsp. ground ginger

Mix cucumbers with onions and salt in a large bowl, covering with 2 inches of ice. Let stand in refrigerator 3 hours, adding more ice as ice in bowl melts. Combine sugar, vinegar, and spices in a large kettle and bring to a boil; boil 10 minutes then add drained vegetables. Slowly reheat to boiling then pack hot into hot, clean pint or quart jars, leaving ½ inch of head space, making sure vegetables are well-covered with syrup. Seal and process 10 minutes in a boiling water bath. Ideal pickle flavor develops after 4 to 5 weeks in jars.

CORA PICKLE'S PICKLES

By Miriam J. Williams

September 1938

The fact that her name was Cora Pickle before she was married probably had little to do with Mrs. Albert Wilson's success in making and marketing pickles from her own farm home and her husband's store near Clarksville, Texas.

But when she was quite young she was made sick on poor pickles and decided to learn to make good ones.

She made a beginning with 46 pounds of brined cucumbers in 1934. Last fall she and her husband brined 3,000 pounds of cucumbers and 350 pounds of white pickling onions. That her results are successful we realized fully when an attractive jar of Orange Ring Pickles came to the Country Kitchen—crisp slices of pickled cucumber with orange rind centers giving them a most intriguing spicy flavor. So fast has the Wilsons' fame spread that they have shipped pickles to no [fewer] than ten states.

Mrs. Wilson does not use alum to make her pickles crisp, but rather depends upon careful curing and gradual concentration of syrup during the sweetening process, which sometimes requires as long as five weeks. Only the best quality vinegar is used, an important factor in Mrs. Wilson's opinion.

When pickles have been canned for 10 days or two weeks, she opens a test jar or two, and if satisfactory in every way, into the store they go for sale. Small jars of from 6 to 11 ounces each, depending on the kind, sell at the store for 15 cents, 20½-ounce jars of sours and dills for 20 cents, and the same size of sweets or chow-chow for 25 cents. Their label, designed by Mrs. Wilson, is registered at the county courthouse.

❦ Dill Pickles

July 1910

Adapted from the NCHFP website

To this recipe, The Farmer's Wife originally added grape leaves (according to the USDA, grape leaves contain an enzyme that prevents softening but removing the blossom end from a cucumber has the same effect), bay leaves, green pepper, horseradish, and dill. This recipe provides a variation to this combination.

4 lbs. pickling cucumbers, 4 inches long
4 to 5 heads fresh dill, divided in half
2 tsp. whole mixed pickling spice, divided in half

½ c. canning or pickling salt
¼ c. vinegar at 5 percent acidity
8 c. water
2 dried red peppers

Wash cucumbers and slice off blossom ends; trim stem to ¼ inch. Place half the dill and half the spices at the bottom of a clean gallon container (see page 171). Add cucumbers and remaining dill and spices. Dissolve salt in vinegar and water and pour mixture over cucumbers. Cover, weight, and cover with a clean towel. Store, maintaining a temperature of between 70°F and 75°F for 3 to 4 weeks, or at temperature of between 55°F and 65°F for 5 to 6 weeks. Check container several times a week and remove any surface scum or mold that develops. However, if pickles become soft, slimy, or foul-smelling, discard them.

Pour brine into a large kettle and bring slowly to a boil; lower heat and simmer 5 minutes. Filter through a coffee filter, then pour over pickles packed into hot, clean pint jars, leaving ½ inch of head space. Seal and process for 10 minutes in a boiling water bath.

TEXTURE TRICKS IN PICKLES

By Miriam J. Williams
September 1935

When is a pickle a good pickle? Let an experienced judge of food products give the answer: "A pickle must have snap," she says. "It should add interest to a meal which already has enough bland, mild-flavored food. It must not be disagreeably sharp, for most people prefer a very slightly sweet taste along with the acid, nor should it be so heavily spiced that the mouth feels puckery. But as for texture, is there anything more sad than a soft, slippery pickle?"

Sometimes, the judge said, vegetables are cooked too long, as in mustard pickles or spiced fruit pickles. More often, the failure to get crispness is due to insufficient curing or perhaps poor vinegar. And remember, pickles need time. Almost all kinds need to stand in the jars to develop flavor before they are opened for use.

Causes of Pickle Troubles

Soft or slippery
Action on bacteria, due to too weak a brine or pickles exposed above brine
Fermentation sets in because of weak vinegar solution

Poor color
Over-dark pickles may be caused by hard water
Dark because of free spice
Light or dull pickles may be due to scalding or poor-colored cucumbers

Hollow
Cucumbers not strictly fresh or poor quality

Shriveled
Too strong a salt or vinegar solution
Too sweet a pickling syrup

❦ Beet Sweet Pickles

September 1911
Adapted from the NCHFP website

7 lbs. beets, 2 to 2½ inches in diameter
4 c. cider vinegar at 5 percent acidity
2 c. brown sugar
1½ tsp. canning or pickling salt

2 c. water
2 cinnamon sticks
12 whole cloves
1 tsp. whole allspice

Trim off beet greens, leaving roots and 1 inch of stem. Wash and sort for size, cooking same-sizes together until tender, 25 to 30 minutes. Drain beets and cool. Peel and trim off roots and stems, slice ¼ inch thick. Combine vinegar, sugar, salt, and 2 c. new water in a large kettle with spices in a spice bag. Bring to a boil then add beets. Simmer 5 minutes, remove spice bag, and pack beets into clean, hot pint jars, leaving ½ inch of head space. Pour over hot syrup, leaving ½ inch of head space. Seal and process 30 minutes in a boiling water canner.

❦ Bean Pickles (Dilly Beans)

September 1911
Adapted from the NCHFP website
Another almost-annual favorite of The Farmer's Wife.

4 lbs. green beans, 5 inches long
8 heads fresh dill
8 cloves garlic
½ c. canning or pickling salt

4 c. white vinegar at 5 percent acidity
4 c. water
1 tsp. red pepper flakes

Wash beans and trim ends to make each bean 4 inches long. Place 1 dill head and 1 clove garlic in each hot, sterile pint jar. Pack in beans upright, leaving ½ inch of head space. Bring remaining ingredients to a boil in a pot and pour over beans, again leaving ½ inch of head space. Seal and process 5 minutes in a boiling water bath.

❦ Apple Relish

Adapted from the NCHFP website

4 lbs. apples, peeled, cored, and thinly sliced, then soaked in 2 qt. water and ½ tsp. ascorbic acid to prevent discoloration
1 c. white vinegar at 5 percent acidity
1¼ c. sugar

½ c. light corn syrup
⅔ c. water
1½ tsp. whole cloves
2 sticks cinnamon, crushed
1 tsp. whole allspice

Combine all ingredients but apples in a large pot and bring to a boil. Drain apples, add them to the syrup, and simmer 3 minutes. Return to boil. Pack apples into hot, clean pint jars, leaving ½ inch of head space. Pour over hot syrup, again leaving ½ inch of head space. Remove air bubbles, seal, and process 10 minutes in a boiling water bath.

Green Tomato Relish

September 1913
Adapted from the NCHFP website

10 lbs. small, hard green tomatoes
3 lbs. mixed green and red bell pepper, diced
2 lbs. onions, diced
½ c. canning or pickling salt
1 qt. water

4 c. sugar
1 qt. cider vinegar at 5 percent acidity
1 tsp. each cinnamon, cloves, and mace in spice bag
⅓ c. prepared yellow mustard
2 tbsp. cornstarch

Wash tomatoes, chop fine, and place in a large pot. Dissolve salt in water and pour over tomatoes. Bring to a boil, lower heat, and simmer 5 minutes. Drain and return tomatoes to pot. Add remaining ingredients, stir, and bring to a boil; lower heat and simmer 5 more minutes. Discard spice bag and pack hot relish into hot, sterilized pint jars, leaving ½ inch of head space. Seal and process 5 minutes in a boiling water bath.

Indian Chutney

September 1918
Adapted from the NCHFP website
This recipe, completely lacking in spice, reflects the farmer's wife's preference for milder foods. You may add 1 tsp. ground ginger and ¼ c. whole mixed pickling spice in a spice bag at the initial boiling stage if you prefer a chutney that is somewhat peppier.

6 lbs. ripe tomatoes, washed, skinned, and chopped (to equal 3 qt.)
5 lbs. sour apples, peeled, cored, and chopped (to equal 3 qt.)
2 c. seedless raisins
2 c. onion, chopped

1 c. mixed green and red bell peppers, chopped
2 lbs. brown sugar
4 c. vinegar at 5 percent acidity
4 tsp. canning or pickling salt

Combine ingredients in a large pot and bring to a boil. Lower heat to boil gently for 1 hour, stirring frequently, til mixture is thick and reduced by one-half. Pack hot into hot, clean pint jars, leaving ½ inch of head space. Remove air bubbles, seal, and process 10 minutes in a boiling water bath.

Baking

The farmer's wife baked for every circumstance and occasion. She baked all the family's bread, to accompany meals, to slice for sandwiches, and, when stale, to grind for crumbs. At a time when "dinner" was called "supper" and no supper was complete without dessert, she baked tarts and pastries to follow up roasts and stews and casseroles. She baked cookies and cupcakes to stick in her children's lunch pails. She baked dainties and muffins to serve at afternoon teas and club luncheons. She baked elaborate cakes for birthdays and weddings. She baked simple pies in great profusion to serve at threshing parties and other large community gatherings. Through the rationing of World War I, the privations of the Great Depression, and the uncertainty of the years leading up to World War II, the farmer's wife baked what she had—sometimes absent wheat and sugar—and she baked it as well as she could. The following recipes are a testament to the durability and ingenuity of the farmer's wife.

Cookies and Bars

❧ Jam Marguerites

Perhaps the fastest, simplest cookies of all time.

2 egg whites
2 drops lemon extract

3 tbsp. raspberry or other jam
Saltine- or Ritz-type crackers

Beat egg whites stiff and gradually add the jam. Mix until thoroughly blended. Add lemon extract. Place by the spoonful on crackers and sprinkle with more nuts. Bake at 350°F until delicately brown.

Variation:

Black Walnut Crisps: Substitute 6 tbsp. chopped black walnuts for jam, and vanilla for lemon extract; add 6 tbsp. sugar.

❧ Marshmallow Marguerites

1 egg white
½ c. marshmallows, cut up

½ c. nuts, chopped
Saltine- or Ritz-type crackers

Beat egg white till stiff. Add marshmallows and nuts. Mix. Drop small spoonfuls of mixture on individual crackers and bake at 350°F until a glaze has formed on top. Serve strictly fresh.

Plain drop cookies are not easy to come by with the farmer's wife—she preferred nuts or molasses in hers, or sour cream to replace the butter. The following two recipes are adapted from Our Favorite Recipes, *a church collection from New Jersey, for those days when you must bake but there's very little in the larder.*

❧ Plain Drop Cookies

½ c. unsalted
  butter, softened
1 c. maple syrup

1 egg
2¼ c. flour

2 tsp. baking powder
1 tsp. salt

Cream butter; add the syrup and egg. Sift in dry ingredients and mix well. Drop by teaspoonfuls onto buttered baking sheets with plenty of room between. Bake at 400°F until golden.

Chewy Drop Cookies

½ c. unsalted butter, softened
1 c. sugar
2 eggs, stiffly beaten
1 tsp. milk

2 tsp. baking powder
pinch salt
1 c. flour

Cream butter and sugar, then add eggs and milk. Sift in baking powder, salt, and flour and mix well. Drop by teaspoonfuls onto buttered baking sheets with plenty of room between. Bake at 400°F for just a few minutes, watching closely to prevent scorching.

Variation:
Orange Drop Cookies: To the above add 1 tsp. grated orange rind and ⅛ tsp. baking soda, and substitute 1 tsp. vanilla for milk.

Sponge Drops
Adapted from Recipes Tried and True by Cooks

3 eggs, beaten light
¾ c. sugar
1 c. flour
⅓ tsp. salt
1 tsp. baking powder

To the eggs add sugar and mix well. Sift in remaining ingredients, then drop by teaspoonfuls onto buttered baking sheets. Bake at 400°F till lightly golden.

Brown Sugar Drops
A very plain cookie.

1 c. brown sugar, firmly packed
1 large egg
¾ tsp. baking powder
¼ tsp. baking soda dissolved in
⠀⠀¼ c. buttermilk

½ c. unsalted butter
1½ c. flour
¼ tsp. salt
1 tsp. almond extract

Cream sugar with butter; add egg. Sift in dry ingredients, then add buttermilk mixture and extract. Drop on buttered baking sheets and bake 8–10 minutes at 325°F until lightly browned at edges.

TABLE TALK FOR THE COUNTRY COOKIE JAR

By Clara E. Wells
October 1914

As the "stolen fruits" from the cookie jar of our far off youth ever seemed "sweetest," I herewith pass on some of my favorite recipes, and those "begged, borrowed or stolen" from country gentlewomen who do not have to economize so rigidly in their land "flowing with milk and honey" as must the city housewife.

These favorites have been served to the past and present generation though they have never appeared in print.

As the nut and fruit cookies "ripen" with age, the recipes for them should be doubled and the extra supply of cookies be hidden away in the large cookie jar for later use.

[Editor's note: More thorough recipes for most of these cookies appear elsewhere in this book. I include these here as they appear in the magazine, as a point of interest. How would you fare baking from these sparse directions?]

Hickorynut Cookies: One cupful of chopped hickory nut meats, one cupful of sweet milk, two eggs, one cupful and a half of maple sugar, teaspoonful of baking powder sifted in two quarts of flour. Bake in a moderate oven and glaze with honey, pressing half a hickory nut meat in center of each cookie.

Walnut Cookies: Half cupful of walnuts meats, cupful of buttermilk, teaspoonful of soda, quart and half of flour, three eggs, two cupfuls of sugar.

Chocolate Cookies: One cupful of sweet cream, half cupful of butter, four eggs, two cups of sugar, teaspoonful of baking powder sifted in quart of flour. Bake in quick oven, glaze with sweetened chocolate or put half cake of sweetened melted chocolate in batter.

Hermit Cookies: One and a half cupfuls of sugar, two thirds cupful of sugar, three eggs, two tablespoons of Orleans molasses, one teaspoonful of soda. Beat soda in molasses. Two cupfuls of raisins, one teaspoonful of spices. Two quarts of flour.

Cocoanut Cookies: One cupful of sweetened cocoanut, whites of three eggs, one cupful of sugar, one cupful of sweet cream, teaspoonful of baking powder. Bake in quick oven, glaze with honey, and sprinkle with cocoanut.

Caraway Cookies: One cupful of sweet milk, one cupful of butter, one teaspoonful of baking powder, half cup of caraway seeds, two cupfuls of maple sugar, quart and half of flour. Roll thin and bake in quick oven.

School Lunch Cookies: One cupful of lard, one cupful of buttermilk, two cupfuls of sugar, one egg, teaspoonful of baking powder, two quarts of flour. Bake in quick oven, ice with pink sugar.

Harvest Ginger Cookies: One pint of Orleans molasses, cupful of lard or butter, cupful of sugar, cupful of buttermilk, teaspoonful of soda, two quarts of flour. Roll and bake in quick oven. They will disappear quickly when served as afternoon lunch in the harvest field.

Nearly every farmer's wife boils down a jug or more of cider for use in her mince pies yet ignores . . . another good use to which it can be put:

Boiled Cider Cookies: One cupful lard and one cupful sugar creamed together. Add one cupful boiled cider, one teaspoonful soda, and a taste of cloves and cinnamon. Beat one egg, adding a little salt, and then beat all together for five minutes. Add flour enough to make a moderately stiff dough and bake in moderate oven.

❧ Ginger Drops

1 c. sugar	2 c. molasses
1 c. sour cream	1⅓ c. unsalted butter
4 tsp. baking soda	2 tsp. ground ginger
1 tsp. cinnamon	4 eggs
flour to make a soft dough—about 5 c.	

Mix all together well and drop onto buttered baking sheets. Bake at 350°F till done. Watch closely to prevent burning.

Variation:
For New Year's Eve Clock Cookies: Make above ginger cookies large. Decorate with a clock face made of an icing of powdered sugar and heavy cream mixed together until smooth; apply with a toothpick twelve dashes around the edge of the cookie, and two hands pointed near the hour of 12:00.

❧ Walnut Cookies

1 tsp. baking soda dissolved in	3 eggs
1 c. buttermilk	2 c. sugar
6 c. flour	½ c. walnuts, chopped

Mix, adding walnuts last, then drop onto buttered baking sheets and bake at 350°F till just done.

❧ Molasses Butterballs

1 c. unsalted butter, softened
¼ c. molasses
2 c. flour

½ tsp. salt
2 c. walnuts, chopped
confectioner's sugar for rolling

Cream butter; add molasses. Sift in flour and salt, then mix in nuts. Form into 1-inch balls and place on unbuttered baking sheets. Bake at 350°F for about 25 minutes, until lightly browned. Remove from sheets and roll in confectioner's sugar.

❧ Almond Butterballs

1 c. unsalted butter, softened
¼ c. confectioner's sugar
1 tsp. almond extract

2 c. flour
1 c. blanched almonds, chopped

Cream butter and sugar; add extract, then sift in flour. Mix in almonds. Form into 1-inch balls and place on unbuttered baking sheets. Bake at 350°F for about 20 minutes.

❧ Date Butterballs

½ c. unsalted butter, softened
⅓ c. confectioner's sugar
1 tbsp. milk
1 tsp. vanilla
1¼ c. flour

¼ tsp. salt
1 c. dates, pitted and finely chopped
½ c. walnuts, finely chopped
confectioner's sugar for rolling

Cream butter and sugar. Mix in milk and vanilla, then sift in flour and salt. Finally, stir in dates and nuts and mix well. Form into 1-inch balls and place on unbuttered baking sheets. Bake at 350°F for about 20 minutes, until lightly browned. Remove from sheets and roll in confectioner's sugar.

❦ Boston Drops

½ c. unsalted butter, softened
¾ c. sugar
I egg
1½ c. flour
½ tsp. baking powder

¼ tsp. salt
I tsp. cinnamon
½ c. chopped raisins
¼ c. walnuts, chopped

Cream butter and add sugar slowly, creaming them together. Add egg, then sift in
I c. flour, baking powder, salt, and cinnamon. Sift remainder of flour into raisins and
nuts, mix, and add to batter. Mix thoroughly and drop from teaspoon I inch apart on
buttered baking sheets. Bake at 400°F
for 10 to 15 minutes.

Variations:

Dutch Drops: Substitute ½ c. blanched
chopped almonds for walnuts, and ½ tsp.
lightly crushed anise seed for cinnamon.
Omit raisins.

English Drops: Add ½ c. cold coffee;
increase sugar to I c. and flour to 1¾ c.
Omit raisins.

❦ Chocolate Drops

I egg, well beaten
I c. brown sugar
½ c. unsalted butter, softened
2 squares Baker's bittersweet
    chocolate, melted
1½ c. flour, or mix equal parts white and
    wheat flour

¼ tsp. salt
2 tsp. baking soda
1½ tsp. baking powder
½ c. buttermilk
½ tsp. vanilla

Combine egg, sugar, butter, and
chocolate. Beat well. Sift in dry
ingredients. Add liquids and nuts. Mix
thoroughly. Drop from a teaspoon
onto buttered baking sheets about
an inch apart. Bake at 350°F for
about 15 minutes.

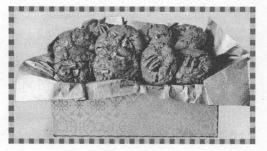

Variation:

Chocolate Nut Drops: Add ½ c. chopped walnuts to the batter.

❧ Iced Chocolate Drops

½ c. unsalted butter, softened
1 c. light brown sugar
1 egg
¼ tsp. baking soda
2 tsp. baking powder

1½ c. flour
½ c. buttermilk
2 squares bittersweet Baker's chocolate,
   melted

Cream butter and sugar; add egg and beat well. Sift baking soda and baking powder with the flour and add alternately with buttermilk. Add the chocolate (and nuts if desired). Drop on buttered baking sheets and bake at 350°F until done. Ice with:

1 egg
2 c. powdered sugar
1 tsp. butter, melted

1 square bittersweet Baker's
   chocolate, melted

Beat the egg slightly and add the sugar, beating until smooth. Add the butter and chocolate and spread on the cookies. If frosting is a bit stiff, add cream to make it the right consistency to spread.

❧ Sour Cream Drop Cookies

Light, puffy cookies. Be sure not to let these brown, since they will dry out quickly in the oven.

¼ c. unsalted butter, softened
1¾ c. sugar
2 eggs, beaten
1 c. sour cream
3 c. flour
½ tsp. baking soda

1 tsp. baking powder
½ tsp. salt
1 tbsp. grated lemon rind
raisins for garnishing
granulated sugar for dusting

Cream butter and ½ c. sugar in a large bowl. Beat eggs with remaining sugar and sour cream and add to first mixture. Sift flour with baking soda, baking powder, and salt. Add lemon rind, then combine with rest of ingredients. Drop small spoonfuls onto buttered baking sheets. Top each cookie with 1 raisin and sprinkle with sugar. Bake at 400°F for 5 to 6 minutes, till very slightly browned at the edges. Remove at once to cooling racks.

Variations—two ways with cinnamon:

Cinnamon Sour Cream Cookies: Add 1 tsp. vanilla and omit lemon rind and raisins; dust with ¼ c. sugar mixed with 2 tsp. cinnamon before baking.

Sour Cream Date Cookies: Substitute 2 c. brown sugar for white sugar, and 1 tsp. cinnamon and ¼ tsp. nutmeg for lemon rind. Add 2 c. chopped dates and 1 c. finely chopped walnuts. Omit raisins.

Fruit Drops

1 c. unsalted butter, softened
3 c. brown sugar
4 tbsp. milk
4 eggs, lightly beaten
2 tsp. baking soda
5 c. flour

2 c. raisins, chopped
2 c. dried currants
1 c. walnuts, chopped
1 tsp. cinnamon
4 tsp. cream of tartar

Cream butter and sugar; add milk and eggs. Sift baking soda and half the flour together and add to the mixture. Add fruit and nuts and work well together, then add cinnamon. To the remainder of the flour add the cream of tartar and sift, then add to the dough. Drop by teaspoonfuls on buttered baking sheets some distance apart and bake at 400°F till done. These are delicious and will keep a long time.

Delicious Drop Cookies

¾ c. unsalted butter, softened
1½ c. brown sugar
3 eggs, beaten
2½ c. flour
pinch salt
1½ c. dates, chopped

1 c. peanuts, skinned and chopped
½ tsp. each cinnamon, allspice, and
   ground cloves
1 tsp. baking soda dissolved in ½ c. hot
   water

Cream butter and sugar; then add eggs, flour, and salt. Mix and add remaining ingredients. Mix well and drop by small spoonfuls onto hot buttered baking sheets. Bake at 400°F till done.

Honey Drop Hermits

1⅓ c. honey
½ c. unsalted butter
1 tsp. cinnamon
½ tsp. cloves
½ tsp. nutmeg
1 egg, beaten

3 to 3½ c. flour
½ tsp. salt
¾ tsp. baking soda dissolved in ¼ c. water
1 c. chopped raisins or ½ c. each nuts
   and raisins

Heat honey and butter together. Add spices to the mixture while it is hot. Cool and add egg. Alternately add flour and salt, sifted together, and baking soda in water, then raisins (and nuts if desired). Beat well. Drop on greased pans and bake at 375°F until just brown.

❦ Peanut Drop Cookies

½ c. unsalted butter, softened
½ c. smooth peanut butter
1 c. brown sugar
1 egg
½ tsp. salt

1⅔ c. flour
1 tsp. baking powder
½ tsp. baking soda
½ c. milk
1 c. salted peanuts, skinned and chopped

Cream butter and peanut butter; add sugar and cream until fluffy. Add egg, beat thoroughly, then add sifted dry ingredients alternately with milk. Divide dough in half; to one half add half of the chopped peanuts. Drop by small spoonfuls on greased tin, pressing lightly with a finger. Drop out the other half of the dough in small spoonfuls, stamp down with a glass covered with a damp cloth, and sprinkle with remaining peanuts. Bake at 375°F for 8 to 12 minutes. This recipe makes 60 cookies. If brown-coated salted nuts are used, put in a salt sack and rub to remove husks. Fan out husks by pouring from one pan to another in the wind.

Variations:

Walnut Drops: Substitute 1 c. chopped walnuts for peanuts and add 1 tsp. vanilla.

Hickory Nut Drops: Same as for Walnut Drops, substituting chopped hickory nuts for walnuts.

Currant Drops: Substitute 1½ c. currants for nuts, dredging them in a little flour before adding to the batter; increase sugar to 1¼ c. and add 1 tsp. vanilla.

❦ Oatmeal Cookies

1½ c. unsalted butter, softened
1½ c. sugar
2 eggs
2 tsp. baking powder

1 tsp. ground cinnamon
2 c. flour
⅓ c. milk or water
2 c. rolled oats

Cream butter and sugar, then add eggs. Sift in baking powder, cinnamon, and flour, then add liquid and, finally, oats. Mix well and drop on buttered baking sheets. Bake at 350°F until browned around edges.

❧ Oatmeal Lace Cookies

A crisp and nearly flourless cookie held together by caramelized sugar. This one is adapted from Cohasset Entertains.

1 c. unsalted butter	1 tbsp. flour
2½ c. light brown sugar	1 egg, beaten
2¼ c. rolled oats	1 tsp. vanilla

Melt butter over low flame. Add sugar and stir until dissolved. Remove from heat and stir in oats and flour. Let stand 5 minutes, then add egg and vanilla. Drop by teaspoonfuls onto well-buttered baking sheets, leaving plenty of room between. Bake at 375°F for 5–7 minutes, until lightly browned at the edges; check often to prevent scorching. Cool on sheets before removing to rack.

Variation:
A slightly chewy, less sweet version of the original. Delicious!

Cocoanut Lace Cookies: Substitute 1 c. shredded unsweetened cocoanut for 1 c. of the oats, and ½ c. honey for ½ c. of the brown sugar. Drop onto well-buttered baking sheets and press lightly with fingers to flatten cookies to the size of silver-dollar coins. Cooking time is slightly less than for Oatmeal Lace Cookies.

❧ Chocolate Oatmeal Drops

Chocolate chip cookies weren't invented till near the demise of The Farmer's Wife. *Here's a version, adapted from* Hot Recipes, *that approximates a cookie that would have come out of the FW kitchen.*

1 c. unsalted butter, softened	½ tsp. salt
½ c. sugar	1 tsp. baking soda
1 c. brown sugar, packed	1 c. rolled oats
2 eggs	1 c. bittersweet chocolate, grated
1 tsp. vanilla	or chopped
1 c. flour	

Cream butter and sugars. Add eggs and vanilla and beat well. Sift in flour, salt, and baking soda and stir to mix. Add oats and chocolate, stir, and drop by spoonfuls onto buttered baking sheets. Bake at 375°F for 8–10 minutes.

❦ Ranch Cookies

Adapted from Recipes from Maa Eway

¼ c. unsalted butter, softened
½ c. brown sugar
½ c. white sugar
1 egg
½ c. flour

¼ tsp. baking powder
½ tsp. baking soda
1 c. rolled oats
½ c. grated unsweetened cocoanut
½ c. pecans, chopped

Cream butter with sugars and add egg. Sift in flour, baking powder, and baking soda. Mix in remaining ingredients and drop by teaspoonfuls on buttered baking sheets. Flatten with fingers. Bake at 350°F for 10–15 minutes.

❦ Wartime Oatmeal Macaroons

A resourceful Farmer's Wife wartime recipe, compensating for a scarcity of sugar.

1 tbsp. unsalted butter,
   melted and cooled
1 egg
½ c. corn syrup

2 c. rolled oats
½ tsp. salt
1 tsp. baking powder

Add egg to butter and beat well, then add corn syrup. Add remaining ingredients and mix. Drop by spoonfuls onto buttered baking sheets and bake at 350°F for about 15 minutes.

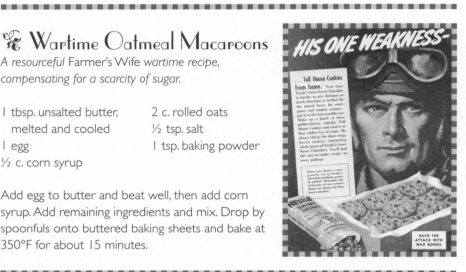

❦ Almond Macaroons

A very delicate, delicious cookie. Recipes nearly identical to this one were the stand-bys in England until the twentieth century, when ingredients other than almonds found their way into the mix, according to the late English food writer and historian Alan Davidson. Cream of tartar will assist in stiffening the egg whites but is not necessary, if you are patient, and adding it will result in an airier cookie.

2 egg whites
⅛ tsp. cream of tartar (optional)
1½ c. confectioner's sugar, sifted

½ c. almond flour, pressed through a
   sieve if grind is not very fine

Beat egg whites till very stiff, with cream of tartar if desired. Very gradually incorporate sugar till the mixture is thick and gluey. Fold in almond flour and drop (or pipe) onto buttered parchment paper–lined baking sheets. Bake at 325°F for 10–15 minutes, until just set—do not allow to brown. Remove immediately from paper.

Variations:

Hickory Nut Macaroons: Substitute 1 c. hickory nuts, ground fine in food processor then sieved, for almond flour.

Pistachio Macaroons: Same as above, substituting 1 c. pistachios for hickory nuts.

Cocoanut Macaroons: Substitute 1 c. cocoanut for nuts.

Fruit Macaroons: Sprinkle up to ½ c. currants or very finely chopped dates or raisins over batter just before spooning onto baking sheets.

Chocolate Macaroons: This (quite toothsome) variation must have appealed to the farmer's wife's sense of thrift; don't throw away those egg yolks—find another use for them! To beaten egg whites, fold in two slightly beaten egg yolks. Mix almond flour with ½ c. grated semi-sweet chocolate (or run ½ c. chocolate chips through the blender, till pulverized) and a few drops of vanilla. Bake 12–15 minutes. This will result in a delicate version of a chocolate chip cookie. Alternately: Melt ½ c. semi-sweet chocolate and allow to cool completely. Mix into egg yolks and fold in.

❦ Simplest Meringue

2 egg whites, beaten stiff
½ c. confectioner's sugar
½ tsp. vanilla

Fold sugar and vanilla into egg whites. Drop in small shapes on buttered waxed paper. Ten or twelve may be made from one white. Bake *very* slowly (*dry* rather than *bake*) at about 225°F for about half an hour or longer.

Variations of the foregoing:
Sprinkle with dessicated cocoanut before baking. Add 2 tsp. cocoa powder with the sugar. Finely chopped nuts may be sprinkled over before baking. Tiny candies, such as sugared caraway seeds, may be put on top before baking. After baking, two may be put together, back to back, with any frosting (or jam).

SAY IT WITH COOKIES
October 1920

There's nothing quite like cookie-baking day. Nothing quite so cheerful in its floury confusion as the cookie-day kitchen, or so compelling as the spicy smell when each pan comes from the oven. Nothing quite so absorbing to the cook as this task which keeps both hands busy and demands a watchful eye on the oven and another on the children making inroads on the freshly baked heap.

There are ways to get around cutting out cookies, unless you want fancy shapes. Then a rich dough is rolled thin on canvas on board. But for plain, round cookies we learned one good method a few years ago—making the dough in a roll, then chilling and slicing it into thin rounds.

Voila! Ice box cookies are born! Or as many of us call them these days, refrigerator cookies.

❦ Chocolate Ice Box Cookies
Kansas

½ c. unsalted butter, softened
1 c. sugar
1 egg, beaten
2 squares bittersweet Baker's chocolate, melted

2 c. flour
¼ tsp. salt
2 tsp. baking powder
¼ c. milk

Cream the butter, add the sugar, and blend well. Add the egg and chocolate and beat. Add the sifted dry ingredients and milk alternately. Chill dough, and when firm, roll out and shape in logs the size of a tumbler. Chill again until firm, then cut into thin slices. Bake on buttered baking sheets at 350°F for about 10 minutes. If dough is put in refrigerator it may be kept several days wrapped in waxed paper.

NUCOA'S DELICIOUS FLAVOR, SO GOOD ON BREAD, *adds richer taste to your cooking, too!*

❦ Apricot Oatmeal Cookies

1 c. unsalted butter, softened
¾ c. sugar
1 c. brown sugar, tightly packed
2 eggs
1 tsp. vanilla
1½ c. flour

1 tsp. salt
1 tsp. baking soda
3½ c. rolled oats
1½ c. dried apricots, finely chopped
1 c. pecans, chopped

Cream butter and sugars; add eggs and vanilla and mix well. Sift in flour, salt, and baking soda. Add remaining ingredients and mix well. Shape into 1-inch logs and wrap in waxed paper. Refrigerate overnight, then slice dough ½ inch thick and place on buttered baking sheets. Bake at 350°F for 10–15 minutes till lightly browned.

❦ Like the Ones Mother Used to Make

Apparently, Mother knew what she was doing—no elaborate instructions for her!

1 c. sour cream
½ c. unsalted butter,
  softened
1½ c. sugar

3 eggs
1 tsp. baking soda
sifted flour enough to roll

Mix, roll out, and bake at 350°F.

❦ Vanilla Cookies

1½ c. sugar
½ c. unsalted butter, softened
1 tsp. vanilla
2 egg yolks
½ c. sour cream

1 tbsp. milk
3¾ c. flour
½ tsp. salt
½ tsp. baking soda

Cream sugar and butter, then add vanilla and egg yolks. Mix in sour cream and milk, then sift in flour, salt, and baking soda. Mix well to make a stiff dough. Cover and refrigerate 1 hour, then roll out very thin on a floured board and cut with cutters. Place on buttered baking sheets and bake at 375°F for about 10 minutes.

❧ Soft Sugar Cookies
September 1931

½ c. unsalted butter, softened
1 c. sugar
2 eggs, well beaten
grated rind of 1 lemon
1 tbsp. milk

2¼ c. flour
2 tsp. baking powder
½ tsp. nutmeg
sugar for dusting

Cream butter thoroughly, add sugar gradually, and cream together until light and fluffy. Add eggs, lemon rind, and milk and beat well. Sift in remaining ingredients a small amount at a time. Beat after each addition until smooth. Roll into thin sheet on slightly floured board. Cut with floured cookie cutter, place on buttered baking sheets and dust with sugar. Bake at 425°F until delicate brown.

❧ The Cookies That Went to Market

2 eggs, well beaten
2 c. white sugar, plus extra for sprinkling
1 c. lard (full)
1 c. sweet milk (scant)
⅓ tsp. nutmeg

1 tsp. vanilla
1 tsp. baking soda
1 tsp. baking powder
4 to 5 c. pastry flour
raisins for decorating

Mix first eight ingredients and let stand overnight if possible (*in the refrigerator!*), since they will not need as much flour if you do. Mix with flour—start with 1 c. and increase gradually as necessary to get a dough as soft as you can easily handle on the board. If too stiff, add cream. Roll out on a floured board and cut with cutters. Lay on buttered baking sheets with two raisins on top of each cookie and a sifting of white sugar. Bake at 400°F till done.

❧ Rolled Fruit Cookies

1 c. unsalted butter, softened
2 c. sugar
3 eggs, slightly beaten
1 tsp. cinnamon
1 tsp. ground cloves
⅓ tsp. baking soda

2 tsp. baking powder
3 tbsp. cold coffee or fruit juice
1 c. raisins, chopped and dredged in a
  little flour
up to 3 c. flour, to make a soft dough

Cream butter and sugar. Add eggs and beat until light. Sift in spices, baking soda, and baking powder with ½ c. flour and beat well. Add the coffee, then the raisins. Beat all together, then add remaining flour, ½ c. at a time, to make a soft dough. Roll out on a floured board and cut. Place on buttered baking sheets and bake at 350°F for 15–20 minutes.

❧ Ginger Creams

2 c. molasses
1 c. unsalted butter
1 tbsp. ginger

1 tbsp. baking soda
4–6 c. flour

Mix ingredients well, being careful not to make dough too stiff. Roll out thick on a floured board and cut with a small cutter. Place on buttered baking sheets and bake at 325°F until just beginning to brown around edges (6–10 minutes)—take care not to scorch. Allow cookies to cool for a few minutes before removing to rack.

Variations:
1 tbsp. orange peel is a nice addition. Some add 1 tsp. black pepper.

Frost all with:

1 c. sugar
3 tbsp. hot water

2 egg whites, beaten

Cook first two ingredients on top of stove until they hair (230–234°F measured on a candy thermometer). When done, pour slowly into egg whites, beating all the while till cool. Spread on cookies.

❦ Orange Butter Thins

Adapted from The Pennsylvania Dutch Cook Book

2 c. unsalted butter, softened
3½ c. confectioner's sugar
5 eggs
4 c. flour

1 tsp. baking soda dissolved in ½ c. sour
cream
1 tsp. orange extract
¼ tsp. salt

Cream butter and sugar, then add eggs. Sift in the flour, then add baking soda in sour cream and extract. Roll out very thin on a floured board. Cut with cutters and place on buttered baking sheets. Bake at 350°F for about 10 minutes.

❦ Lemon Snaps

1 c. sugar
⅔ c. unsalted butter, softened
½ tsp. baking soda

2 tsp. hot water
flour, about 3 c.
lemon extract

Mix well, adding only enough sifted flour to make a dough stiff enough to roll. Roll thin on a floured board. Cut with cutters and bake at 325°F until golden.

❦ Oatmeal Snap Cakes

½ c. fine oatmeal
2 c. flour
pinch of salt
2 tbsp. sugar

2 tsp. baking powder
1 egg, beaten light
½ c. heavy cream
½ c. milk

Put oatmeal and flour in a bowl with the salt, sugar, and baking powder. Add cream and milk to the egg and stir together. Add to flour mixture. With a fork, make all into a light dough. Roll out on a floured board till thin and bake at 350°F till done. On account of the natural heaviness of the oatmeal, the baking powder is necessary.

☙ Sour Cream Molasses Cookies

1 c. unsalted butter
1 c. brown sugar
1 c. molasses
3 eggs, beaten
1 c. sour cream
2 tsp. baking soda
1½ tsp. salt
1½ tsp. ground ginger
3 tsp. cinnamon
up to 6 c. flour

Cream butter with sugar, then add molasses, eggs, and sour cream. Sift baking soda together with salt, ginger, cinnamon, and 1 c. flour and mix into dough. Add more flour 1 c. at a time to make a soft batter. Chill dough several hours, then roll out on a floured board and cut with cutters. Place on buttered baking sheets and bake at 350°F for 12–15 minutes.

To vary you may ice with:

½ c. sugar
1½ tbsp. water

1 tbsp. unsalted butter
few drops vanilla

Boil together the first three ingredients to soft-ball stage (234–240°F registered on a candy thermometer). Whisk until cool and creamy, then add vanilla and spread on cookies.

For Sour Cream Molasses Bars: Spread the batter without chilling in a shallow buttered pan and bake at 350°F. While still warm, dust with powdered sugar. Cut in bars when ready to serve.

☙ Cinnamon Shortbread

Adapted from The Meetinghouse Cookbook

1 c. unsalted butter, softened
½ c. sugar
3 c. flour
¼ tsp. nutmeg

3 egg yolks
1 egg white, lightly beaten
½ c. sugar mixed with 1 tbsp. cinnamon, for dusting

Cream butter and sugar. Sift in flour and nutmeg and mix until smooth, then add egg yolks. Roll thin on a floured board and cut with cutters. Place on buttered baking sheets, brush with egg white, and sprinkle with cinnamon and sugar. Bake at 375°F for 12–15 minutes until lightly browned around edges.

❦ Filled Cookies

1 c. sour cream	½ tsp. baking soda
2 c. sugar	¼ tsp. salt
3 c. flour	1 tsp. vanilla

Blend the sour cream and sugar; sift in flour, baking soda, and salt, then add vanilla. Place a portion of the dough on a well-floured board and roll thin. Cut to desired size with a cutter that has been dipped in flour. Do not put the floured scraps together at the last. The flour that adheres to the scraps will make a stiffer dough and a less tender cooky.

A large variety of filled cookies may be made by using this recipe with different cooked fillings. After the cookies have been cut, put a small amount of cooked filling in the center of one cooky and place another cooky on top of it. Press the edges together and bake at 400°F till nicely golden.

Raisin Filling:

1 c. raisins, chopped	½ c. water
½ c. sugar	1 tsp. flour

Cook in a double boiler until thick. Cool before spreading on cooky.

Fig Filling:

1½ c. dried figs, chopped	⅓ c. sugar
½ c. water	

Mix in the order given and cook in a double boiler until thick. Cool before spreading.

Date Filling:

1½ c. dates	¼ c. water
⅓ c. sugar	

Wash dates and remove pits, if there are any. Add sugar and water and cook as above. Cool before spreading.

Apricot Filling:

1 c. dried apricots, chopped	¾ c. water
¼ to ⅓ c. sugar, depending on how tart you like it	

Place ingredients in saucepan and cook over low heat until thick and smooth, adding more water if necessary. Cool before spreading.

Jam Filling:

Use spoonfuls of jam or preserves of your choosing.

Apple Filling:

1 c. apple, chopped

1 tbsp. preserved ginger, chopped

½ c. sugar

juice and grated rind of 1 orange

½ c. nuts, chopped

Mix and cook until thick and apples are clear. Roll out dough thin and cut half in rounds, half in 2½-inch squares. For the round cookies, put filling on half of the circles and top with the other half, crimping the edges with a fork. Of the squares, make filled crescents. Put a strip of the filling across one corner. Roll the dough over and over to make a filled roll. Shape as a crescent, with the filling showing at each end.

❦ Snickerdoodles

Adapted from Hot Recipes

A nineteenth-century Pennsylvania Dutch specialty, with possibly ancient origins. Some versions resemble Jumbles, others, Sand Tarts. According to the Penguin Companion to Food *by Alan Davidson, to be authentic they should contain nutmeg, nuts, and raisins.*

1 c. unsalted butter, softened

1½ c. sugar

2 eggs

2¾ c. flour

1 tsp. baking soda

2 tsp. cream of tartar

½ tsp. salt

¼ tsp. nutmeg

1 c. walnuts and raisins, chopped fine

½ c. sugar mixed with 1 tbsp. cinnamon, for dusting

Cream butter and sugar, then add eggs. Sift in dry ingredients, then mix in nuts and raisins. Form into small balls, place on buttered baking sheets, and flatten; dust with cinnamon and sugar. Bake at 400°F for 8–10 minutes.

TABLE TALK

Conducted by Mrs. Sarah A. Cooke
February 1913

Mrs. Woodrow Wilson's Old-Fashioned Cakes, Gingerbread and Cookies. The charmingly domestic future mistress of the White House understands the art of cooking as well as she does the art of painting, the art of landscape gardening and the art of fine needlework, for which she is proficient in all these arts, which goes to prove that she is a marvelously well-rounded woman. Her domesticity is one of her chief charms, she is a homemaker in every sense of the word and a fine feminine figure, worthy to stand forth as an example to the women of the land.

She typifies to perfection the spirit of a great republic and is the ideal woman of democracy: many-sided, accomplished to a rare degree, gracious, warm-hearted and home-loving.

She is a southerner by birth, but has lived over half her life in the north. She, however, retains her native southern love of cooking, for in the South cooking is regarded as a fine art. She can make the most delicious things to eat and when she was first married she did her own cooking. Her cooks she trains herself, for her recipes are very fine and she knows exactly how they should be carried out.

Her cakes, cookies and gingerbread are delicious and here are the recipes.

Old-Fashioned Cream Cookies

⅓ c. unsalted butter, softened
½ c. sugar
2 eggs
½ c. light cream

3–5 c. flour
2 tsp. baking powder
1 tsp. salt
2 tsp. ground ginger

Cream the butter, add the sugar, eggs, and cream. Into the mixture add 3 c. flour sifted together with the remaining ingredients, adding more if necessary to make a stiff dough; chill 20–30 minutes. Roll on a floured board as thin as possible, using a small part of the dough at a time. Cut into shapes and bake in a moderate oven (325–350°F) till done.

Cinnamon Cookies

4 c. molasses
4 oz. unsalted butter
2 tbsp. cinnamon
2 c. buttermilk

1 tbsp. baking soda dissolved in
    ¼ c. cold water
8 c. flour

Put the molasses, butter, and cinnamon into a saucepan; heat gently, then add the buttermilk. Add baking soda. Remove from fire and when cool, add the flour. Roll out, using enough flour to prevent sticking. Cut into shapes, lay on buttered sheets, and bake till ready in a moderate oven (350°F).

Maple Syrup Cookies

3 c. maple syrup
heaping cupful unsalted butter
4 eggs, separated

1 c. milk
2 tsp. baking powder
flour

Warm the maple syrup until it will melt the butter. Allow to cool, then add beaten egg yolks and milk. Finally, sift in baking powder with some flour, then fold in the egg whites beaten stiffly, then the remaining flour to make a stiff dough. Roll out, cut with cutters, lay on floured sheets, and bake in a moderate oven (350°F) till golden.

❦ Norwegian Krum Kake

Contributed by Mrs. W.J., Minnesota

This recipe requires a krumkake iron, a contraption resembling a waffle iron that sits atop a stove burner and embosses a slight design on the cookie as it "bakes." The cookie is then rolled into a cone shape while warm. Not just for Christmas—but the holidays are a good excuse for the effort.

1 c. unsalted butter, melted
1¾ c. sugar
2 c. flour

6 eggs
1 tsp. vanilla
1 c. cold water

Mix ingredients to remove lumps and bake on krumkake iron until golden. Remove and roll out right away.

❦ Swedish Spritz Cookies

Contributed by Mrs. A.J., Iowa

1 c. unsalted butter, softened
1 c. sugar
1 egg

2 tsp. almond extract
2½ to 3 c. flour to make a
stiff dough

Cream butter and sugar; add egg, extract, and flour. Force through a cookie press to form into rings or fancy shapes. Place on unbuttered baking sheets. Bake in a hot oven (400°F), taking care not to burn.

❧ Sandbakels

1 lb. unsalted butter, softened	4 c. flour
1⅛ c. sugar	½ tsp. salt
1 egg	1 c. almond flour

Cream butter and sugar, then add egg. Add remaining ingredients. Press small bits into cookie forms [traditionally, small fluted tart-like tins] and place on baking sheets. Bake at 350°F until delicately browned.

❧ Swedish Allspice Cookies

This recipe makes a lot of cookies!

¾ lb. unsalted butter, softened	1 tbsp. ground cloves
2½ c. sugar	2 tsp. allspice
1 c. dark corn syrup	1 tbsp. baking soda
1 c. heavy cream	12 c. flour, approximately
1 tbsp. cinnamon	

Cream butter and sugar. Add corn syrup and mix in cream alternately with dry ingredients sifted together. Chill in refrigerator, then roll out very thin. Cut in Christmas trees, diamonds, or rounds, and place on buttered baking sheets. Bake at 375°F for about 10 minutes.

❧ Rich Peanut Butter Cookies

November 1934

½ c. lard	2 eggs, beaten
½ c. butter	3 c. flour
1 c. white sugar	1 tsp. baking soda
1 c. brown sugar	½ tsp. salt
1 c. peanut butter	1 tsp. vanilla

Cream fats and sugars, then add peanut butter and mix well. Add eggs, then dry ingredients, sifted together, and vanilla. Mix well and shape in balls. Place about 2 inches apart on sheet and press two ways with a fork to flatten and mark. Bake in a moderate oven (375°F) until delicately browned.

❦ Coconut Flake Macaroon
April 1931

2 egg whites
1 c. sugar
1 c. shredded coconut
1 tbsp. flour

½ c. chopped nuts
2 c. crisp corn flakes
1 tsp. vanilla

Beat eggs; add sugar, coconut, flour, nuts, cornflakes, and vanilla. Drop by spoonfuls on buttered pans. Bake in moderate oven (350°F) until lightly golden. Serves 30.

❦ Oatmeal Macaroons
March 1910

Put ¼ cup of rolled oats into a bowl and cover it with 1 egg and 2 tbsp. each of cream, milk, and water, or 3 tbsp. rich milk. *[Editor's note: rich milk is equivalent to un-homogenized, creamline milk—where the cream rises to the surface—which is available at some health food stores and farmer's markets. Be sure to shake the milk well before use.]* Let it stand until the oats have soaked up all the moisture, then add 1 c. powdered sugar, 1 tbsp. melted butter, and a little cinnamon. Sift 2 tsp. baking powder with 1 cup of flour and add it to the mixture with enough additional flour to make a stiff dough. Shape into balls as large as walnuts and bake in a moderate oven (350°F).

❦ Love Krandse (Danish)
March 1927
Contributed by Miss S.R., Nebraska

4 hard cooked egg yolks
1 c. butter
½ c. sugar, plus extra for dipping

3 c. flour
1 tsp. vanilla
1 egg, lightly beaten

Rub the egg yolks through a sieve. Cream the butter and sugar, and mix with the flour. Add the egg yolks and vanilla. Roll the dough thin and form in small wreaths. Dip in beaten egg and sugar. Place in pan and bake at 350°F.

❦ Scotch Short Bread
April 1923

3 c. flour
1 c. sugar
2 c. butter
1 oz. blanched almonds

Sift the flour twice and rub in the butter with the hands. Add the sugar and knead and mix either on a board or in a bowl until a dough is formed. Do not add either egg or milk, as the butter softens the mixing and will bind the ingredients together. Roll the dough rather thinly, cut into rounds or ovals, and press a few almonds onto each. Bake in a pie pan in a slow oven (300°F) until golden brown.

❦ Spiced Oatmeal Cookies
1934

That old stand-by, with variations.

1 c. shortening (½ lb.)
2 c. brown sugar
2 eggs
1 c. buttermilk
2½ c. flour
1 tsp. baking soda

¾ tsp. salt
3 tsp. mixed spice (taken from a mixture made from 4 tbsp. cinnamon, 2 tbsp. nutmeg, and 2 tbsp. ground allspice or cloves)
2 c. rolled oats
2 c. raisins

Cream shortening with sugar. Beat eggs and mix with buttermilk. Mix flour well with baking soda, salt, and spices, and then with the rolled oats and raisins. Add liquid and dry ingredients alternately to the creamed shortening and sugar. Drop on greased pans and bake about 15 minutes in moderate oven (375°F). This makes 4 dozen large cookies. Divide in half for smaller amount.

Variations:
Use 3 c. whole wheat flour instead of white flour.

Use a scant cup of sweet milk instead of buttermilk; decrease baking soda to ½ tsp.; add 2 tsp. baking powder.

Grind rolled oats and raisins to get a finer texture.

Substitute bran for oats for a bran drop cookie. *[Editor's note: Oat bran flour can be purchased at health and kitchen specialty stores, and some supermarkets.]*

Add 1 c. chopped nuts.

❦ Ice Box Cookies
1934

1 c. butter or part other fat	1 tsp. cinnamon
½ c. lard	½ tsp. baking soda
1 c. granulated sugar	1 tsp. baking powder
1 c. brown sugar, firmly packed	1 c. nut meats
3 eggs	4½ c. flour
½ tsp. salt	

Cream the fats and sugars. Add the slightly beaten eggs and beat well. Sift the salt, cinnamon, baking soda, and baking powder with 1 c. flour; add to first mixture and beat well. Add the nut meats mixed with the rest of the flour. Mold into two well-shaped loaves and set in a cold place overnight. In the morning, slice and bake in a moderately hot oven (450°F).

Variations:
Use 1¾ c. white sugar and omit brown. Omit spice if desired

Divide dough into two parts and add sliced dates to one part and cocoanut to the other.

❦ Viennese Almond Cookies
December 1936

½ c. butter
1¾ cups sifted flour
½ c. sugar
½ c. finely ground, blanched almonds
2 egg yolks
2 to 2½ tbsp. cream

Work butter into flour until mealy (finer than for pie crust). Add sugar and nuts and mix well. Add beaten yolks, then cream. Dough should be soft enough to handle without breaking. For "horseshoes," roll in long strips about the thickness of a pencil. Cut in 3-inch lengths and shape each piece as a crescent or horseshoe. Bake in a moderately hot oven (400°F), about 15 minutes. While warm, roll in a mixture of sugar and ground nuts. Cover ends with a thin chocolate icing.

Variation:
For jelly circles, roll dough quite thick, about ½ inch. Cut out very small rounds with a tiny cutter or wine glass. Make a dent in the center and put in a fleck of bright jelly. Sprinkle ground nuts and sugar around edge. Bake 10 to 15 minutes at 400°F.

❦ Spritsbakelser (Swedish)

February 1928
Contributed by Mrs. A.J., Iowa

1 c. butter
1 c. sugar
1 egg

2 tsp. almond extract
flour to make a stiff dough, from 2½ to 3 c.

Cream the butter and sugar; add the beaten egg, extract, and flour. Force through a cookie press to form into rings or fancy shapes. Bake in a hot oven (400°F), taking care not to burn.

❦ Sand Tarts

December 1930
Contributed by a reader in Ohio

½ c. butter
1½ c. brown sugar
2 eggs
3½ c. flour

½ tsp. cinnamon
2 tsp. baking powder
¼ c. granulated sugar mixed with ¼ tsp. cinnamon

Cream butter and sugar, add the beaten eggs, and sift in dry ingredients. Roll ½ inch thick, and sprinkle with cinnamon sugar. Cut out and bake quickly. Citron, raisins, orange peel, nuts, or maraschino cherries make good decorations for these if wished.

❦ Honey Cakes (German Christmas Cookies)

1 lb. sugar
1 lb. honey
1 tsp. baking soda dissolved in 2 tbsp. water
1 lb. flour
¼ tsp. cloves

¼ c. water
1 tsp. cinnamon
ground cardamom seed from 3 pods
juice and grated rind of 1 lemon
1 lb. pecan meats
¼ lb. ground citron

Put the sugar and honey in a saucepan, heat until the sugar is dissolved and the boiling point is reached. Remove from the fire and pour the mixture into a large bowl. Add the baking soda, dissolved in the water, immediately. Then stir in the flour and spices, which have been sifted together, and the lemon juice and rind. Add the nuts and citron (all chopped fine), mix well, roll very thin, and cut. If dough is allowed to cool before rolling, the process will be very difficult. Allow cakes to stand, covered, overnight before baking. Bake at 350°F.

❦ Gingernuts (Old English)

½ c. butter
2 c. sugar
2 eggs
4 c. flour
2 tsp. ground ginger

1 tsp. each of cinnamon and
    ground cloves
½ c. chopped nuts
sugar for rolling
citron pieces or walnut halves for garnish

Cream the butter and sugar; beat in the eggs, then the flour sifted with the spices. The dough will seem quite stiff. Shape into little balls with the fingers, roll them in granulated sugar and press a piece of citron or half an English walnut into each and bake in a moderate oven (350°F).

❦ German Springerle

February 1928
Contributed by Mrs. A. W., Illinois

7 eggs
3 c. powdered sugar
1 tsp. grated nutmeg
1 tsp. cinnamon
1 tsp. vanilla

1 square unsweetened chocolate, grated
2 tbsp. butter
1 tsp. baking powder
1 c. flour

Separate whites and yolks of eggs; beat yolks and sugar, spices, vanilla, chocolate, and butter, which has been slightly softened to facilitate mixing. Fold in beaten egg whites.

Mix baking powder with ½ the flour and stir or knead into mixture. Turn onto well-floured board and knead in as much flour as dough will hold. Roll very thin and mold over single springerle mold or mold of any kind. Press dough on mold to make design distinct. Cut cakes out and lay on the table. Cover with clean cloth and let dry until morning. Bake in moderate oven (350°F) for about 20 minutes.

Chocolatey Fruit & Nut Squares

1 c. dates, chopped fine
1 c. boiling water
1 tsp. baking soda
1 tsp. salt
1 tsp. vanilla
1 c. unsalted butter, melted
1 c. sugar
2 eggs
1⅓ c. flour
12 oz. semi-sweet chocolate chips
¼ c. walnuts, chopped

Mix all ingredients but chocolate and nuts and spread in buttered 8x10-inch baking pan. Cover with chocolate and nuts and bake at 350°F for 40 minutes. Cool and cut in bars to serve.

Brownies I

1 c. sugar
¼ c. unsalted butter, melted
1 egg
2 oz. bittersweet Baker's chocolate, melted
¾ tsp. vanilla
½ c. flour

Mix ingredients in order given. Spread mixture evenly in buttered square baking pan. Bake at 350°F for 25–30 minutes. Turn out and cut in squares to serve.

Variation:
Add ½ c. chopped walnuts.

❦ Brownies II

Chocolate-free brownies! Today we'd call these blondies.

⅔ c. brown sugar
⅔ c. unsalted butter, softened
4 eggs
⅔ c. molasses
2 c. flour
2 c. walnuts, chopped fine

Cream the sugar and butter, add the eggs and molasses, then the flour and nuts. Bake in a buttered square or small oblong pan at 350°F for 15–20 minutes. Cut in squares to serve.

❦ Apple Blondies

Adapted from Favorite Recipes of the King's Daughters and Sons

½ c. unsalted butter, softened
¾ c. sugar
1 egg
1 c. flour
½ tsp. baking powder
½ tsp. baking soda

1 tsp. cinnamon
⅛ tsp. nutmeg
1 c. apples, cored, peeled, and finely chopped
1 c. walnuts, finely chopped

Cream butter and sugar, add egg, then sift in flour, baking powder and soda, and spices. Mix in apples and walnuts and pour into buttered 8-inch-square baking pan. Bake at 350°F for 30–35 minutes. Cool and cut in squares to serve.

❦ Cocoa Sticks

Contributed by H.R., Wisconsin

½ c. unsalted butter, softened
1 c. sugar
2 eggs
1 c. flour

3 tbsp. unsweetened cocoa powder
2 tbsp. milk
1 tsp. vanilla

Cream butter and sugar, then add eggs. Sift together flour and cocoa; add alternately with milk to butter mixture. Lastly add vanilla. Bake in a large, shallow, buttered pan at 400°F for about 30 minutes or until done. Cut in oblong sticks to serve.

❦ Banana Bars

Adapted from **Favorite Recipes of the King's Daughters and Sons**

½ c. unsalted butter, softened
1 c. sugar
2 eggs
1 c. sour cream
2 ripe bananas, mashed
1 tsp. vanilla

2 c. flour
1 tsp. salt
1 tsp. baking soda
confectioner's sugar and chopped walnuts,
     for sprinkling

Cream butter and sugar; add eggs, then sour cream, bananas, and vanilla. Mix well. Sift in dry ingredients and mix. Pour into buttered jelly-roll pan and bake at 350°F for about 20 minutes. Cool and cut in bars, then dust with confectioner's sugar and nuts to serve.

❦ Frosted Creams

⅓ c. unsalted butter, softened
½ c. sugar
1 egg
½ c. molasses
1½ c. flour

½ tsp. baking soda
2 tsp. baking powder
½ tsp. cinnamon
½ c. buttermilk

Cream butter with sugar; add egg. Mix in the molasses. Sift in dry ingredients, adding alternately with the buttermilk. Spread in buttered 9x12-inch baking pan and bake at 350°F till cooked through. Cool and frost with:

1 egg white
⅛ tsp. cream of tartar

1 c. sugar
⅓ c. water

Beat egg white with cream of tartar till stiff. Boil sugar with water till it spins a thread (230–234°F on a candy thermometer). Pour slowly over egg white and beat until smooth. Spread over cookie and cut in squares to serve.

❦ Frosted Nut Cookies

½ c. unsalted butter, softened
1 c. sugar
2 eggs, well beaten
½ tsp. vanilla

1½ c. flour
½ tsp. salt
1 tsp. baking powder
1 c. walnuts, chopped

Cream butter; add sugar and mix together well. Add eggs, vanilla, and flour sifted with salt and baking powder. Spread ¼-inch thick on buttered baking sheet. Sprinkle with chopped nuts and frost with:

1 egg white
1 c. brown sugar

½ tsp. vanilla

Beat egg white till stiff, then fold in sugar and vanilla. Spread over cookie and bake at 375°F for 20 minutes. Cut in squares before entirely cool.

❦ Frosted Honey Fruit Cookies
Contributed by B.N., Nebraska

½ c. unsalted butter, softened
1 c. brown sugar
1 egg
½ c. honey
2½ c. flour
1 tsp. baking soda
½ tsp. salt

1 tsp. cinnamon
¼ tsp. allspice
¼ tsp. ground cloves
½ c. buttermilk
¼ c. raisins, dredged in a little flour
1 c. walnuts, chopped
¼ c. unsweetened shredded cocoanut

Cream butter and sugar; add egg and honey. Sift in flour, baking soda, salt, and spices, adding alternately with buttermilk; then add raisins, nuts, and cocoanut. Mix all together well and spread thinly in two well-buttered 8-inch-square baking pans. Bake at 375°F for about 20 minutes. While still warm, frost with:

½ c. confectioner's sugar
milk to make a thin, smooth paste

few drops vanilla

Spread thinly over cookie and allow to cool. Cut in squares or diamonds to serve.

❧ Apple Oatmeal Torte

1 c. flour
½ tsp. salt
½ tsp. baking soda
1 tsp. cinnamon
1½ c. rolled oats
½ c. brown sugar
½ c. unsalted
  butter, melted
1 egg
1 tsp. vanilla
3 sour apples, cored,
  peeled and sliced

Sift together first four ingredients, then mix in oats, sugar, butter, egg, and vanilla. Press half the mixture into a buttered 9-inch-square baking pan and arrange apple slices over it. Roll out remaining dough and press lightly over apples. Bake at 350°F for 25–30 minutes, till done. Cool and cut in bars to serve.

❧ Lemon Bars

Adapted from The Meetinghouse Cookbook

2¼ c. flour
½ c. confectioner's sugar, plus more for
  dusting
1 c. unsalted butter, softened
4 eggs
2 c. sugar
⅓ c. lemon juice
½ tsp. baking powder

Sift together 2 c. flour and confectioner's sugar. Cut in butter, then press dough into buttered 9x13-inch baking pan. Bake at 350°F for 20–25 minutes, until just done. Beat together eggs, sugar, and lemon juice. Sift in remaining flour and baking powder and mix well. Pour over cake and return to oven for an additional 25 minutes. Dust with confectioner's sugar and cool. Cut in bars to serve.

❧ Apricot Bars

½ c. unsalted butter, softened
¼ c. sugar
1 c. flour

Mix butter, sugar, and flour and press into buttered 8-inch-square baking pan. Bake at 350°F for 15 minutes. Top with:

1 c. water
⅔ c. dried apricots
2 eggs
1 c. brown sugar
¼ tsp. salt
⅓ c. flour
½ tsp. baking powder
½ c. walnuts, finely chopped
½ tsp. vanilla

Cook apricots in water for 10 minutes, then drain, cool, and chop. Beat eggs, then add apricots and all remaining ingredients. Spread over cookie, then return to oven for an additional 30 minutes. Cool and cut in squares to serve.

 Filled Date Torte

Crumb mixture or streusel:

1½ c. flour	1½ c. rolled oats
½ tsp. baking soda	1 c. unsalted butter, melted
½ tsp. salt	1 c. walnuts, chopped
1 c. brown sugar	

Sift together flour, baking soda, and salt, then mix in sugar and oats. Add butter and nuts and mix thoroughly with the hands. Pat half of the crumb mixture in a fairly shallow buttered baking pan. Top with:

40 dates, chopped	1 c. sugar
1 c. water	½ tsp. vanilla

Filling:

Cook filling until thick and smooth, add vanilla, then cool. Spread over cookie, then add remaining crumb mixture, patting down well. Bake at 350°F for 45 minutes. Cool and cut in strips or squares to serve.

❦ Raspberry Meringue Bars

Meringue was a great favorite of the farmer's wife, allowing her to use up egg whites she might otherwise have discarded. This recipe using meringue is adapted from The Meetinghouse Cookbook.

½ c. unsalted butter, softened	2 egg yolks
½ c. confectioner's sugar	1 c. flour

Cream butter and sugar, then add egg yolks. Sift in flour and mix. Press into unbuttered 9x12-inch baking pan and bake at 350°F for 10–15 minutes. Remove from oven and top with:

1 c. raspberry jam	½ c. sugar
2 egg whites	1 c. almond flour

Spread cookie with jam, then beat egg whites until stiff, gradually adding sugar. Fold in almond flour and spread over jam. Return to oven and bake 25 more minutes, till golden. Cool and cut in squares to serve.

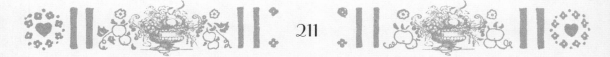

THE SECRET OF GOOD GINGERBREAD

By Jeanette Beyer and Eleanor Murray
September 1930

A good deal is to be said in favor of gingerbread. It is not only a simple sweet, which adds interest to a meal, but it will also furnish many economical and delicious calories, and there is abundant iron in its molasses to build bones and red blood.

If you have wondered at all the colors of gingerbreads, the black, the dark brown, the cinnamon, and all shades ranging to yellow, let me tell you the secret. Aside from molasses—of course the light or dark does make a difference—the leavening is the "x" in the recipe which accounts for the color variations. Since molasses and sour milk contain acid, soda is needed to neutralize and sweeten them, and this union of soda and acid produces the carbon dioxide gas (the same that comes from baking powder) which bubbles through the cake to make it light.

Now if you use very much soda, say two teaspoons in the recipe which I shall give you, your gingerbread will be very dark, of good volume, and flat on top. It will be wonderfully tender, but the texture will be coarse and the cell walls thick, because the excess soda has dissolved the thin walls. The flavor is fine, but slightly alkaline.

If you use just enough soda to neutralize the acid, about three-fourths teaspoon is added, the gingerbread will be good but not so large. The top will be rounded, the color lighter, and the texture not so coarse. But it will not be as tender as a cake, and will have more of the molasses flavor.

When no soda is added, but three teaspoons of baking powder used instead, the color is still lighter, the volume small and the texture fine. But the gingerbread will be tough and have a strong molasses flavor.

Three teaspoons of baking powder and sweet milk instead of sour milk will give about the same color, size and flavor as the gingerbread just above, but it is far tougher than any of the others.

So what does the gingerbread artist do? If she wants very dark tender cakes she uses soda, and for very light tough ones, baking powder. But for the perfect gingerbread, tender, mild in flavor, good texture and of medium color, she uses both baking powder and soda. Here is the recipe which can be mixed in ten minutes. You will go far to find a better:

Perfect Gingerbread

2 c. flour
½ c. sugar
1½ tsp. ground ginger
½ tsp. cinnamon
2 tsp. baking powder
⅔ tsp. baking soda

¼ tsp. salt
¾ c. molasses
1 c. buttermilk
1 egg
¼ c. unsalted butter, melted

Sift all dry ingredients. Put wet ingredients in mixing bowl. Mix in dry ingredients and beat until smooth. Fill well-buttered shallow pan one-half full. Bake at 350°F, from 20 to 40 minutes depending on size. This makes a loaf 7½ inches square. Cut in squares.

The flour, as for all baking, should be sifted before measuring. An all-purpose flour is entirely satisfactory. If the molasses is very strong, sugar can be substituted for part of it. Instead of buttermilk, whey is good, and this same rule can be used with sweet milk, although the gingerbread will not be as tender.

With pungent molasses and spice, the flavor of the shortening is overcome so that drippings, lard, or any of the butter substitutes will make good gingerbread.

Probably there are hundreds of ways to serve gingerbread in all its varieties. Perhaps you have found how good it is hot with butter, or as a dessert topped by a fluff of whipped cream. Maybe you already vary it with nuts and raisins, or have tried adding ¾ c. cocoanut to the batter and sprinkling some over the top about 15 minutes before it is finished baking. Or maybe you eat it hot with lemon or hard sauce, or cover it with grated cheese and put the gingerbread in the oven long enough for the cheese to melt, serving it immediately.

❦ Old English Gingerbread with Fruit Filling
Contributed by Mrs. H.E.C., Nebraska

1 c. unsalted butter, softened	1 tbsp. ground ginger
1 c. molasses	3½ c. flour
1 c. sugar	1 tsp. cinnamon
1 c. buttermilk	1 tsp. baking soda
2 eggs	1½ tsp. nutmeg

Cream butter; add molasses and sugar. Add remaining ingredients and mix well. Bake in two 8-inch-square buttered baking pans at 325°F for about 30 minutes, until firm. Fill with:

1½ c. water (with a little grated lemon rind)	½ c. sugar
1 c. raisins	1 tbsp. cornstarch
1 tbsp. lemon juice	½ c. each walnuts, dried figs, and
¼ c. dried apricot pulp	dates, chopped

Soak the raisins in the water, which has a little grated lemon rind in it. Marshmallows may be added, too. Add the rest of the ingredients. Cook until thick and spread between gingerbread layers. Ice or not, as preferred. Cut in squares to serve.

Cakes

❦ Orange Sunshine Cake with Whipped Cream Topping

February 1936
Contributed by L.H., Colorado

5 eggs, separated
1½ c. sugar
½ c. orange juice
1½ c. cake flour

¼ tsp. salt
½ tsp. baking powder
¾ tsp. cream of tartar

Beat yolks until thick and light, adding half of the sugar. Add orange juice and beat. Sift flour, salt, and baking powder together three times and add. Beat whites until foamy, add cream of tartar, then rest of sugar gradually. Fold into other mixture. Bake in an ungreased tube pan in a very slow oven (325°F) for 1 hour. Cool, remove from pan, and ice with whipped cream, very slightly sweetened. Sprinkle with grated orange rind.

❦ Kiss Cake

June 1936

3 large egg whites
dash salt
few drops lemon juice or vinegar
1 c. finely granulated sugar

1⅓ c. powdered sugar
whipped cream
strawberries

The success of meringues depends upon thorough beating of sugar into egg whites and slow baking. Whites whip up best at room temperature. Beat until stiff and dry, adding salt. Add vinegar or lemon, then add sugar gradually, beating after each addition. When finished, the meringue will be very stiff and satiny in appearance. Cover a greased baking sheet with parchment paper. Shape meringues into 3 round, flat layers, making them graduated in size with the largest one about 9 inches across. Bake in a very slow oven (250°F to 275°F) for 45 minutes. They will be a very pale brown. Pile whipped cream and strawberries between layers, and whipped cream over the top.

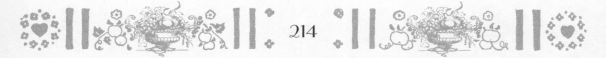

❦ Lemon Roll

March 1936
Contributed by Mrs. W.K., Minnesota

Cake:

6 eggs, separated
½ c. sugar
1 tbsp. lemon juice
1 tsp. grated lemon rind

½ c. cake flour
½ tsp. baking powder
¼ tsp. salt
½ pt. heavy cream, whipped

Beat egg whites, adding sugar gradually until stiff and smooth. Beat yolks, add lemon juice and rind, and fold into whites. Sift flour, baking powder, and salt two or three times and fold into egg mixture. Line a 10x15-inch pan with waxed paper, which has been greased, and spread in sponge mixture. Start in a very slow oven, bringing up to 250°F. Bake just until firm but not brown. If a regulated oven, bake until cake is raised, then turn off heat and let cake stay in oven until firm. Turn onto a clean towel, sprinkled liberally with powdered sugar and remove waxed paper. Let stand about 30 minutes until cool, then roll cake up in cloth like a jelly roll, rolling it the long way of the cake. Let stand 10 minutes. Unroll, spread with part of whipped cream (unsweetened) and roll up. Sprinkle roll with powdered sugar, wrap in waxed paper and store in cool place until used. Serves 8.

Sauce:

1 c. sugar
grated rind and juice of 1 lemon
3 tbsp. cornstarch

⅔ c. water
1 egg or 2 yolks, beaten
½ tbsp. butter

Mix sugar, lemon rind, and cornstarch, add water and cook 10 minutes in double boiler, stirring until thickened. Add eggs and butter. Add lemon juice and cool. To serve, slice roll. Top each piece with a spoonful of whipped cream and over that a spoonful of lemon sauce.

THE CAKE THAT PHOEBE JANE BAKED
Another Champion Visits the Country Kitchen
By Miriam J. Williams
April 1937

This is a house-that-Jack-built kind of story because the events which led to Phoebe Jane Huff's coming to the Country Kitchen to bake angel food cake unfold on paper like a nursery rhyme. But this story runs back aways in time. It begins with a 14-year-old club girl's wish to do her part, and keeps on to a 20-year-old college junior's thrill in a trip to St. Paul.

It was all because a 4-H Club leader near Leesburg, Ohio, asked one of her girls if she would exhibit an angel food cake at the country fair. When Mrs. Allen left instructions with this inexperienced fourteen-year-old club member, she knew that it would take some practicing at home to make a successful cake. But since Phoebe Jane was in foods club work to learn, she and her mother immediately went into conference. Mrs. Huff answered her daughter's questions as best she could and then suggested that she consult a neighbor who had a reputation for angel food. In Phoebe Jane's own words, "Mrs. Moore laughed when I told her what the club leader had asked me to do. Right that afternoon she took me to her kitchen and there my cake career began, when she began telling me many things about angel foods that I should remember.

"The first afternoon I did not do a thing but watch. The second afternoon I was allowed to measure some of the ingredients and do part of the mixing. On the last afternoon I mixed the cake and regulated the oven by myself."

The exhibition at the country fair was a success. Then later, in high school, an enterprising young brother suggested that Sis advertise in the school paper, of which he was business manager. Surprisingly enough, the orders which came in a few weeks also took care of all the extra Huff eggs. In that school year, 120 cakes were sold, almost entirely by favorable comment where these cakes were served.

Phoebe Jane's Angel Food Cake

1 c. sifted cake flour
1⅓ c. sugar
1¼ c. egg whites
½ tsp. salt

1 tsp. cream of tartar
2 tbsp. water
1 tsp. vanilla

Sift flour once before measuring, then sift 4 times with ⅓ c. of the sugar. Beat egg whites with a rotary beater, adding salt, cream of tartar, water, and vanilla when they are foamy. Beat whites just until they peak, and are still moist and shiny. With flat beater or mixing spoon, fold in remaining sugar, sifting one or two tbsp. at a time over surface and gently folding it in (about 50 strokes). Fold sifted flour and sugar mixture in the same way (about 90 strokes). Pour into ungreased angel food cake pans, and bake immediately in slow oven (325°F) for 1 hour or until surface of cake, when pressed lightly with finger, springs back into place. It should be at its full height and have a delicate brown color, and be shrunken slightly from the pan. Let cool in the inverted pan an hour before removing.

❧ White Cake with Cherry Frosting
February 1936

½ c. butter or part other fat
1 c. sugar
3 egg whites, unbeaten
1 tsp. vanilla

2 c. cake flour
3 tsp. baking powder
¼ tsp. salt
⅔ c. milk

Cream shortening; add sugar slowly, beating until fluffy. Add unbeaten whites, one at a time, beating very thoroughly after each addition, then add vanilla. Sift together dry ingredients and add alternately with milk to first mixture. Make into a large loaf or two layers. Bake in a moderate oven (375°F). A slightly less moist but lighter cake results if whites are folded in last. Frost with Cherry Frosting (page 225).

❧ Whipped Cream Cake with Boiled Marshmallow Icing
February 1939

1 c. heavy cream
2 eggs
1 c. sugar
1 tsp. vanilla

1½ c. sifted cake flour
2 tsp. baking powder
½ tsp. salt

Whip cream until stiff. Drop in unbeaten eggs, one at a time, and sugar, beating after each addition. (If eggs are large, one white may be omitted and used for a Seven-Minute Icing.) Add vanilla. Put dry ingredients into a sifter and fold lightly, blend well. Bake in a 9-inch square pan or 2 small layers or cupcakes for 25 to 30 minutes in a moderate oven (350°F to 375°F). Let cool on rack, un-mold, and ice with Boiled Marshmallow Icing (page 224).

Variation:
Frost with Caramel Nut Icing (page 225).

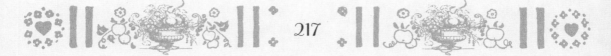

Cocoanut Cake with Seven-Minute Icing

February 1936
Contributed by Mrs. J.M., New York

⅓ c. butter or part other fat
1 c. sugar
1 whole egg and 2 yolks, unbeaten
2 c. cake flour

2 tsp. baking powder
¼ tsp. salt
¾ c. milk
¼ tsp. lemon extract or ½ tsp. vanilla

Cream butter thoroughly; add sugar gradually and cream again. Add egg and yolks and beat until creamy and light. Add dry ingredients, sifted three times, alternately with milk. Flavor and beat until smooth. Bake in two 9-inch layers in moderate oven (350°F). Put layers together with Seven-Minute Icing (page 224) from 2 egg whites reserved, sprinkling each layer thickly with unsweetened grated cocoanut.

Raspberry Cake (Two-Layer)

December 1930
Contributed by a reader from New York

½ c. butter
1 c. granulated sugar
2 eggs
2 tbsp. buttermilk

1 tsp. baking soda
1 c. raspberries
2 c. flour
½ tsp. cream of tartar

Cream the butter, add the sugar, and blend well. Add eggs, well beaten, and the buttermilk in which the baking soda has been mixed. Add raspberries and flour and cream of tartar, which have been sifted together. Use any Boiled Icing (page 223).

German Apple Cake

May 1927
Contributed by Mrs. E.I.K, North Dakota

2½ c. flour
pinch of salt
1 tsp. baking powder
2 tbsp. butter or lard

1 c. milk
6 tart apples
cinnamon, sugar, unsalted butter

Mix the first five ingredients into a dough; roll out to ½ inch thick. Line a square tin with dough to 1 inch from top. Pare and core and quarter apples to fill in, standing apples on ends. Sprinkle with sugar, cinnamon, and bits of butter. Bake and serve as any cake (350°F until cooked through).

❦ Lemon Layer Cake
February 1913

3 eggs
6 tbsp. sugar
grated rind of 1 lemon

6 tbsp. flour
1 tsp. baking powder
1½ oz. butter, melted

Put the eggs, sugar, and grated lemon rind into a basin, stand it over a pan of boiling water, and whisk until warm. Then remove and continue whisking until quite cold and stiff. Then add the flour mixed with the baking powder, and the melted butter, taking care to stir it very gently, but on no account to beat it. Pour into cake pans that have been buttered and floured; bake 10 minutes in a moderate oven (350°F). Before turning out, allow the pans to stand 2 or 3 minutes. When cold, spread each thickly over with lemon mixture (see below); lay the rounds together, divide into 12 pieces, dust with powdered sugar, and serve.

Lemon Mixture:
Put into a saucepan ¾ c. sugar, yolks of 4 eggs, white of 1 egg, grated rind and strained juice of 1 large lemon, and 2 oz. butter. Stir over a gentle heat until it thickens. Pour onto a plate, and when cool use.

❦ Gingerbread Banana Shortcake
June 1928

1¾ c. flour
1 tsp. ground ginger
½ tsp. cinnamon
½ tsp. salt
½ tsp. baking soda
3 tbsp. shortening

½ c. sugar
1 egg
½ c. molasses
½ c. boiling water

Sift dry ingredients together. Mix as for cake and bake in a pan where the dough will be about 1 inch thick. It will take from 25 to 30 minutes in a moderate (350°F) oven. While slightly warm, cover with sliced bananas and pile with whipped cream.

UPSIDE-DOWN CAKE

September 1938

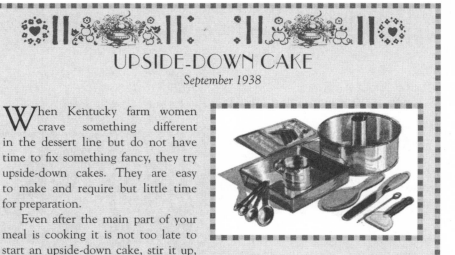

When Kentucky farm women crave something different in the dessert line but do not have time to fix something fancy, they try upside-down cakes. They are easy to make and require but little time for preparation.

Even after the main part of your meal is cooking it is not too late to start an upside-down cake, stir it up, put it in the oven and let it bake while the rest of the meal is being eaten. And you may use your fruit "leftovers" to a good advantage.

The following recipe is one that has been successfully tried by women of rural Kentucky with different toppings.

Cake:

1½ c. flour
1 c. sugar
2 tsp. baking powder
½ tsp. salt

2 eggs broken into a cup which is
    then filled with rich milk or cream
1 tsp. vanilla

Sift dry ingredients together, add liquids and beat hard for five minutes. Set aside.

Pineapple Topping:

1 small can pineapple, crushed or
    sliced, ¾ c. juice reserved

4 tbsp. butter
¾ c. brown sugar

Place pineapple juice, brown sugar, and butter in a skillet. Bring to a boil and boil for 2 minutes. Place pineapple in the juice and cover with the batter, spreading it so it covers all the fruit. Bake in a moderately hot oven (375°F) for 30 minutes. Let stand until partly cool, turn upside down on cake plate or platter to serve. Accompany with unsweetened whipped cream.

It is essential to beat the batter until it is smooth and fluffy for a light cake of fine texture. In blending the brown sugar, butter, and fruit juice, do not boil the syrup until it becomes thick and candy-like. Let it boil only long enough to blend together well.

If you like a richer cake sprinkle a few nut meats in the syrup.

Orange Topping:

juice of one large orange
¾ c. brown sugar

4 tbsp. butter
2 oranges sliced in rings

Put juice, sugar, and butter in skillet. Bring to a boil. Slice the oranges in fairly thin rings and boil for 2 minutes. Arrange slices, overlapping if necessary, pour on batter. Bake in a moderate oven 35 to 40 minutes.

Spice Cake with Prune Topping:
In the above cake recipe, omit vanilla and add ½ tsp. each allspice, cinnamon, and ground cloves, sifting them with the dry ingredients. For the topping use:

4 tbsp. butter
¾ c. brown sugar
¾ c. prune juice

2 c. cooked and pitted
prunes, unsweetened

Boil sugar, juice, and butter for 2 minutes in a skillet. Place in prunes which have been well drained, with the uncut, skin side down. Pour in the batter and bake 30 minutes in a moderate oven.

❦ Upside-Down Strawberry Crumb Cake

June 1936
Contributed by Mrs. G.A.C., Louisiana

½ c. butter or part other fat
1 c. sugar
3 eggs, beaten
2 c. dry sifted breadcrumbs
½ c. flour

1 tsp. baking powder
⅛ tsp. salt
1 c. milk
½ tsp. almond extract

For mold:
3 tbsp. melted butter
¾ c. brown sugar

fresh strawberries

Cream fat and sugar together thoroughly. Add eggs, then crumbs and dry ingredients alternately with milk and extract. Prepare mold or baking pan with melted butter, then sprinkle with sugar and whole or sliced strawberries to cover thickly. Pour on batter and bake in a moderate oven (350°F) for 40 minutes. When done, let stand a few minutes, unmold, and cool. Serve with unsweetened whipped cream.

🌿 Fruit Roll

February 1933
Contributed by A.B.M., Indiana

I pt. canned peaches mixed with:
½ tsp. ground cinnamon

½ c. brown sugar
I tsp. lemon juice

Rich biscuit dough:
Mix and sift 2 c. flour, 3 tsp. baking powder, and I tsp. salt; quickly work in 4 tbsp. fat with a fork or dough blender. Add ⅔ c. milk all at once and stir lightly to make a soft dough. Turn out onto a slightly floured board and knead lightly for a few seconds.

Roll to ½-inch thickness and spread with seasoned peaches. Roll as for jelly roll. Bake in hot oven (425°F). Cut into individual servings. Serve with whipped cream.

🌿 Apple Roly-Poly

February 1925

2 c. bread flour
5 tsp. baking powder
½ tsp. salt

2 tbsp. each butter and lard
⅔ to ¾ c. milk, depending on stiffening
    qualities of flour

Mix and sift dry ingredients, work in the fat and add milk to make dough to be handled as soft as possible. Turn on a floured board and pat into an oblong I inch thick. Brush with soft butter, sprinkle with I tbsp. sugar mixed with ½ tsp. cinnamon. Over this, sprinkle 3 or 4 sour apples that have been pared, cored, and chopped. Roll like a jelly roll and cut into eight slices. Place cut side up in a buttered acid-proof baking dish 2 inches deep, leaving a little space between them. Make the following brown sugar sauce and pour half of it over the dumplings. Bake 40 minutes at 350°F. Serve with other half of the sauce. Dried apples, soaked and chopped, may be used.

Brown Sugar Sauce:
Mix and boil 6 minutes.
¾ c. white sugar
½ c. light brown or maple sugar
I ½ tbsp. flour

I ½ c. boiling water
I ½ tbsp. butter
¾ lemon, grated rind and juice

❦ Buttermilk Cupcakes
October 1914

½ c. sugar
½ c. butter

1 egg, beaten light
1 c. buttermilk

Beat the first three ingredients together, and in the buttermilk dissolve 1 tsp. baking soda, a little salt, ground cloves, allspice, and cinnamon to taste. Pour the buttermilk into the sugar and butter and add 1 c. molasses and 2 c. sifted flour. Bake in a moderate oven (350°F) in cupcake cups and frost with chocolate (try Easy Fudge Icing, page 224).

❦ Plantation Cupcakes
April 1930

½ c. shortening
¼ c. brown sugar
2 eggs
½ c. molasses

1¾ c. sifted flour
¼ tsp. baking soda
1 tsp. baking powder
1 tsp. cinnamon

¼ tsp. mace
½ tsp. salt
½ c. milk

Cream the shortening and sugar together, and gradually work in the eggs, one at a time, until the mass is fluffy. Add the molasses. Mix and sift the dry ingredients and add, alternately with the milk, until they are all blended. Bake in muffin pans (or paper cupcake cups) at about 350°F for 20 minutes.

❦ Boiled Icing
December 1925

1¾ c. sugar
¾ c. boiling water
3 egg whites

1 tsp. any desired extract
1 level tsp. baking powder

Reserve 1½ tbsp. sugar. Dissolve remaining sugar in boiling water—if cover is placed over saucepan for a few minutes it will prevent sugar from adhering to the sides of pan. Let this boil very rapidly. When heavy drops fall from a spoon when spoon is held high above saucepan, then it is time to beat egg whites—a tiny pinch of salt may be added to whites before beginning to beat. Wait until syrup begins to thicken before beating egg whites because if beaten egg whites stand, they will liquefy. When eggs are well beaten, add the reserved sugar and beat well into egg whites until stiff but not dry. Test boiling syrup again. If it silks to a long thread that flies out, it is ready to be poured very slowly over beaten egg whites mixed with extract—beating vigorously. After beating about 5 minutes, add baking powder. Continue beating until it is cool and you have a smooth, creamy filling that should stand up well.

❧ Boiled Marshmallow Icing

February 1939

2½ c. granulated sugar
½ c. light corn syrup
¼ tsp. salt
½ c. water

2 egg whites
1 tsp. vanilla
8 marshmallows, cut in quarters

Cook sugar, corn syrup, salt, and water together in a saucepan to the firm ball stage. *[Editor's note: 250°F registered on a candy thermometer.]* Pour the hot syrup slowly into the well-beaten egg whites, beating constantly. Add vanilla extract and continue beating until the frosting will hold its shape when tossed over the back of a spoon. Add marshmallows.

❧ Seven-Minute Icing

February 1939

1 c. sugar
1 egg white
¼ c. water

1 tbsp. syrup or honey
few grains salt
½ tsp. vanilla

Put all ingredients except vanilla in the top of a double boiler. Cook over boiling water 7 to 10 minutes, beating all the while with a rotary beater. When ready to remove from the stove, the icing will be thick and almost ready to spread. Add vanilla and beat until cool and ready to spread. Double the recipe for all but a small cake.

❧ Easy Fudge Icing

February 1936

2 tbsp. softened butter
1 whole egg or 2 yolks
few grains of salt
1 square melted unsweetened chocolate

½ tsp. vanilla
2 c. powdered sugar
cream as necessary

Put first four ingredients in bowl and beat with rotary beater until creamy. Add vanilla and powdered sugar and enough cream to spread easily. Put on with even strokes, leaving a slightly ridged appearance.

❦ Caramel Nut Icing
February 1936

2 c. sugar
1 c. thin sweet or sour cream
3 tbsp. Caramel Syrup (see below)

1 tbsp. butter
1 tsp. grated orange rind
nut meats

Boil sugar, cream, and syrup until the mixture forms a soft ball in cold water (candy thermometer reading of 234–240°F). Remove from fire, let cool, add butter and grated orange rind, and beat until thick and creamy. Spread on cake. Decorate top with whole nut meats.

Caramel Syrup:
Make a syrup by melting 2 c. white sugar in a smooth, heavy skillet until golden brown. Avoid overheating or the syrup will have a burned taste. Add 1 c. hot water, stir until caramel is dissolved, and boil until a heavy syrup. Cool, store in a jar until needed.

❦ Cherry Frosting
February 1936
Contributed by A.A.F., Wisconsin

1 c. sugar
½ c. water
⅛ tsp. cream of tartar
1 egg white, beaten

few drops almond flavoring
⅓ c. drained chopped cherries (preserved or maraschino)

Put sugar, water, and cream of tartar in a saucepan to cook, stirring until dissolved. Then cook without stirring until the syrup spins a good thread. *[Editor's note: 240°F registered on a candy thermometer.]* Pour over egg white slowly, beating meanwhile. Add flavoring and cherries which must be well drained of extra juice or the frosting will be too soft. Continue to beat until thick and ready to spread.

Pies, Tarts, and Other Pastries

❦ Plain Pastry—Two Crusts
1934

½ tsp. salt
1½ c. sifted flour

½ c. lard
3 or 4 tbsp. ice cold water

Add salt to flour and cut in shortening with a dough blender, sharp-tined fork, or fingertips, until pieces are size of small peas. Add a little water at a time, mixing with a fork lightly until it can be shaped into a ball. Divide dough and roll out one crust at a time. Avoid overhandling the dough either in mixing it or in rolling out the crust. Work quickly, especially in warm weather so that fat doesn't melt. To bake single crusts, lay in pie tin quite loosely and prick well over bottom or fit over the bottom of an inverted tin. Bake in a hot oven (450°F).

    Tough crust may be due to too much water and too little fat, overhandling, or too slow an oven. Soggy undercrust may be due to not having the oven hot enough to bake the under crust before the filling soaks in, or to having the crust so rich or rolled so thin that the filling breaks through.

❦ To Make Flaky Pastry
April 1923

Have all ingredients very cold. Pat and roll the pastry in rectangular shape. Spread with ½ tbsp. fat. Fold to make three layers. Pat gently with rolling pin, then roll up like jelly roll. Butter is often used for this dressing-up process. To make it spread easily, wash it in cold water to remove all buttermilk and to make it waxy and pliable. Pat in a cloth to remove excess moisture before spreading. Pastry may be wrapped in wax paper (to keep from drying out) and kept in a cool place for several days.

❦ Meringue

2 egg whites
2 tbsp. sugar

¼ tsp. vanilla

Beat the whites until stiff but not dry. Add sugar and beat until smooth and glossy. Add vanilla, spread on top of pie, and bake.

❧ Angel Pie
April 1939

Crust:

6 tbsp. butter
1 c. flour

3 tbsp. sugar

Filling:

¾ c. sugar
3 tbsp. cornstarch
1 c. hot water
1 lemon, juice and grated rind

3 egg whites
¼ tsp. salt
⅓ c. whipping cream
⅓ c. crushed peanut brittle

Blend together softened butter, flour, and sugar. Put into a pie pan and bake 15 minutes in a moderately hot oven (400°F). Cool. For the filling, combine sugar and cornstarch, add hot water and cook 10 minutes, stirring until thick. Add grated rind of lemon, cool slightly, add juice. Fold in whites beaten until stiff with salt. Pour in shell and let stand until firm. Spread top with whipped cream and sprinkle with crushed peanut brittle. (Or a color scheme may be carried out with the use of other crushed candy.)

❧ Chess Pie
April 1931
Contributed by Mrs. D., Tennessee

8 egg yolks
3 c. white sugar
¼ c. cream

1 tsp. vanilla or lemon extract
rich pastry crust (such as Flaky Pastry, page 226) in muffin tins

Mix together in order given. Fill unbaked pie crusts. Bake in slow oven (300°F) for 20 minutes to ½ hour.

❦ Cream Pie
1934

2 c. rich milk
½ c. sugar
¼ c. cornstarch or ⅓ c. flour
¼ tsp. salt

2 egg yolks, beaten
1 tsp. vanilla
Meringue (see page 226)

Scald 1¾ c. milk in top of double boiler. Mix remaining ¼ c. milk with sugar, cornstarch, and salt and add to milk. Cook 10 minutes, stirring constantly. Add egg yolks to mixture, stirring a little of the hot custard into eggs first. Cook 3 to 5 minutes; add vanilla and cool slightly. Pour in baked shell, cover with meringue and bake 20 minutes at 425°F.

Variations:

Banana Cream Pie: Slice bananas into baked shell, pour on custard, and finish as directed.

Strawberry or Pineapple Cream Pie: Fresh sliced strawberries or canned pineapple may be used in place of bananas.

❦ Lattice-Top Strawberry-Cherry Pie
June 1936

1 c. fresh strawberries, sliced
1½ c. sour red cherries, drained and ¼ c.
   of juice reserved
2½ tbsp. fine tapioca

1 c. sugar
dash of salt
1 tsp. butter

Combine reserved cherry juice, tapioca, sugar, and salt and let stand. Line a pie tin with pastry and have ready pastry cut in strips for lattice top. Fresh or canned cherries, pitted and unsweetened, may be used. Combine fruit and juice mixture and pour in pie shell. Dot with butter, and top with pastry strips. Seal edges, building up a rim or binding with parchment pie tape—a special bit of equipment readily available from kitchen supply stores that helps prevent juice overflow and reduces edge darkening. Bake in a very hot oven (450°F) for 10 minutes, then 25 minutes in a moderate oven (350°F).

❦ Pear Coronet Pie
April 1938

½ c. flour
⅔ c. sugar
⅛ tsp. salt
2 c. milk, scalded
2 tsp. butter
3 egg yolks

¾ tsp. vanilla
2 to 3 drops almond extract
6 to 8 canned pear halves, well drained
cherries, preserved ginger, or red jelly
    for garnish

Combine flour, sugar, and salt thoroughly in top of double boiler. Add scalded milk slowly, stirring well. Cook over hot water, stirring often, until mixture is thick and smooth; add butter. Beat egg yolks slightly; add a little hot mixture; stir quickly into filling. Stir and cook until eggs thicken. Remove from heat and cool. Add flavorings. Fill cooled baked pastry shell. Arrange pears, rounded end toward rim of pastry, pressing lightly so that surface of pears is flush with filling. Fill hollows of pears with whole or chopped cherries, chopped preserved ginger, bit of red jelly, etc. Fill space between pears and in center with meringue: 3 egg whites left-over from filling, beaten with sugar until stiff. Bake in a very slow oven (325°F) to brown the meringue.

Two Reader-Testers comment in this fashion:
"I have rated this pie for special occasions, but my boys disagree with me and say it should be every day." "Whether I make the topping the same way or not, I shall always use [this] recipe for cream filling; [it] is perfect."

❦ Rhubarb Pie
April 1925

3 c. diced and scalded rhubarb
1 c. sugar
⅛ tsp. salt

1 tsp. cinnamon
1 tbsp. butter

Follow recipe for Baked Rhubarb (below) and when cooked, place in a baked pie shell and serve hot.

Baked Rhubarb:
Mix rhubarb, sugar, and salt; sprinkle with cinnamon and dot with butter. Place in uncovered baking dish and cook slowly (300°F) until rhubarb is tender and some of the juice has evaporated.

Variation:
Add ½ c. raisins to 2 c. rhubarb and proceed as above.

CHEERS FOR CHERRY PIES
May 1938

One cheer goes for the good-looking cooks themselves—eight of them from eight different states—who entered this national cherry pie baking contest held recently in Chicago.

A second cheer goes for the delectable pies which these girls baked from cherries grown and canned in their states. Flaky brown crusts bursting with cherry-red fruit and oozing a bit of crimson juice! That tart-sweet flavor of cherries enhanced with a bit of butter and a meltingly-rich pastry!

A third cheer goes to the country kitchen cooks among them, for six of eight got their start in pie baking in a kitchen whose windows framed a view of the red barn and silo or perhaps a wheat field or cherry orchard.

Here are recipes for . . . three different fillings, each distinctive in its own way. You will notice that all of the recipes call for unsweetened canned red cherries, drained. Drain first, then measure cherries and juice as directed.

Indiana Cherry Pie
Contributed by Mary Wien, Indiana

3 tbsp. cornstarch (5 tbsp. if pie will
  be served warm)
½ c. juice
1 c. sugar

1 tbsp. butter
few grains salt
3 c. unsweetened red canned
  cherries, drained

Mix cornstarch and juice in top of double boiler. Cook until thick, stirring constantly. Add sugar and cook 5 minutes longer. Remove from fire, add butter and salt, then cherries, stirring carefully. Let stand while the crust is mixed and rolled [*such as Plain Pastry, page 226*], pour into pastry-lined tin. Cover with top crust, and cut to allow for escape of steam. Seal edges, bake 15 minutes in a hot oven (425°F) and 30 minutes in a moderate oven (350°F).

Ohio Cherry Pie
Contributed by Eleanor Enos, Ohio

3 c. drained, unsweetened canned
  cherries
1 c. sugar

sprinkle salt
2 tbsp. flour
¼ c. juice

Line plate with pastry [such as Plain Pastry, page 226]. Sprinkle bottom crust with a little flour. Spread half of cherries in, then sprinkle over them half of the sugar, salt, and flour mixed well together. Cover with remaining cherries and juice, and rest of sugar mixture on top. Put on upper crust. Brush top with milk, then sprinkle lightly with sugar. Bake at 425°F for 10 minutes, then reduce heat to 350°F and bake 30 to 40 minutes longer, till crust is nicely golden and filling is set.

Michigan Cherry Pie
Contributed by Annabelle Jones, Michigan

3 c. cherries, canned without sugar,
    drained
1 c. juice
1¼ c. sugar

3½ tbsp. cornstarch
2 tbsp. butter
½ tsp. almond extract

Mix cherries, cherry juice, and sugar. Allow to stand 5 minutes while crust is being made [such as Plain Pastry, page 226]. Drain juice from cherries. Mix cornstarch with a little of the juice until smooth. Bring remaining juice to a boil; stir in cornstarch mixture. Boil, stirring constantly, for 1 minute. Remove, add butter. Let cool until crust is rolled out. Add cherries and  almond extract to thickened juice; pour into pastry shell. Adjust top crust; press down edge with tines of a fork. Cut off excess pastry. Bake in a hot oven (425°F) until crust is golden brown, about 45 minutes.

Variation:
To any of the cherry pie recipes above, substitute 1 c. blueberries or raspberries for 1 c. cherries.

❦ Raspberry Pie
May 1910

Put a pint of berries in a granite saucepan, add 2 tbsp. water and 3 tbsp. of sugar and shake over the fire until the juice flows freely, but do not let the berries lose their shape. Skim them out and boil the syrup until clear. Cream together butter the size of an egg with 1 tbsp. of powdered sugar, add 1 tbsp. fine breadcrumbs, a few drops of almond flavoring, and the well-beaten yolks of 2 eggs. Lastly stir in the whites, whipped stiff. Line plates with a nice unbaked pastry and spread with the raspberries, pour over them the syrup, and spread with the egg mixture. Bake in a hot oven (400°F) until baked through.

Individual Pumpkin Pie
November 1921

⅔ c. brown sugar
½ c. steamed and
   strained pumpkin
2½ c. milk
2 eggs

1 tsp. cinnamon
½ tsp. ground ginger
½ tsp. salt
1 tsp. grated lemon peel

GRANDMA'S PUN'KIN PIE

Mix the ingredients and turn into individual unbaked pie shells—between 4½ and 5 inches around, readily available at bakers' supply shops. Bake in a slow oven (275°F to 300°F) and when cold serve with whipped cream. Will make about 6 small pies.

Sweet Potato Pie
February 1910

Make a custard of 1 pt. milk, 3 eggs, and ½ c. sugar. Beat yolks until light; add milk and sugar. Press the sweet potatoes, which have been peeled and steamed, through a sieve, and stir into milk and eggs. *[Editor's note: about 1 to 2 medium to large sweet potatoes, enough to yield 1 c.]* Season with cinnamon and 1 tbsp. melted butter. Put in unbaked crust before baking at 350°F. When done, make a meringue out of the whites of eggs, spread over the top of the pie, and return to oven to brown.

Apple Tart
February 1937

pastry-lined tin (see recipe for Lemon
   Tart Crust, page 233)
4 apples
3 tbsp. flour mixed with 2 tbsp. sugar

½ c. sugar mixed with cinnamon
butter
3 tbsp. water

Peel and core apples. Halve lengthwise, from stem to blossom end. In the bottom of the pastry-lined tin, sprinkle sugar and flour. Put in apples, round side up. Sprinkle sugar and cinnamon over top, dot with butter. Pour in water and put in a moderately hot oven (375°F to 400°F). Bake until apples are soft, about 40 minutes. As soon as removed from the oven, pour in about ¼ c. boiling water, shaking until it is absorbed. Serve slightly warm, plain or with ice cream or whipped cream as a special treat.

☙ Colonial Innkeepers Pecan Pie
March 1938

3 eggs
½ c. sugar
¼ tsp. salt
1 tsp. vanilla

1 c. dark corn syrup
1 c. melted butter
1 c. whole pecan meats

Beat eggs; add sugar, salt, and vanilla and beat lightly. Add syrup and butter. Place pecans in bottom of unbaked crust, add filling. Bake in moderate oven (350°F) for 50 to 60 minutes.

☙ Cranberry Molasses Pie
November 1929

1 qt. ripe cranberries
1 c. brown sugar
1 tbsp. butter

1 c. white sugar
1 c. molasses

Cook ingredients over a slow fire for 10 minutes. Line a deep pie dish with piecrust. Fill with cranberry mixture. Cover with strips of crust, criss-cross. Bake in a slow oven (300°F) for 45 minutes to 1 hour, or until the berries are thoroughly cooked.

☙ Lemon Tart
February 1937

Filling:
6 tbsp. flour
2 c. sugar
2 c. milk

2 lemons, juice and grated rind
2 eggs, lightly beaten

Crust:
3½ c. sifted flour
½ tsp. baking soda
½ tsp. salt

1 c. sugar
¼ c. butter and lard
⅔ to ¾ c. buttermilk

For filling, mix flour, sugar, and milk together and cook in a saucepan until thick and smooth. Add lemon juice and rind and pour over eggs. Cool slightly. Mix crust by sifting together dry ingredients. Work in fat as for pie crust, add milk to make a soft dough. Roll out, making two rounds and extra for top strips. Fit rounds into two small pie tins. Put half of filling in each and lay strips, 3 inches wide, across the top. Bake in a hot oven (400°F) until brown.

❦ Cream Puffs
March 1931

1 c. boiling water	1 c. flour
½ c. butter	4 eggs

Heat the water and butter in a sauce pan until the water boils, then add the flour all at once and stir vigorously. Cook over the fire until the mass is thick and smooth. When it is thick enough it will ball up on the spoon. Remove from fire when it has reached this stage and add the eggs, unbeaten, one at a time. Drop by spoonfuls on an oiled baking sheet. Bake in a moderate oven (350°F), from 25 to 30 minutes. When puffs are cool, make an incision in the side and fill with cream filling or whipped cream.

Cream Filling:

¾ c. sugar	1 square unsweetened chocolate, melted
½ c. flour	2 eggs
⅛ tsp. salt	1 tsp. vanilla
2 c. milk	

Mix sugar, flour, and salt together. Add milk, which has been heated. Boil, add melted chocolate if desired, add slightly beaten eggs, and cook for a few minutes in top of double boiler. Cool and flavor with vanilla.

Variation:

Whipped Cream Filling for Cream Puffs: A filling of flavored and sweetened whipped cream may be used in the cream puffs if desired.

❦ Cherry Turnovers
June 1910

Rub 1 c. butter into 1 lb. flour. When like coarse meal, moisten with 1 c. or less ice water and work to a paste, handling as little as possible. Roll out on a floured board, fold up, and roll for the second and third time. If still very cold, use at once, if not, set in the ice box until chilled. Roll out and cut into rounds the size of large biscuits. Drain juice off sweetened canned or freshly stewed stoned cherries and chop. Mix with 2 well beaten eggs and a little lemon juice, put 1 tbsp. of the cherry mixture on ½ each round of the crust, fold other half over, and pinch edges together. Lay these half-circles on a floured or buttered tin and bake to a golden brown at 375°F. Sift sugar over them and serve either hot or cold

❦ Southern Apple Dumplings
October 1938

Dumplings:

2 c. flour
2 tsp. baking powder
½ tsp. salt
2 tbsp. butter

¾ c. milk
1 c. chopped, peeled apple
2 tsp. lemon juice (not if apples are tart)

Sift flour, measure, and resift with baking powder and salt into mixing bowl. Work in butter with fingertips; when well blended, add milk and stir vigorously until dry ingredients are wet. Turn out on floured board, knead very slightly to make dough smooth, and roll out to ¼-inch thickness. Cut in six to eight squares and in the center of each piece place 2 to 3 tbsp. of chopped apple, moistened with lemon juice. Wet edges of dough and pinch together around apple. Drop dumplings, seam side down, into boiling hot sauce made as follows:

Sauce:

2 c. white sugar
½ c. brown sugar
2 tbsp. flour
½ tsp. salt
dash nutmeg, if desired
2 c. water
½ c. butter

Mix dry ingredients in deep skillet or baking pan (about 10 inches in diameter), add water and butter, and cook with constant stirring until thick. When dumplings are added, cover and place in a hot oven (425°F) for 30 minutes. Then remove cover, baste dumplings with sauce, and continue cooking uncovered until dumplings are golden brown. Serve with sauce and a scoop of vanilla ice cream.

Pasties

September 1932
Contributed by Boscastle

The Cornish pasty is the staple dish of the country. When the pasties are being made, each member has his or hers marked at one corner with the initial of the prospective owner. The true Cornish way to eat a pasty is to hold it in the hand and begin to bite it from the opposite end to the initial so that should any of it be uneaten, it may be consumed later by the rightful owner.

Any good pastry may be used but it should not be too flaky, not too rich. A very useful pastry is:

1 lb. flour, ½ lb. lard and suet *[Editor's note: substitute butter or shortening]*, ½ tsp. salt, mix with water. When pastry is made, roll out about ¼ inch thick and cut into rounds with plate to size desired.

Lay the rounds on the pastry board with half the round over the rolling pin and put in the fillings; damp the edges lightly and fold over into a semi-circle. Shape the pasty nicely and crimp the extreme edges where it is joined between the finger and thumb. Cut a slit in the center of the pasty, lay on a baking sheet, and bake in a quick oven (450°F).

Variations:
Chicken Pasty: Cooked, boneless chicken cut up in small pieces.

Herby Pasty: Well wash equal quantities of parsley, shallots, and a half quantity of spinach. Prepare some slices of bacon, cut into small pieces, and an egg, well beaten. Pour boiling water over parsley and spinach and let sit for ½ hour; well squeeze all moisture out. Put on pastry with the shallots cut finely and the bacon, pinch up the edges of the pasty, allowing a small portion for the egg top be added, finish pinching, and bake.

Fried Treats

❧ Pumpkin Doughnuts

Built-In Fryer
**Lets You French Fry
Like The Finest Chef!**

3 eggs, beaten light
1 c. sugar
1 c. sour cream
1 scant tsp. baking soda
pinch salt

2 tsp. cinnamon
1 tsp. nutmeg
1 c. pumpkin puree
4–6 c. flour, to make a
   rollable dough

Mix well and roll out ½ inch thick. Cut in strips, twist, and fry in deep, hot lard. While hot, roll in powdered sugar and cinnamon.

❧ Molasses Doughnuts

2 eggs
1 c. molasses
2 tbsp. shortening, melted
1¼ tsp. baking soda
½ tsp. salt

¼ tsp. nutmeg
¼ tsp. ginger
½ tsp. cinnamon
5 to 6 c. flour, sifted
1 c. buttermilk

Beat eggs and stir in molasses and shortening. Sift in baking soda, salt, spices, and 2 c. flour, adding to eggs alternately with buttermilk. Add more sifted flour to make a stiff dough. Roll out to ⅜ inch and cut in strips. Twist strips, fold in half, twist again, and pinch ends together. Fry in deep, hot fat. Drain on brown paper.

❧ Grandmother's Crullers

2 c. sugar
4 eggs, or less if they are scarce
1 c. buttermilk

½ tsp. baking soda
4 to 6 c. flour, enough to make a smooth
   paste

Mix, roll out thin, and cut into 3-inch squares. Beginning half an inch from one end, cut the squares into three or four strips. Braid these, or twist them into fancy shapes, and fry in hot lard. Drain on paper and sprinkle with confectioner's sugar, if desired.

❧ Banana Fritters

Contributed by L.S., Nevada

4 large, firm bananas
confectioner's sugar
lemon juice
1 c. flour

½ tsp. salt
2 eggs
⅔ c. milk

Remove banana skins, then cut in halves lengthwise and crosswise. Sprinkle each piece with confectioner's sugar and a little lemon juice and let them stand for an hour. Have ready a well-beaten batter made of remaining ingredients. Dip bananas into this, fry in hot, deep fat, and drain on brown paper.

❧ Apple Fritters

2 eggs, separated
½ c. honey
1 c. sour cream
2 c. flour
½ tsp. nutmeg

½ tsp. salt
½ tsp. baking soda
1 tbsp. unsalted butter, melted
4 sour apples, peeled, cored and sliced
    into ¼-inch rings

Beat egg yolks and honey till smooth, then mix in sour cream. Sift in flour, nutmeg, salt, and baking soda, then stir in butter. Beat egg whites till stiff and fold into batter. Dip apple rings in the mixture and fry in deep, hot fat, turning once to brown on both sides. Drain on brown paper.

❦ Funnel Cakes

Adapted from The Pennsylvania Dutch Cook Book

4 c. milk
4 eggs
½ tsp. baking soda dissolved in 1 tsp. water

2 tbsp. sugar
4 c. flour, approximately
pinch salt

Mix ingredients using enough flour to make a batter that will run smoothly through a funnel (hence, the name!) into deep, hot fat. Twist and turn funnel to make shapes. Drain on brown paper.

❦ Snowballs

Contributed by Mrs. Tschida

2 egg yolks
1 tbsp. heavy cream
few drops vanilla
pinch salt

1 tsp. cider vinegar
1 tsp. confectioner's sugar, plus extra for
  dusting
flour to stiffen—approximately to 2 c.

Blend yolks, cream, and seasonings. Add flour to stiffen. Roll out on floured board and cut in 1-inch circles. Drop in hot fat to cover, and with fork, lift up points as the ring fries to make it like a rosette. Fry a very light brown, drain, and sprinkle powdered sugar over to serve.

Yeast Breads, Rolls, and Cakes

❦ Whole Wheat or Cracked Wheat Bread
1934

1 qt. milk
⅓ c. brown sugar or honey
6 tbsp. butter
2 tbsp. salt
2 cakes compressed yeast *[Editor's note: substitute 2 packages active dry yeast]*

¼ c. lukewarm water
3 c. white flour and 6 c. whole-wheat flour
-or-
4 c. white flour and 4 to 5 c. coarser wheat flour

Scald milk in a double boiler with sugar, butter, and salt. Cool to lukewarm. In a large bowl, soak yeast in water and add milk. Add enough whole-wheat flour to make a batter. Beat thoroughly; add rest of whole-wheat and white flour to knead. The dough should be of a softer consistency than for white bread but not actually sticky. Knead for 10 to 15 minutes; put into a greased bowl; cover; let rise at a temperature of 80°F to 85°F until double in bulk. Knead down slightly without adding more flour; cover; let rise again until double. Make into loaves and put in well-greased individual bread pans. Brush top with melted fat. Cover and let rise until double in bulk. Bake until a golden brown in a moderately hot oven (400°F). Yield: three loaves of 1¾ lbs. each before baking.

"I made it *all myself*"

Bread—what home of hard-working people can do without it even to three times daily? Great variety is possible with a little alteration of foundation recipes. Mastery of good standard recipes . . . will open the door to an endless variety, and establish a firm reputation for good cooking.

❦ Hot Cross Buns
March 1910

Take a bowl of bread dough after the first kneading. Set it aside to rise like the other bread dough; when light, knead into it ½ c. currants that have been washed and dried, ½ c. sugar, and nutmeg to flavor. Knead no more than is necessary to mix the ingredients. Form into round biscuits, and place in a baking pan about ½ inch apart. Cut two deep gashes on top of each, crossing each other, and set to rise in a warm place. Just before putting into the moderately hot oven (400°F), brush the tops with melted butter or white of egg. Bake 10 minutes, then reduce heat to 350°F and bake about 15 minutes more, until golden.

PUT YOUR EQUIPMENT TO WORK . . . .

The Country Kitchen finds it helpful to
USE A RING MOLD FOR—

- Coffee cake or pecan roll
- Upside-down cake; fruit cake
- Steamed pudding or ice-box pudding
- Chilled potato salad garnished with quartered tomatoes and deviled egg halves
- Meat, chicken or fish loaf with creamed vegetables
- Noodle, macaroni or rice ring with creamed meat or chicken
- Vegetable souffle with cheese or bacon sauce
- Jellied salad or dessert

For baked things, first grease or oil the mold thoroughly. For jellied dishes, first rinse in cold water and to unmold, set in lukewarm water a few minutes. Turn ring mold out on chop plate or platter. Garnish appropriately, serve at the table. Just the thing for club luncheons or guest dinners.

❦ Ice Box Rolls
1934

1 qt. milk, scalded and cooled
1 c. mashed potatoes
½ to ¾ c. sugar
¾ c. melted shortening
1 cake compressed yeast dissolved in ¼ c.
   lukewarm water *[Editor's note: substitute*
   1 package active dry yeast]

1 tsp. baking powder
1 tsp. baking soda
1 tbsp. salt
about 2¾ c. flour

Mix the ingredients together, adding enough flour to make a thin batter or sponge. Let it rise until it is full of bubbles. Add more flour to make a dough as stiff as would be desirable for Parker House rolls—light, fluffy, oval-shaped dinner rolls that originated at the Parker House hotel in Boston in the mid-nineteenth century. Knead thoroughly; put in a large covered container; grease top of dough and lid together. Put in ice box for 24 hours before using. This mixture will keep for several days. When ready to use, take as much dough as desired; let it stand in a warm room for about 2 hours; make into rolls. Let rolls rise for 1 hour; bake in a hot oven (425°F) for about 20 minutes. This will make 96 small rolls.

❦ Butterhorn Rolls
April 1937

1 c. milk, scalded
2 tbsp. sugar
1 c. lukewarm water
1 cake compressed yeast *[Editor's note:*
   substitute 1 package active dry yeast]
7 to 8 c. sifted flour

½ c. fat
½ c. sugar
6 egg yolks
1 tbsp. salt
1 egg, beaten with 1 tbsp. cold water

Scald milk with 2 tbsp. sugar and cool to lukewarm. Add water and yeast that has been mixed with part of the water. Add 3 c. flour to make a spongy batter. Beat, let stand until light. Cream fat and sugar, add egg yolks, and beat until light and fluffy. Add to sponge with rest of flour and salt. Knead lightly, cover, and let stand in warm place until double in bulk. Divide in three pieces, roll out each one in ⅓-inch thick rounds. Spread with soft butter, cut in 16 pie-shaped pieces. Beginning at large end, roll up each section with point at top, place on greased tin, brush top with egg beaten with water, and let stand, covered, until double in bulk. Bake 20 minutes in a hot oven (425°F).

❦ German Kuchen (Coffee Cake)
April 1938

1 package active dry yeast	1 tsp. salt
¾ c. sugar	1 egg
¼ c. water	½ tsp. nutmeg
3½ c. flour, sifted	½ c. raisins
1 c. milk	¼ c. shortening

Topping:

1½ tbsp. butter	1 tbsp. brown sugar
2 tbsp. granulated sugar	½ tsp. cinnamon, if desired

Dissolve yeast and 2 tbsp. sugar in lukewarm water. Scald milk and cool until lukewarm. Add dissolved yeast and sugar mixture. Sift flour before and after measuring. Add ½ of the flour and beat thoroughly. Cover, and allow sponge to rise in a warm place until full of bubbles, about 45 minutes. Add remainder of sugar, salt, slightly beaten egg, nutmeg, raisins, and melted shortening. Add remainder of flour gradually and beat thoroughly after each addition. Let stand 10 minutes. Turn onto lightly floured board and knead until smooth and elastic. Place in bowl, cover, and let rise until double in size, about 1½ hrs. Shape into two loaves to fit greased pans. Let rise until light—about 45 minutes. For topping, spread with soft butter. Sprinkle with sugars and cinnamon. Bake in moderately hot oven (400°F) for 30 minutes. Remove from pans and allow to cool before storing.

Mrs. W.B. [a reader-tester] from Illinois: *"I'm calling on some friends this afternoon and one of these coffee cakes is going along with me because I'm eager for others, too, to learn of the fine qualities of this nice product and the good work the Reader Test Department of your magazine is doing for the public. I am so enthusiastic about this entire affair that I do want you to know and feel I am 100 percent heart and soul in it and I'll probably be a reader of* The Farmer's Wife Magazine *until I'm so old I can't read anymore."*

Quick Breads and Muffins

Banana Loaf

March 1939
Contributed by Mrs. E.O. Park

1 c. sugar
¼ c. fat
1 egg
3 mashed bananas
2 c. sifted flour
1 tsp. baking soda
½ tsp. salt
1 c. nut meats

Cream sugar and fat, add egg and bananas, and blend well. Sift together dry ingredients, add nuts and combine with the batter. Stir just until flour is dampened and put in greased loaf pan. Bake 1 hour in very moderate oven (350°F).

Old-Fashioned Pound Cake

March 1938

This lovely all-over flower-and-leaf design—the Shalimar—is adapted from an ancient Persian print

PHOTOGRAPH COURTESY DU PONT STYLE NEWS SERVICE

1¾ c. butter
2 c. fine granulated sugar
8 eggs
2 tbsp. brandy
1 tsp. mace or nutmeg
1¾ c. sifted cake flour
1 tsp. salt
¼ tsp. baking powder

Cream butter very thoroughly and add sugar gradually. Cream together until light and fluffy. Add 1 egg at a time without separating, and beat after the addition of each egg. Add brandy and spice. Add sifted dry ingredients and beat until light and fluffy. Bake in a well greased tube pan in a very slow oven (300°F) for 1¼ hours. The heat should be turned off the last ¼ hour of baking. Pound cake is not usually iced. Store in the pan in which it is baked.

❧ Bran Muffins

October 1927

2 tbsp. shortening
¼ c. sugar
1 egg
1 c. bran
1 c. flour

½ tsp. salt
½ tsp. baking soda
1 tsp. baking powder
1 c. buttermilk

Cream together shortening and sugar; add egg and bran. Add flour sifted with other dry ingredients and buttermilk. If sweet milk is used, omit baking soda and use 2 tsp. baking powder. Bake 20 minutes in moderate oven (375°F).

❧ Cranberry Muffins

November 1933

2 c. flour
2½ tsp. baking powder
½ tsp. salt
2 tbsp. sugar

½ c. ground cranberries
1 c. milk
1 egg, beaten
2 tbsp. melted butter

Sift flour, baking powder, salt, and sugar together, then add cranberries. Add beaten egg to milk, then melted shortening. Beat liquids together. Add liquid to dry ingredients all at once. Combine in about 3 seconds, mixing until ingredients are just dampened. Fill greased muffin tins a little over ⅓ full. Bake in hot oven (400°F) about 20 minutes.

❧ Blueberry Muffins

August 1923

3 tbsp. butter
½ c. sugar
2 eggs
1½ c. flour (sifted)
3 tsp. baking powder
½ tsp. salt
1 c. milk
1 c. blueberries

Cream butter; add sugar and well-beaten eggs. Mix and sift flour, baking powder, and salt, reserving a small amount of flour to dust over berries. Add flour mixture and milk alternately to butter mixture. Stir in berries last, being careful not to crush them. Bake in a moderately hot oven (400°F).

🐝 Scotch Scones
March 1933
Contributed by B.W., Massachusetts

2 c. flour
2 tsp. baking powder
2 tsp. sugar
¾ tsp. salt
4 tbsp. butter
2 eggs
⅓ c. milk (approx.)

Sift together flour, baking powder, sugar, and salt. Work in the butter. Save out a small amount of egg white. Beat the rest of the 2 eggs and add to milk and beat again. Add to the dry ingredients and mix lightly and quickly. Toss on floured board, roll out to 1 inch in thickness and cut in triangles with a knife. Brush with the saved egg white, sprinkle with sugar, and bake in a very hot oven (450°F) from 10 to 15 minutes. This makes a nicely glossed scone. They also may be cut out in squares and folded over to form three-cornered shapes if you prefer.

🐝 Orange Rolls
December 1932

2 c. flour
2 tsp. baking powder
½ tsp. salt
1 tbsp. shortening
1 egg
½ c. milk
1 c. unsalted, creamed butter
12 sections orange pulp

Sift flour, baking powder, and salt together; add shortening, mixing with a fork. Beat egg slightly and add with milk to first mixture. Roll into an oblong piece about ¼ inch thick. Cut into 3-inch circles; spread with creamed butter and place a section of fresh orange coated with granulated sugar over half the circle. Fold over other half to completely cover orange and pinch edges together. Place rolls in greased baking pan and bake in moderate oven (350°F) about 20 minutes. Just before removing, brush tops with melted butter.

❦ St. Paul Popovers
November 1936

4 eggs, beaten slightly
1 c. milk
1 c. water
2⅓ c. sifted bread flour
1 tsp. salt
2 tsp. sugar

To eggs add ⅔ of liquid, then all of flour, salt, and sugar. *[That's right, there's no baking powder.]* Beat until smooth; add rest of liquid. When blended, pour in warm, thoroughly greased pans. Fill muffin pans half full, deep custard cups or popover pan scarcely more than ⅓ full. Bake smaller tins, as muffin pans, for 25 to 30 minutes, deeper tins for 35 minutes at 450°F to 475°F, a really hot oven. Serve piping hot with butter. The popovers will pop up in 15 or 20 minutes, and the additional baking makes the thin walls crisp and brown. Serve as breakfast or hot supper bread. On occasion, fill with creamed chicken or chipped beef in cream.

❦ Mammy's Corn Bread
March 1921

1 c. cornmeal
1 c. flour
1 tbsp. sugar
1 tsp. baking soda

1 tsp. salt
buttermilk (approximately 1½ c.)
1 egg

Sift well together. Then work in 1 tbsp. shortening. Mix to a medium batter with buttermilk. Whip in 1 well-beaten egg and bake in a hot oven (400°F).

Resources

Alley, Lynn. *The Gourmet Slow Cooker, Volumes I and II*. Berkeley, CA: Ten Speed Press, 2003, 2006.

American Cooking: New England. New York: Time-Life Books, 1970.

Berolzheimer, Ruth, ed. *United States Regional Cook Book*. Garden City, NY: Garden City Publishing, Inc., 1939.

Cohasset Entertains. Cohasset, MA: The Garden Club of Cohasset, 1979.

Cooking Favorites of Vergennes. Vergennes, VT: Students Going to Europe, date unknown.

Davidson, Alan. *The Penguin Companion to Food*. New York: Penguin Books, 2002.

Favorite Recipes of the King's Daughters and Sons. Chautauqua, NY: International Order of the King's Daughter's and Sons, 1978.

Hot Recipes. Georgia, VT: Georgia Firewoman's Auxiliary, date unknown.

Hutchinson, Ruth. *The Pennsylvania Dutch Cook Book*. New York: Harper & Brothers, 1948.

Kaufmann, Beth and Julie. *Not Your Mother's Slow Cooker Cookbook*. Hensperger, Boston: The Harvard Common Press, 2005.

The Meetinghouse Cookbook. Concord, MA: Women's Parish Association, 1974.

Our Favorite Recipes. Metuchen, NJ: Women's Guild of the Presbyterian Church, date unknown.

Out of Vermont Kitchens. Burlington, VT: Women of St. Paul's Cathedral, 1999.

Recipes from Maa Eway. Evening Department Women's Club of Mahwah Cook Book Committee, 1958.

Recipes Tried and True by Cooks. Windsor County, VT: Members of the Home Demonstration Clubs of Windsor County, 1941.

Soper, Musia, ed. *Encyclopedia of European Cooking*. London: Spring Books, 1962.

Additional Resources for Canning and Pickling

The science of preserving is ever-changing, with experts at federally funded university extension services testing and making updates to existing recommendations on a regular basis. There is, therefore, an abundance of information available to the home canner. To find the extension service for your area, visit **www.csrees.usda.gov/ Extension**.

Additionally, your local extension service will have information on preserving products native to your area—wild fruits, for example—and may also be testing updates for products similar to those that are now recommended in this book for refrigeration only. They can answer any questions you have about methods and safety, such as how to test a pressure canner, how to make adjustments for altitude, and how to dispose of food that is potentially contaminated.

The USDA's National Center for Home Food Preservation is another excellent resource: **www.uga.edu/nchfp/publications/publications_usda.html**. *(This link allows you to download and print the USDA's "Complete Guide to Home Canning.")*

The University of Georgia's (UGA) cooperative extension service for food preservation is a helpful site as well: **www.fcs.uga.edu/ext/pubs/food/canning.php**.

Additionally, the UGA's "So Easy to Preserve"—a print version with more than 185 tested recipes that includes the USDA's latest recommendations, as well as a series of demonstration DVDs, are available from **www.uga.edu/setp**.

Other sources consulted for this book: The Clemson University Extension Service Food Safety & Preservation website (**hgic.clemson.edu/food.htm**) and the University of Minnesota Cooperative Extension Service website (**www.extension.umn.edu/ distribution/nutrition/DJ1089.html**).

Index

Jams, Preserves, and Other Spreads

Main Courses

Soups